Explorations in Managerial Economics

Productivity, Costs, Technology and Growth

Explorations in Managerial Economics
Productivity, Costs, Technology and Growth

Bela Gold, B.S., Ph.D.
Timken Professor of Industrial Economics,
Case Western Reserve University, Cleveland, Ohio

BASIC BOOKS, INC., Publishers
New York

Preface

The basic purpose of this volume is to help call attention to the under-developed state and to the exciting potentials of managerial economics. This does not involve any invidious reflections on achievements to date in what is still a newly emerging field. Rather, it seeks to highlight some of the intriguing gaps between the available theory and tools and the major problems pressing for more effective analytical treatment.

Instead of concentrating on the simplified abstractions which are commonly regarded as less frustrating for beginners than the direct confrontation of complex realities, it has been assumed that a partial reversal of this emphasis might prove more attractive to the graduate students and to the corporate as well as governmental personnel most likely to be interested in exploring and applying managerial economics.

Some of the following material has been published previously, scattered among professional journals in economics, operations research, management and statistics edited in England, France, Italy and India as well as the United States. But this is the first appearance of the analytical framework as a whole.

During the ten years of research underlying this volume, a formidable array of debts has been accumulated for intellectual stimulus, for critical comment and for financial assistance. It is a pleasure, therefore, to express my warm appreciation to the Warden and Fellows of Nuffield College, Oxford, for inviting me to join them for the greater part of a year; to Samuel Eilon and his colleagues in the Imperial College of Science and Technology, London, for allowing me to serve with them as a Visiting Professor, and to P. W. S. Andrews and Elizabeth Brunner, now of the University of Lancaster, for their unstinting friendship and partnership in research. I am indebted to the Ford Foundation and to Resources for the Future, Inc. for needed support and for the helpful interest of Marshall A. Robinson and Hans H. Landsberg. And I am most grateful indeed to the Timken Foundation for helping to establish the Research Programme in Industrial Economics to continue development of the lines of research presented in the following pages.

March 15, 1970 BELA GOLD

v

Contents

vii

1 Economic Analysis and Managerial Decision Making: Some Conceptual Perspectives

The development of managerial economics has been stimulated by increasing pressures for more effective guidance in the making of major corporate and governmental decisions. Although its contributions have fallen short of needs so far, as might be expected in any relatively new field, substantial progress is being made in identifying the sources of past inadequacies and in formulating approaches to overcoming them. Resulting advances are likely not only to enhance the direct applicability of economic analysis at the decision-making level, but also to strengthen the theoretical structure of economics by filling in some of the voids underlying its generalised concepts and models.

Early writings implied that managerial questions concerning demand, input factor requirements, output levels, pricing and capital investments could be answered by the routine application of already-developed microeconomic theory to the relevant data. And this impression was reinforced by using simple illustrative exercises and carefully selected case studies, as well as references to empirical findings ostensibly demonstrating the relevance to actual experience of the theoretical models which had been presented. Such efforts have provided a useful introduction to the problems involved. But most of the exercises tend to be trivial and most of the cases have obviously been severely truncated or cannot be resolved through economic analysis alone. Moreover, careful analysis reveals that few of the empirical studies cited conform rigorously to the restrictive assumptions of the formal theory which they are supposed to be testing or applying. It should be emphasised, however, that such limitations are not attributable to the textbook authors; on the contrary, most provide a reasonably correct reflection of the major gaps between the analytical framework of available theory and that within which most significant decision issues arise and have to be resolved.

Accordingly, efforts to build more effective bridges between economic theory and managerial decision making are likely to require the development of successive intermediate frameworks increasingly closer to the managerial definition of issues and evaluative criteria. Each of the exploratory undertakings presented in the following chapters involves such revisions of prevailing ideas about economic processes, the most promising foci of economic analysis, the most relevant methodologies and the nature and processes of decision making. A brief review of these may help.

1.1 REVISING SOME VIEWS ON THE NATURE OF ECONOMIC PROCESSES

1.1.1 Economics is not Simple—it is Extremely Complex

Although many students think that stabilising cyclical fluctuations, increasing economic growth rates, controlling inflation, and overcoming balance-of-payments problems merely require the manipulation of a few simple equations, the hard evidence does not support such views. The processes by means of which the efforts of tens of millions of people are interwoven to convert raw materials into hundreds of thousands of changing goods and services and to distribute them all over the earth are not likely to be either few or simple. Indeed, one can readily sympathise with Nobel Laureate Max Planck's decision to renounce his early interest in economics in favour of the less appalling complexities of theoretical physics [9].*

All sciences place a premium on simple generalisations, of course. But they place an even heavier premium on wide applicability for purposes of explanation and prediction. As a result, the simplicity of the Greeks' hard little atoms and earth, air, fire and water have been disregarded in favour of complex atomic structures, more than 100 chemical elements, and concepts of intricately structured macro-molecules and cells which all but stagger the imagination. The formulation of simple generalisations in economics has been encouraged by a crusade to promote economic literacy through concentrating on its rudiments, by a desire to emulate the success of the hard sciences, and perhaps by the temptations to gain a role in policy formulation with an apparently applicable body of expertise. Most of the resulting generalisations have taken two forms: those representing essentially logical deductions on the basis of highly restrictive assumptions; and those seeking to rationalise relatively stable statistical relationships found to be applicable to past data. Either of these could, of course, provide important contributions to the understanding of economic processes—and often has. But the infrequency with which the former have

* References are given at the end of the book, see pp. 275–88.

proved applicable to actual economic experience, and with which the latter relationships have continued to be stable, cannot but reinforce doubts concerning the array of simple generalisations currently available.

One implication of the foregoing is the need to gradually reduce the array of reasonable assumptions which facilitate the derivation of simple generalisations and also protect them from serious testing. Instead, it may be necessary to probe actual experiences in such areas and even to learn enough about the technicalities involved to prevent focusing on peripheral rather than strategic factors, as is illustrated in Chapter 3. And a second implication would seem to be the need to reduce the value placed on the aesthetics and methodological convenience of simplicity relative to that placed on demonstrable and widespread applicability [10]. That such a shift from the continued pile-up of simple but untested hypotheses is likely to engender far more complex models is suggested by the major macro-economic models being developed in the United States and abroad, as well as by the analyses presented in each of the following chapters.

1.1.2 In Any Given Period, Economic Relationships may Differ Substantially not only from Economy to Economy, but also among Major Sectors within an Economy

All horses look alike only to those who are quite unfamiliar with horses. And the generalised treatment all industries receive in economic textbooks would seem to indicate comparable ignorance. Drawing on different factor markets, using diverse technologies, and selling to dissimilar product markets, industrial sectors are far more likely to differ than to be alike in respect to production and cost functions, scale economies, pricing practices and demand characteristics. It may properly be contended, of course, that the usual graphical representations of short-term and long-run cost functions, for example, represent only one among the wide variety of possible shapes encompassed by theory, the latter requiring only a minimum point somewhere. But the usefulness of such theories gains little support from demonstrations of wide applicability at the expense of admissions that they have little to say. It is far more constructive to explore the comparative economics of industries—along lines illustrated in Chapters 7 and 9—as a belated parallel to our long active concern with the comparison of different economies.

1.1.3 Economic Systems are Hierarchical rather than Homogeneous

Instead of representing domains uniformly dotted with decision points which are independent of one another, economies are extremely intricate structures of successively larger networks reaching from individuals through organised groupings of individuals and then through loose as well as tight clusters of organised units, eventually emerging as industry, regional and larger components of the national economy. As a result, although input, output and other data can be accumulated at innumerable levels representing progressively larger sectors of the economy, many of these statistical aggregates may represent only the passive result of heterogeneous decisions and adjustments actually made at lower levels of aggregation, as discussed in Chapter 3. To understand such changes, and to influence them, it is necessary to identify the decision points involved as well as the objectives, incentives and penalties considered by the decision maker. For example, since investment decisions are made at the level of the firm, and the employment effects of such decisions may differ widely among industries depending on the relative pressures of labour-displacing technologies and of expanding product markets, the use of national aggregates to estimate the effects of adjustments in investment on employment levels may be of limited value. A second implication is that commonly used variables need not be equally meaningful at different levels of aggregation. For example, profit rates tend to be more relevant to performance evaluation at the level of the firm than at the level of the industry. The most effective levels of aggregation for analysis are examined in the following chapters for a wide array of other variables including input and output quantities, factor and product prices and productivity measures.

1.1.4 All Economic Relationships Tend to Change Through Time

Because of changes in consumer tastes, resource availabilities, technological potentials, governmental pressures and institutional arrangements, relatively few economic relationships have been found which have been stable over extended periods. And even these cannot be projected with any assurance either into previous or into subsequent periods. But neither are all economic relationships turbulent. Analysis suggests rather that there is a wide range; from sectors of stability which have persisted over periods of several decades (as illustrated in Chapters 6, 9 and 11) to sectors seemingly devoid of even short term stability (as illustrated in Chapter 7). Of particular interest in this connection is that neither of these sets of findings conformed to prior theoretical expectations. Another important aspect of this generalised process of progressive re-creation in economics is that some of the most serious problems faced in given periods may be traced to the very successes achieved in coping with other problems in earlier periods: e.g. recent problems of agricultural surpluses, inflation, balance-of-payments and environmental pollution are obviously rooted in some of the past successes of agricultural production, industrialisation and foreign reconstruction and development.

1.1.5 Economies Represent Open and Reactive Systems, rather than the Closed, Passive Systems of the Physical Sciences

For example, in accounting for the trajectory of an artillery shell, mechanics deals with a system closed to all forces other than those of the propellant, gravity and atmospheric friction—and regards the shell itself as indifferent to the outcome. In economics, however, the firm or industry facing a declining market may fight back instead of accepting its predicted fate. And it may do so by introducing such new forces as new management, new capital and new products as well as marketing innovations. As shown in Chapter 11, the smooth growth paths drawn on the basis of hindsight through the jagged ups and downs of past production tend to imply a continuity, and even an inevitability, in strong contrast to managerial expectations and attendant policy manipulations during the course of negotiating such intermittent threats and stresses.

1.1.6 Economic Problems are Inextricably Imbedded within Larger Political and Social Frameworks which must be Recognised as Influencing Economic Analysis

At the very least, this means that economic alternatives must be formulated within explicitly defined political and social constraints, as indicated in Chapter 3. Thus, the prospective cost savings of new technologies cannot be appraised without regard to established safety regulations or governmental sensitivity to attendant pollution and other social costs. More seriously, recognition of these larger frameworks serves as a reminder that economic problems which remain unsolved for too long may lead to political action which permanently reduces the domain left solely to managerial decision. This has been illustrated not only by the sharply increased amount of governmental intervention introduced during the 1930s and their further extensions thereafter in the United States, but even more dramatically by the expansion of socialised sectors in all western European countries. And still another implication of these larger frameworks is that political and social pressures may interact with economic considerations even in the making of ostensibly private economic decisions, as illustrated by decisions involving plant location, overseas investment and the introduction of technological innovations on railroads.

1.2 STRENGTHENING SOME UNDER-DEVELOPED AREAS OF ECONOMIC ANALYSIS

As in other scientific disciplines, the very successes of economics which result from heavy concentrations of effort in some sectors emphasise the relative under-development of sectors attracting less interest. There have been economists in every period, of course, who have been concerned with public issues. But the central development of economics was long dominated by academic efforts to integrate the short- and long-term production and consumption alternatives of individuals, households, firms and larger economic sectors through exchanges involving factor and product price adjustments within an essentially static analytical framework derived through deductive logic. That tremendous advances in concepts and tools were achieved is apparent from any history of economic thought [12]. But most of these gains emerged within restrictive premises which continued to insulate resulting hypotheses from rigorous testing under real-life conditions (although that has always been proclaimed as the eventual objective of these theoretical explorations).

1.2.1 For Fuller Coverage of Economic Interactions

Partly because of the growing intellectual attraction of under-developed fields and partly because of the pragmatic pressures generated by increasing public concern, the thirty years following the First World War were marked by a significant diversion in economics from traditional emphases to the exploration of business cycles. And, as might be expected, sharply expanded theoretical and empirical work led in time to quite remarkable improvements in the analytical models and tools relating to short-term economic fluctuations, along with the formulation of a variety of policy-oriented hypotheses considered applicable to real life conditions. After the Second World War, economic growth emerged as a new major focus of economic analysis. Interest in this area may have been stimulated partly by the urgent problems of rebuilding war-torn economies and accelerating the growth of under-developed economies. But additional attractions were surely that here was another *terra incognita* within economics, that it provided further opportunities for involvement in policy issues, the appetite for which had been whetted by the work on business cycles, and that the problems of stabilisation were believed to have been largely solved except for the details of 'fine tuning' left to be worked out by econometricians.

As seems to be characteristic of each shift to a new, under-developed sector of economics, however, the concepts, models and tools which yielded such gratifying results in respect to cycles proved much less fruitful in coping with the problems of growth. Among the re-orientations in analytical foci which seem necessary in order to encompass the central problems of growth, the following are also basic to another under-developed sector of economic analysis of particular concern here, i.e. managerial economics:

(1) from the national economy viewed as a coherent entity to its major industrial and regional components;
(2) from a monopolising concern with aggregate demand levels to a balanced consideration of the composition of supply as well;
(3) from a primary concentration on the financial level of analysis (incomes, expenditures, investment and price levels) to a complementary concern with the physical resource flows underlying them; and
(4) from explicitly excluding technological innovations to including them not merely as an addition to the traditional inputs of natural resources, labour and capital, but rather as an integral component of the interactions affecting the nature and price as well as the magnitudes of input requirements and output potentials.

Business cycles are currently seen as fluctuations pervading the entire economy, with attempts made to reduce them through stabilising aggregate demand. The most influential sources of such stabilising pressures are thought to be adjustments in governmental fiscal policy, in interest rates and, more recently, in the money supply—thus implying that supply arrangements, including the technologies in use, are essentially satisfactory and unchanging. However, it is not possible to expand the entire economy merely by increasing aggregate demand. Moreover, persistent economic growth almost invariably involves changes not only in the level of output, but also in its product composition. And these, in turn, require corresponding changes in the magnitude and allocation of input factors and in the distribution channels. Although economic growth need not involve the development of new technologies, changes in the level and composition of inputs and outputs can hardly avoid affecting, and being affected by, the diffusion of technological improvements. Furthermore, the creation and application of new technologies can seriously alter product characteristics, productive capacity and the nature of inputs required, as well as cost and price levels. Thus a fuller understanding of economic growth may be gained by extending the most commonly used analytical frameworks to provide fuller coverage of supply as well demand and the physical as well as the financial characteristics of resource flows at successive disaggregated levels.* The need for similar contributions in the development of managerial economics is illustrated in the following chapters.

* To extend an earlier illustration, macro-economic analysis might suggest a need to increase capital investment by say $10 billion to promote specified growth objectives. But this cannot be done at a generalised level; it can only be effected through specific facilities and equipment in given plants producing certain products. The resulting adjustments in employment, output, costs and other aspects of economic activity depend on the particular allocations made rather than on the sheer magnitude of the total investment.

1.2.2 For Fuller Coverage of Managerial Needs

The emphasis in managerial economics on decision making calls attention to several other relatively under-developed sectors of economic analysis. First, it requires more comprehensive identification of the decisions which are made at each level of aggregation, the time perspectives within which each is implemented and reconsidered, and the constraints applicable to each. One may note in this connection that there is no decision to be made if there are fewer than two rational alternatives [6], as is frequently the case in elementary models of the firm. Second, it urges increasing efforts to reach beyond the deduction of laws and persistent empirical adjustment patterns to the engineering of new relationships. Possible alternatives for given operating units under various conditions should be explored and means devised for effecting them. For example, Chapter 7 discusses the possibility of designing and implementing desired cost functions for given firms or industries instead of merely adapting to those which happen to prevail in a particular period.

A third area deserving more intensive development involves supplementing past efforts to guide optimal decision making with respect to one variable at a time—as reflected by the usual textbook treatment of each in a separate chapter. This would require serious efforts to integrate alternative combinations of input factors, alternative output and product-mix policies, and alternative pricing, investment and marketing strategies, into top management decisions—perhaps along such lines as are explored in Chapter 2 and thereafter. And what is probably the most perplexing, as well as the most important area in need of extensive development concerns bases for making truly major decisions in the face of seriously limited information, as is discussed in Chapter 10.

1.3 MODIFYING SOME ANALYTICAL METHODS

The unavoidably pragmatic thrust of managerial economics also reinforces familiar pressures for the modification of certain foundations of the methodologies in economic analysis which have become pervasive in academic settings.

1.3.1 On the Range of Permissible Assumptions

As is discussed in greater detail in Chapter 7, scholars ordinarily concentrate their analytical efforts within a domain defined by methodological premises and by substantive assumptions. The former specify which variables and relationships are to be covered as well as the conditions within which the inquiry is to be restricted. In thus limiting his target area, the scholar is free to focus on broad or narrow problems, on real or imaginary relationships and on common or improbable conditions. With respect to the variables in this target area, the scholar is similarly free to make substantive assumptions concerning those characteristics or adjustment patterns which underlie the central focus of his planned analysis (e.g. assuming the shape of fixed and variable cost functions as a basis for estimating the shape of total unit cost functions). It should be emphasised, however, that the results would obviously be applicable only to situations which correspond with these premises and assumptions, although they may provide useful elaborations or extensions of previous academic findings in closely related areas of inquiry. It should also be emphasised that the resulting body of theory may grow indefinitely, rarely making contact with the questions, conditions and substantive behaviours actually confronting managers.

On the other hand, efforts to develop sectors of economic analysis which would be directly applicable to a reasonable array of common management decisions would seem to impose serious restrictions on the methodological premises and substantive assumptions by requiring conformity with those characterising the intended areas of application. Progress in this direction need not require immediate confrontation with the bewildering difficulties which could result from discarding all traditional simplifying conditions, including the restriction of analyses to a moment of time, assuming all variables outside the immediate focus of analysis to be fixed, requiring full information and, sometimes, free competition, etc. But neither is much progress likely to result from passively awaiting chance advances in this direction. Rather, it may well be necessary to attempt systematic extensions of various sectors of current theory through the progressive relaxation of premises and assumptions which prevent or seriously limit their relevance to the forms in which real decision issues are posed. This approach is attempted in Chapter 7. This need not restrict the development of economics, for managerial economics constitutes only one sector of the discipline. On the contrary, this may provide a valuable challenge. In theoretical physics, for example, empirical findings have been enormously stimulating while not preventing speculative forays into areas not yet subject to empirical approaches.

1.3.2 On Rational Models

Enthusiastic efforts to emulate the success achieved in some of the natural sciences seem to have encouraged a rush to present economic speculations in a mathematical form without serious evaluation of the resulting contribution to understanding. Some have dryly labelled such activities as SONK-ing, the acronym referring to the *scientification of non-knowledge* [5].

Oskar Morgenstern warned, in this connection, that 'the primary task is to discover the true nature of the underlying economic phenomena and to concentrate efforts in that direction instead of stopping short and branching out into the mathematical treatment of an ill-defined and vaguely described situation' [11].

The main point in this connection is that a rudimentary (or even an advanced) knowledge of mathematics and statistics is not much of a substitute for expertise in the theories, findings, tools and related experiences representing major disciplines. Physics and chemistry have managed to remain reasonably distinguishable from mathematics, although making heavy use of it; and it is probable that economics will also remain distinct, despite its eager reliance on any tools likely to further its inquiries. Hence efforts to throw all managerial problems into a generalised format labelled 'decision making under uncertainty' do not really contribute much to their resolution. Nor is this achieved by labelling each of the seemingly relevant variables about which nothing is known and adding it to a bag of independent variables. Expanding an equation by adding T for technology is of little help if one does not understand the nature of the particular technology involved, or how it affects inputs and outputs as well as other process characteristics and outcomes. This is discussed in Chapters 3 and 10. In short, the usefulness of a model is likely to depend more on the effectiveness with which comprehensive knowledge about the phenomena involved has been distilled so as to reveal the strategic determinants of its behaviour, than on the elegance of the mathematical formulation in which it is expressed.

Careful analysis of managerial decision-making processes has another major implication for the development of rational models: specifically, most managerial decisions are not single actions which remain unalterable thereafter. On the contrary, they represent one of a series of successive judgements and partial commitments responsive to any additional information and experience accumulated, and also influenced by any adjustment in goals and resources during the intervening period. As a result, to construct rational models *ex post* by assuming that the final outcomes of such sequential decision processes agree with the original intentions, or with a deductive judgement concerning what management was probably trying to accomplish, involves serious hazards. In the last analysis, then, the development of managerial economics is quite likely to depend on the extent to which economists move out of their classrooms into factories and executive offices to study decision making in its native habitat [8] instead of imaginatively simulating it. In this respect, the emergence of behavioural models of certain kinds of decision making [4, 13] are a hopeful sign because they demonstrate the possibility of gaining new insights through field studies, especially on the carry-over of habit patterns formed by previous economic conditions and also, as shown in Chapter 9, on the interaction of economic and organisational pressures.

1.3.3 On the Time Foci of Analysis

The most commonly employed methods of time series analysis, which were largely developed during the period of central preoccupation with cyclic fluctuations, involved the separation of statistical series into trend, seasonal and cyclical components plus a residual. This approach is based on three assumptions which tend to minimise rather than to reveal the rich texture of adjustments underlying macro-economic issues as well as those to be dealt with in managerial economics:

(1) that these four categories of adjustment through time encompass areas of economic behaviour which are exclusive of one another;
(2) that trend, cyclic and seasonal components combined account for all 'meaningful' economic change; and
(3) that the stable adjustment pattern characterising each of these three major components is due to a fixed array of persistent forces interacting with one another in some orderly manner.

The first tends to obscure both the possibility of interactions among these supposedly mutually exclusive categories of change (e.g. between cyclic patterns and growth trends) and the need for a wider array of time foci between the stroboscopic glimpses of static analysis and the long term perspectives reflected by trends. Even in macro-economic analysis, 'the' business cycle cannot be regarded as anything more than one conception of the central tendency of a wide distribution of fluctuations among the various sectors of the economy ranging from some arbitrary boundary line for seasonals to cycles of eight years or more in length (e.g. in housing) [1, 2]. And trend lines are no less vague in conception, ranging from perhaps five years (or less than the period of some cycles) to thirty years and longer.

In actual industrial operations, too, there is considerable range in the frequency with which operating variables are likely to require managerial review and decisions. Production levels may change within periods of a few weeks or less, generating comparably frequent adjustments in labour, and material and shipping requirements. Price adjustments are subject to change within periods of a few months in many areas of manufacturing and much more frequently in retailing. Product specifications, wage rates, salary levels and productivity relationships are likely to change substantially over somewhat longer periods, perhaps of the order of a year or more. Plant capacity, basic production processes, capital equipment and primary materials used are likely to undergo major adjustments over still longer periods. Inasmuch as actual industrial operations are invariably the product of a variety of such changes recurring at different rates, economic analyses intended to help in the making of each of a wide variety of decisions may well require the development of a more flexible set of time-oriented analytical concepts, some of which are illustrated in Chapters 6 to 11.

By assuming the dominance of trends, cycles and seasonals, assumption (2) above tends to discourage direct determination of the proportion of total change in any given period *not* accounted for by these persistent adjustment patterns and thereby also diverts attention from the need to uncover the elements of such residual change. At the macro-economic level, this tends by definition to leave substantial proportions of the change in any abnormal period unaccounted for. The significance of this shortcoming is readily evident from the anomalous rarity of normal periods except on the basis of long hindsight. In managerial economics, however, the primary focus must be on the total change in any period, rather than on those portions of it which may be identified as having recorded stable patterns over several decades. Therefore, after the latter have been identified, measured and separated off by some means, the remainder must remain a central focus of analysis in the interests of making recommendations for adaptation to expected changes beyond the control of managerial efforts.

But it is the third of the above assumptions that lies at the heart of economic interpretations of statistical findings—and it gives rise to a variety of troublesome questions. Perhaps the simplest of these would involve the identification of particular forces which tend to yield reasonably consistent growth trends and those which tend to yield consistent cycles. Although population, capital formation and technological progress are frequently alluded to in discussions of long-term forces, there is ample basis for questioning both the steadiness of changes in each of these and the likelihood that such changes would yield consistent effects in economies undergoing major changes in values, institutions and controls. As a second question, it seems worth asking whether the effects of sporadic forces are clearly distinguishable from those of persistent forces. In other words, what basis is there for assuming that trends reflect only a fixed array of persistent forces unalloyed by more transitory stimuli? At a still more fundamental level, one may inquire: can there be an adequate theory of economic change which concentrates on the influence of persistent pressures to the comparative neglect of such patently irregular but powerful forces as those unleashed by war, major technological innovations and the wide variety of governmental measures designed to remould economic relationships in accordance with political urgencies? Some further explorations in these areas are presented in Chapter 11.

In short, economic change may be considered the result of various combinations of interacting forces—periodic and spasmodic, slow moving and volatile, widespread and narrowly localised. Concentration on selected components of total change offers the advantage of simplifying analysis, but only at the cost of dealing with fragments of the contexts in which they are shaped and with which they interact. More serious still, although the theorist may isolate particular forces for speculative analysis, he usually cannot extricate reliable measures of the effects of such forces from the composite product of all forces represented by statistical aggregates. Indeed, many of the regularities in economic behaviour suggested by statistical analysis may have been abstracted from measures of total economic change primarily by using statistical tests of conformity rather than by applying clearly formulated theories of the loci of significant clusters of behaviour. Under such conditions, statistical regularities may be merely a summation of homogeneous adjustment patterns, whatever their causes, rather than a measure of the changing effects of some theoretically meaningful grouping of economic forces. And projections of past trends into the future may have no roots whatever in economic analysis, often reflecting a mechanistic view of economic systems overlaid with some casual rationalisations rather than serious efforts to identify the influential forces in the past and the probable course of each in the future.

To help in responding to the needs of managerial economics, a variety of supplementary analytical approaches might be encouraged. Efforts to simplify analysis by sacrificing close approximations to reality might be paralleled by attempts to hold tight to reality even at the cost of analytical simplicity. The search for uniformities need not preclude intensive examination of sectors lacking this characteristic. And the uncovering of broad, persistent uniformities might well be accompanied by the study of localised and temporary uniformities. The thorough explanation of the complex of changes within a particular period might be as valuable an objective of economic theory as the explanation of some narrower segment of change over longer periods. Even variables and relationships which apparently do not undergo uniform movements may become the foci of meaningful research by concentrating such efforts on the analysis of processes of interaction and sequences of change. Moreover, analysis of the possibility that much of the regularity in economic change is simply the result of conflicting irregularities may be as fruitful as the hypothesis that such regularities are attributable essentially to component regularities. Illustrations of the latter two points are provided in Chapter 9.

1.3.4 On Relevant Measures

The requirements of managerial economics also tend to intensify the effects of some of the conceptual weaknesses of measurements already becoming apparent in macro-economic analyses. Among these, two of the most significant centre around changes in the nature of particular resources or outputs through time and changes in the composition of aggregate measures of such inputs or outputs. In both cases, the pressure for statistical comparability over time encourages under-estimating the significance of such changes, whereas the pressure for increasing precision in measurement tends to undermine statistical comparability. The resulting compromises represent errors whose significance depends on the purpose for which the measurement is made as well as on the theoretical basis for linking the particular variable which has been measured to the analytical concept by means of which such adjustments are interpreted.

Changes in the nature of products may affect the two most fundamental measures in economics: quantity and unit value or price. If a product has changed in size, complexity or other characteristics, a basic judgement must be made concerning the significance of these modifications. If these are regarded as significant, output levels can no longer be compared with previous periods on the basis of the number of units produced, because each unit now represents either more or less output than before—nor are prices comparable any longer if they refer to product units representing changed levels of output. Thus, determinations of the magnitude of changes in output and price levels depend on the criteria of significance which are employed. And this obviously raises the question of what aspects of output should be measured in order to accord with the analytical models used in interpreting such output variations. All data depend on the theory underlying their measurements [3, pp. 96–7]. From the producer's viewpoint, output may be measured in terms of the volume or value of the resources absorbed into production, or in terms of the physical quantity of products. From the consumers' viewpoint, output might be measured in terms of the expected volume of service values to be obtained over the life of the product as modified by considerations of attractiveness, reliability, safety and operating costs. Inasmuch as the criteria specified in defining output then provide the yardstick for determining whether product changes are significant, it is apparent that considerable differences could result in the output and price adjustments found through shifting from one criterion to another. Perhaps the most extreme form of this problem occurs in seeking to differentiate between changes in the quantity and in the price of services such as medical care.

Even more serious differences in evaluations of the significance of changes in the nature of inputs and outputs may be expected as such evaluations reflect progressively greater involvement in the direct application of resulting measurements. Thus, while many macro-economic analysts seem quite content to measure outputs in terms of kilowatt-hours of electricity generated and tons of steel products shipped, and inputs in terms of tons of iron ore and coal consumed, managers in the electric power and steel industries need far more detailed measures to appraise input–output relationships, unit costs, prices and other bases for performance evaluation—as is discussed in Chapter 3. It should also be emphasised, however, that over-generalised judgements about the significance of changes in the nature of outputs, whether attributable to inexpertness or casual expediency, may seriously undermine the validity of macro-economic analyses of annual rates of change in outputs and product prices, where differences between 2 and 4 per cent may be of critical significance for the shaping of public policies on such issues as growth and inflation.

A similar array of problems must be faced in measuring changes in aggregates of inputs or outputs or prices, or in seeking to interpret changes in such statistical series. In this case, one set of difficulties concerns the selection of some common denominator for encompassing otherwise heterogeneous elements. This may be illustrated by efforts to measure changes in aggregate output by using relative prices to weight the changes in each of the constituent product categories—as discussed in Chapters 3 and 9—with consequent problems for interpreting resulting changes and for measuring the effects of resource-saving innovations. A second set of problems is faced in seeking to differentiate between the effects of parallel changes in all components and shifts in the proportions represented by the various components. Cyclical and long-term adjustments in wage rates for given industries provide quite common examples of the differential role of these two influences—and the need for operating managements to uncover both as a basis for cost control and pricing purposes. A third set of problems, which deserves fuller recognition, concerns the hazards of seeking to establish relationships among aggregates which may be analytically untenable except at the levels where such variables interact directly. Analysis of the relationship between industry aggregates for profits and growth, or the adoption of technological innovations with a view to determining the relative incentives and rewards for expansion and innovation in different sectors of industry, would seem to illustrate such a dubious approach. It is apparent, for example, that decisions to adopt given innovations must be made at the level of the firm and can be implemented only at the level of the plant, thus emphasising the likelihood of differences among the plants and firms constituting the industry. Moreover, the profit effects of such decisions (or of others seeking to promote growth) are felt at the level of the firm, and gains by some firms frequently involve losses by their competitors. Thus, the relationships between these industry aggregates would seem to be the passive resultant of an array of heterogeneous relationships actively moulded by managerial decisions and market responses at the level of the constituent firms. This is discussed in Chapters 9 and 11.

In addition to the preceding areas of measurement problems which reach beyond managerial economics alone, attention should be drawn to others more narrowly concerned with the development of this field. One of the most worrying difficulties involves the continuing absence of reasonably effective and measurable surrogates for some of the central concepts in the ostensibly relevant sectors of economic theory. Aside from the frequently cited instances of marginal costs and marginal productivity, these include input factor isoquants, scale economies, the price elasticity of demand and similar bases for decision making. Although some of the preceding instances may yet prove viable, experience to date casts even stronger doubts on the operational usefulness of another group of theoretical concepts, including physical capital, real costs and embodied as against disembodied technical progress. If these and related concepts continue to defy efforts to contrive useful approximations, the direct contributions of extant micro-economic theory to the further development of managerial economics may be severely limited. On the other hand, the vigorous development of the industrial and other economic sectors subject to complex trains of managerial decisions opens the possibility that comprehensive field studies of what decisions are made, how they are made, and the means by which they are rendered reasonably consistent with other decisions, may help to enrich the theoretical structure and analytical tools of micro-economics—just as has been the case in other scientific disciplines which have objectives reaching beyond logical consistency alone.

1.3.5 Other Analytical Needs of Managerial Economics

Empirical studies in economics have been dominated by the search for reasonably stable relationships among statistical series representing the variables in *ex ante* or *ex post* models. Despite the endlessly repeated *caveats* in statistical theory (for a recent expression of despair about the disregard of such *caveats*, see [7]) these are then used either to imply causal sequences with obvious implications for control efforts, or to estimate the effects of changes in the independent variables on the dependent variable as the basis for forecasting or planning. While these approaches may be useful at certain levels of aggregation, they fall far short of the requirements of managerial economics. Specifically, such studies sample intricate activity systems rather than providing rounded descriptions of the whole.

But correlation ratios do not provide any sound bases for describing the linkages among the test samples taken, nor for evaluating the relationships between the measured and the unmeasured components of the system. The manager, on the other hand, realises that most of the ostensibly independent variables are strongly or weakly coupled to other elements of the system, that some activity sectors are more responsive to changed instructions than others, and that intervening linkages need not adjust automatically to shifts in intended outcomes. Hence the analytical objectives in managerial economics tend to press for increasingly detailed elucidation of the successive steps and processes whereby changes in major aspects of performance are effected.

This discussion is also relevant to a second set of problems commonly faced in managerial economics: the difficulty of determining the specific outcomes of given decisions as the basis for testing or modifying the analytical models used. One reason for this, noted immediately above, is the multiplicity of intervening linkages between the application of a given decision and its eventual results. A second reason is that the management of complex systems involves a continuous flow of problems and decisions with differing but overlapping sectoral and time foci. A third reason is that the implementation of decisions in real time involves responsiveness to changes in objectives, information and operating conditions, as well as learning from the early and continuing feedback of experience with the new decisions. Such considerations reinforce earlier warnings about the dangers of inferring managerial intentions from actual results and about the difficulties of interpreting the implications of statistical correlations for decision making. In addition, however, they also strengthen the case for developing more comprehensive information networks encompassing physical and financial measures at multiple levels of aggregation over a wide range of time periods. This would provide sounder bases for tracing the effects of particular decisions over progressively broader, and hence increasingly entangled, domains of activity and time, as indicated in Chapter 9.

The need to integrate the findings of managerial economists with those of engineering, finance, marketing and other specialists as part of the larger decision-making process is likely to encourage one more change in analytical methods. In place of the usual practice of sealing off his model from disturbing influences via reasonable assumptions, often generated by a desire for analytical convenience combined with ignorance about the forces being excluded, the managerial economist may find it more fruitful to formulate such assumptions with the advice of such experts. Doing so may not only enhance management's responsiveness to his recommendations, but, more important, may open the way for the gradual development of models encompassing an expanding array of specialised models and thus provide sounder bases for integrated decision making.

In short, these introductory observations have suggested that the development of managerial economics is hardly out of its infancy and have called attention to some of the areas in which development efforts might prove fruitful. Before proceeding to explore some of these areas further, it may be worth repeating the judgement that most advances required are likely to enrich economics as a whole as well as to strenghten the decision-making processes by which resources are allocated and utilised.

2 Managerial Control Ratios: an Integrated Analytical Framework

Economic development rests heavily on two closely interrelated processes: specialisation and integration. The increasing specialisation of human capacities, organisational functions, productive facilities and other resources offers the enticing prospect of still further gains in efficiency along with reductions in cost. But these potentials can be realised only if the growing multiplicity of specialised operations can be effectively fitted together so as to minimise overlapping, conflicts and dislocations among the parts. For many years now the largely technical developments which underlie specialisation have been forging ahead more rapidly than the capacity of industrial establishments to utilise fully the advances which they offer. One of the major reasons for this lag has been the failure to improve managerial control techniques, which are the tools of integration.

This generalised pressure for more effective integrated decision making has been intensified by progressive increases in the size and complexity of major firms in most industries. Whether such expansion has been due to expected gains in efficiency or to market power, one obvious result is that increasing arrays of economic resources are being allocated on the basis of intra-firm decisions. Such choices commonly cover different product lines, different functional fields (e.g. procurement, production, pricing, finance) and different time cycles for effecting decisions (ranging from setting weekly output schedules to planning long-term capacity increases).

Under these conditions, some companies have frankly given up the struggle to develop the more advanced control techniques needed to integrate vast operations effectively. Instead, they have granted increasing autonomy to their major divisions, thus resigning themselves to foregoing those additional benefits of specialisation which would flow from operating each division as part of an organic whole. This may well represent a defensible position for the moment, in view of the obvious shortcomings of available control techniques. But such a policy tends to prove increasingly costly as technical progress continues to expand the potentials of further specialisation.

2.1 MANAGERIAL REQUIREMENTS

The most significant progress achieved so far in the development of more effective managerial controls centres around the collection of increasing information about the details of inputs, outputs and costs at all levels of operation, and this approach has been sharply stimulated by the availability of computers. But more information is not enough, no matter how prompt and accurate it may be. Indeed, as current operating information becomes more voluminous, management is in danger of being engulfed by a mass of findings whose significance for current decision making is not readily apparent. As a result, top management may either disregard such material, hoping that it is somehow proving useful in the lower echelons, or it may be led into making piecemeal decisions on the piecemeal problems reflected in each of the numerous operating reports.

What, then, is the most serious obstacle to the development of more effective techniques of managerial control? Curiously enough, in view of the constant emphasis on the need to be practical in business, the urgent need is for a theory, or a framework of ideas, which will indicate what aspects of operations constitute the strategic core of operations planning and analysis. Stated somewhat differently, we need a basis for selecting from among the thousands of possible measures which may be employed, some small number which will identify the major determinants of success.

In the final analysis, top management cannot evaluate past results, or formulate effective new policies, merely by considering each sector of operations by itself. Its basic problem is to integrate, rather than to collate, the policies guiding component operations. And this undertaking involves not only the appraisal of alternative price policies, output policies, or means of raising productivity. Top management also faces the more difficult and more important task of analysing the interacting effects of particular policies in each sector. Specifically, top management must seek not the best policy in each area of operations, but rather the best combination of component policies—those which most effectively reinforce one another in promoting the objectives of the firm.

The basic purpose of this chapter is to present a new conception of the strategic areas of decision making. Every effort will be made to use variables which approximate as closely as possible to the recognised foci of managerial data collection and policy formulation. Experience to date suggests that the resulting measures are generalised enough to permit wide application, and yet specific enough to yield directly useful results when applied to actual plants and firms.

2.2 INTEGRATING PHYSICAL AND FINANCIAL
RESOURCE FLOWS

Efforts to dig beneath the final measure of business performance represented by the rate of profit on investment have long been dominated by various sets of financial ratios. Relationships among items in the income statement and balance sheet seem to have been developed into tools for appraising the soundness of the underlying structure by prospective lenders and investors. The influence of these viewpoints on capital markets and the corporate financial officers who deal with them has ensured continued reliance on such diagnostic tools and even their further elaboration. Like other special purpose tools, however, their usefulness drops off rapidly when forced into alien tasks. And the responsibilities of operating management are sufficiently different from those of lenders and investors to require a comparably differentiated structure of evaluative criteria.

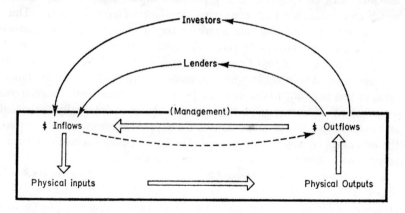

Fig. 2.1   Physical and financial resource flows within the firm

Fig. 2.1 helps to clarify some of these differences. It shows business activity as a four-stage process consisting of: (a) inflows of financial resources from investors and lenders; (b) the conversion of these into physical inputs; (c) the transformation of such inputs into physical outputs; and (d) the conversion of physical goods and services through sales into financial outflows which are allocated to lenders and investors, and fed back into the business. Investors and lenders virtually monopolise the upper, or financial, level of these flows—substituting for the actual conversions into physical resources and eventually back into financial flows a phantom (broken line) line running directly from dollar inflows to dollar outflows.

The financial ratios favoured by suppliers of funds depend, of course, on the nature of their involvements. Short-term lenders are understandably preoccupied with the security of their commitments as reflected by such ratios as current assets to current liabilities, inventories to sales and net working capital to sales. Long-term lenders are similarly concerned with the security of their resources as reflected by such ratios as sales to fixed investment and long term debt to net worth. Similarly, investors concentrate on the relationships between financial inflows and outflows which affect their prospective shares, as measured by such ratios as profit to total investment and to equity investment. But all of these interests are encompassed by the financial level of flows and, therefore, financial evaluations dominate the annual reports of corporate performance from which these ratios are determined.

Although committed to certain of the same objectives as investors, management's primary responsibilities centre around the adjustment of the level and composition of the physical inputs and outputs through which financial inflows are converted into larger financial returns. Thus, as indicated in the figure, management requires criteria of performance relating financial outlays to physical input quantities, physical output quantities to physical input quantities, and the financial value of outputs to their physical volume. In addition, management needs sufficient elaboration of this network to differentiate between short-term and longer-term determinants of aggregate performance, and between internally controlled and externally imposed adjustments. Finally, management would require the extension of such an integrated structure of performance criteria to progressively lower levels of organisational activity.

The resulting framework would help to trace changes in aggregate levels of performance back through intervening linkages to the initiating units. It would guide efforts to explore the likely ramifications of prospective changes in specified operations. Moreover, it would assist planning by specifying the magnitudes of component adjustments necessary to achieve proposed aggregate advances, and by highlighting the interactions likely to be triggered by prospective innovations.

2.3 BASIC AREAS OF DECISION MAKING

In accordance with common practice, the present analysis will begin with the assumption that management's primary measure of aggregate performance is the rate of profit on investment. This assumption is wholly incorrect, of course, only if emphasised to the exclusion of all other objectives (see, for example [1, Chapter 4]).

The areas of decision making which affect this objective may be identified by proceeding through the five simple stages of analysis reviewed below. In each case, the verbal description of relationships will be supplemented by their translation into algebraic identities in order to highlight the specific measures which are applicable.

The ratio of profit (before income tax) to total investment may be regarded as determined by the ratio of profit to physical output and by the ratio of output to total investment:

$$(1) \qquad \frac{\text{Profit}}{\text{Total Investment}} \equiv \frac{\text{Profit}}{\text{Output}} \times \frac{\text{Output}}{\text{Total Investment}}$$

But profit per unit of output (the middle term in (1)) is determined by the difference between the average gross receipts per unit of output (i.e. average realised price) and average total costs per unit of output:

$$(2) \qquad \frac{\text{Profit}}{\text{Output}} \equiv \frac{\text{Value of Products}}{\text{Output}} - \frac{\text{Total Costs}}{\text{Output}}$$

In seeking the determinants of changes in the ratio of output to total investment (the final term in (1)) one may follow the process whereby the latter is linked to the former. Specifically, part of total investment is allocated to facilities and equipment which determine productive capacity and it is the latter which determines output potentials. Hence, changes in the ratio of output to total investment may be regarded as determined by the ratios of output to productive capacity, of productive capacity to fixed investment, and of fixed investment to total investment:

$$(3) \qquad \frac{\text{Output}}{\text{Total Investment}} \equiv \frac{\text{Output}}{\text{Capacity}} \times \frac{\text{Capacity}}{\text{Fixed Investment}} \times \frac{\text{Fixed Investment}}{\text{Total Investment}}$$

Thus, changes in the ratio of profit to total investment may be attributed to five areas of performance: product prices (Total Product Value/Output); unit costs (Total Costs/Output); utilisation of facilities (Output/Capacity); productivity of facilities and equipment (Capacity/Fixed Investment); and the allocation of investment resources between capital goods and working capital (Fixed Investment/Total Investment):

$$(4) \qquad \frac{\text{Profit}}{\text{Total Investment}} \equiv \left(\frac{\text{Product Value}}{\text{Output}} - \frac{\text{Total Costs}}{\text{Output}} \right)$$
$$\times \frac{\text{Output}}{\text{Capacity}} \times \frac{\text{Capacity}}{\text{Fixed Investment}} \times \frac{\text{Fixed Investment}}{\text{Total Investment}}$$

2+

Moreover, a shift in focus to the ratio of profit to equity investment would add a sixth area of decision making concerned with the structure of financing:

$$(5) \quad \frac{\text{Profit}}{\text{Equity Investment}} \equiv \frac{\text{Profit}}{\text{Total Investment}} \div \frac{\text{Equity Investment}}{\text{Total Investment}}$$

Useful bases for the planning and evaluation efforts of top management seem to be provided by these six managerial control ratios, for they represent a blend of physical and financial aspects of resource flows, of short- and long-term perspectives, and of the stock and flow components of the system. Specifically, since capacity, fixed and total investment tend to change very much more slowly than sales (or value of product), costs and output, the first three ratios in expression (4) above would tend to determine-short term changes in Profit/Total Investment. Long-term changes in the latter would be traceable, in turn, not only to the remaining two control ratios, but also to persistent trends in the first three. Both the physical and financial aspects of stocks and flows are accordingly encompassed.

Application of this network of managerial control ratios to the performance records of particular firms or plants can reveal which of the strategic areas of decision making contributed most or least to observed adjustments in the rate of profits on investment. Moreover, if the analysis is applied to records covering a long period, the findings may be expected to reveal any persistent trends in the sources of upward and downward pressures on the rate of returns, and also to spotlight the sectors most likely to shift between exercising favourable and unfavourable effects.

This analytical framework may also be used in forward planning to help analyse either the probable effects of expected changes on the rate of return or the alternative combinations of adjustments needed to achieve specified profits.

All of the data required for applying the proposed control ratios are readily available in most companies, with the possible exception of appropriate measures of aggregate physical output and of productive capacity. The first of these presents no problem, however, because all industrial establishments have complete information about the volume and value of all products so that the aggregate can readily be calculated. Briefly, the change in the physical volume of total output between two periods may be determined by weighting the change in the output of each product category with the average price of the category in the two periods, and then averaging the results. A further explanation is offered in Chapter 3. For a detailed discussion, see [2, pp. 92-97].

Although the precise measurement of productive capacity presents serious problems in theory, reasonably acceptable estimates of practical capacity can generally be made without too much effort. The basic data required are usually available as the by-product of various plant operation and control functions, including engineering, production control and the establishment of cost and production standards. Moreover, rough estimates at least of productive capacity are also required for production planning, capital goods procurement, the balancing of work loads and other areas of decision making. In developing such estimates, the task is usually simplified by concentrating on the level of capacity which can be attained under practical operating conditions for the dominant product-mix patterns on the assumption that products and processes will remain unchanged, that sufficient labour and materials will be available to fully utilise capital facilities, and that prices and costs will be such as to encourage the efficient utilisation of all except clearly marginal and obsolete resources [3, pp. 101–4].

2.4 COMPARISON OF MANAGERIAL CONTROL RATIOS AND FINANCIAL RATIOS

The traditional array of financial ratios centres around total sales, total costs and total profits from the income statement, and around fixed investment, working capital, total investment and net worth from the balance sheet. Differences may be observed, however, in the detailed subdivisions of costs and investment used by analysts [3, 5, 7]. In evaluating general performance, the ratios used most commonly relate: profit and sales to total and equity investment; profit and costs to sales; and working capital and net worth to total investment. Models used by well-known industrial corporations for top management control purposes follow closely parallel lines. DuPont emphasises Profit/Sales, Sales/Total Investment and Profit/Total Investment as well as the composition of cost of sales, of working capital and of total investment [7]. Monsanto concentrates on Profits/Investment, Net Income/Investment, Sales/Property, and the ratios of selling expense, operating expense and cost of goods sold to sales [8]. Armstrong Cork and West Virginia Pulp and Paper reflect essentially similar patterns [4].

Comparisons reveal that the managerial control ratios cover most of the basic variables entering into these financial ratios and would cover most of their key relationships as well, if—as shown in Figure 2.2—the network of managerial control ratios was elaborated to include the following three intermediate relationships:

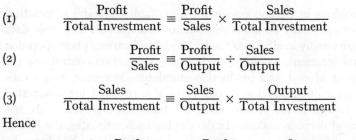

$$(1) \quad \frac{\text{Profit}}{\text{Total Investment}} \equiv \frac{\text{Profit}}{\text{Sales}} \times \frac{\text{Sales}}{\text{Total Investment}}$$

$$(2) \quad \frac{\text{Profit}}{\text{Sales}} \equiv \frac{\text{Profit}}{\text{Output}} \div \frac{\text{Sales}}{\text{Output}}$$

$$(3) \quad \frac{\text{Sales}}{\text{Total Investment}} \equiv \frac{\text{Sales}}{\text{Output}} \times \frac{\text{Output}}{\text{Total Investment}}$$

Hence

$$(4) \quad \frac{\text{Profit}}{\text{Total Investment}} \equiv \frac{\text{Profit}}{\text{Output}} \times \frac{\text{Output}}{\text{Total Investment}}$$

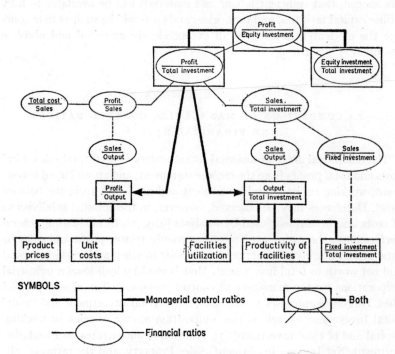

Fig. 2.2   Comparison of managerial control and financial ratios

In addition, the managerial control ratios include consideration of changes in prices, output, capacity, facilities utilisation and investment requirements per unit of capacity—and delineate their interactions with one another and with solely financial aspects of operations in shaping adjustments in measures of aggregate performance. These additional bases for managerial control obviously cannot be used in place of the financial ratios. But it seems reasonable to suppose that, in most industrial situations, management would secure additional, practically useful guides to control with a system of managerial control ratios supplementing pure income, outflow and investment relationships with a variety of measures designed to represent the physical side of production and to bridge the gap between the physical and financial aspects of operations.

2.5 ELABORATIONS OF THE NETWORK OF MANAGERIAL CONTROL RATIOS

Managerial control ratios also lend themselves to further disaggregation, identifying performance criteria for successively more specialised sectors of activity and permitting appraisal of the relative dominance of such results by internally controlled and by external forces, as shown in Figure 2.3.

For example, changes in Product Value/Output, or the average price received for all products, are traceable to adjustments not only in the price of each product but also in the relative volumes of different products sold—the former often being more responsive to direct management controls than the latter. Thus, an increase in each product price may be accompanied by a decrease in the average price received for all products, if sales of the lower priced products increase relative to sales of the higher priced products. Similarly, changes in average total costs per unit of output (Total Costs/Output) are determined not only by current changes in unit material, unit wage and each of the other component unit costs, but also by their respective proportions of total costs.* In turn, changes in each of these unit cost categories may be attributed to changes in the factor price and in the amount of that input required per unit of output, with the latter probably more responsive to direct managerial controls than the former.†

$$* \quad \left(\Delta \frac{\text{Total Costs}}{\text{Output}} \right)_{1-2} = \left[\left(\Delta \frac{\text{Materials Cost}}{\text{Output}} \right)_{1-2} \left(\frac{\text{Materials Cost}}{\text{Total Cost}} \right)_1 \right]$$

$$+ \left[\left(\Delta \frac{\text{Wages}}{\text{Output}} \right)_{1-2} \left(\frac{\text{Wages}}{\text{Total Cost}} \right)_1 \right]$$

$$+ \left[\left(\Delta \frac{\text{Other Costs}}{\text{Output}} \right)_{1-2} \left(\frac{\text{Other Costs}}{\text{Total Costs}} \right)_1 \right]$$

where 1 and 2 signify the beginning and end of the period. Other relevant models will be reviewed in Chapter 8.

† For example,

$$\left(\frac{\text{Materials Cost}}{\text{Output}} \right) = (\text{Materials Price}) \left(\frac{\text{Materials Quantity}}{\text{Output}} \right)$$

For further exploration of the factors affecting the productivity of each input factor, see [2, Chapter 7].

Continuing with this process of unravelling complex performance
measures into their components, changes in Output/Capacity may be
traced to two sets of factors. The firm's output adjustments may be due to
changes in the total market for such products and in the firm's share of
that total. Capacity adjustments may be due to technological advances,

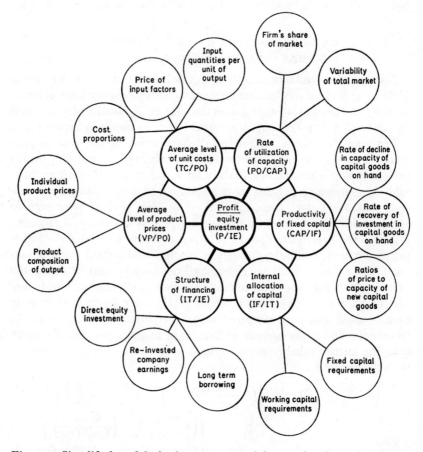

Fig. 2.3   Simplified model of primary managerial control ratios and of factors
affecting them

to wear and obsolescence of the facilities and equipment, and to changes
in the stock due to acquisitions and retirements.

Following this line of reasoning, changes in Capacity/Fixed Investment
reflect adjustments in capacity relative to changes in net investment resulting from depreciation and obsolescence charges as well as payments for
newly acquired additions to the stock. Changes in Fixed Investment/Total

Investment reflect managerial estimates of the relative need for productive capacity and for working capital to promote and finance capacity utilisation.

Finally, managerial control ratios also encourage analysis of the continuous interaction of physical and financial aspects of operations in shaping aggregate performance adjustments in any sector. The successive linking of control ratios (each having one term identical with the ratio on either side) means that adjustments in output, capacity or fixed investment play inverse roles in adjacent ratios and thus cancel each other out, unless the initiating adjustment exercises differential effects on the two variables with which it interacts in these ratios. Thus, increases or decreases in capacity can affect Profit/Total Investment only if they induce differential changes in output and fixed investment, with which capacity is linked in the third and fourth control ratios. Any resulting changes in output and in fixed investment must then be traced through the remaining control ratios to assess the final effects of the capacity adjustment on Profit/Total Investment. Application of these managerial control ratios should reveal the relative contributions of the six strategic decision-making areas to observed adjustments in Profit/Total Investment.

2.6 DEVELOPING MORE EFFECTIVE THEORETICAL GUIDES FOR MANAGEMENT

Managerial control ratios can also help the development and utilisation of theoretical guides for shaping strategies to cope with the complexities of actual business systems. Only by replacing endless intuitive judgements by an analytical framework refined by empirical testing and adjustment can the foundations of decision making be strengthened.

One part of this process may be illustrated by recalling that, in the short term, changes in Profit/Total Investment are traceable to changes in product prices, total unit costs and output. Consideration of alternative decisions in these different sectors of performance must begin by recognising their interactions: prices affect output; output affects costs; and costs affect prices. This demonstrates the direct relevance for managerial evaluation of such traditional economic concepts as the price elasticity of demand and production cost functions—and also encourages efforts to determine the specific parameters of these functional relationships which apply to given industrial settings.

Managerial control ratios can also stimulate extensions of economic analysis. The traditional approach, for example, considers the relationship between adjustments in price and output, or between costs and output, assuming that all else remains unchanged. The managerial decision-making focus, however, stresses that any change in one determinant of Profit/ Total Investment tends to affect the others. It emphasises that management does not seek to maximise output or price alone, nor to minimise unit costs alone, but rather seeks to adjust each of these so as to optimise the net result of their interactions. Such needs are likely to encourage the development of more broadly inclusive theoretical models and, through their increased relevance, are likely to induce increased managerial interest in such guides.

In addition, managerial control ratios also suggest new foci for the shaping of economic concepts and analytical frameworks as well as for empirical research designed to clarify major patterns of industrial change. Further development of the concept of a functional relationship between productive capacity and fixed investment, for example, would seem to offer a useful supplement to prevailing preoccupations with the scale and capital-output ratio concepts. And managerial decision-making alternatives might be usefully clarified by developing average product price, average unit cost and physical output concepts for application to multi-product firms. Additional targets for analytical advances might include the patterning of long-term changes in unit profits, in the utilisation of capacity, in the productivity of capital, in the internal allocation of investment and in the structure of financing. (The latter might invite applications of recent work on the cost of capital and suggest extensions of such efforts.)

Finally, the object of extending the structure of managerial control ratios to progressively lower levels of organisational activity poses the problem for economic theory of developing guides to promote the most efficient allocation of resources *within* individual firms as well as between the resource aggregates comprising separate firms. It is apparent from the preceding discussion, of course, that the usual resort of minimising unit costs cannot offer an adequate guide to resource allocation within the firm since the means of adjusting unit costs may also affect the market demand for, and the price of, the products involved.

At the level of empirical research, the preceding analysis raises a wide range of questions which have a direct bearing on long-range planning for individual companies as well as on the comparative analysis of the cyclic and growth characteristics of different industries. Such questions might concern the nature and extent of stable adjustment patterns for individual and groups of managerial control ratios; the causes and effects of major changes in particular control ratios; and the relative magnitude and durability of the effects on Profit/Total Investment of changes in various control sectors as a guide to developing effective strategies in different industries.

In any event, the provision of a framework for planning and appraising performance which permits integrated consideration of different operating components from the standpoint of central management, and invites theoretical treatment as well as empirical testing, represents an additional important potential of the suggested structure of managerial control ratios.

This introductory discussion of managerial control ratios will be followed by detailed exploration of the productivity and cost relationships underlying them. After that there will be a presentation of the results of some empirical applications of the original model along with some further extensions which have been found useful in applications to large, multi-divisional firms.

3 Productivity

Changes in productivity levels are being increasingly recognised as a major influence on a wide range of managerial problems, including wage levels, cost–price relationships, capital investment requirements, labour utilisation and even competitive standing. The very importance of these problems, however, emphasises the seriousness of continued widespread misunderstanding of the nature and effects of productivity adjustments.

Productivity analyses have been undertaken by such a variety of specialists and in such differing contexts that few can cope with the broadly dispersed literature. It is not surprising, therefore, that the same problems are rediscovered time and again, that faulty concepts remain in use and that empirical findings are often misinterpreted. Such shortcomings will continue to hamper the development of this field until previous advances are more effectively consolidated and the current frontiers more clearly delineated. In this chapter, therefore, certain past findings will be used as points of departure for considering the problems and means of effecting further gains.

One comprehensive exploration of productivity analysis [5] (see also [4, 7, 9, 15]) suggested four general conclusions, along with their analytical foundations, which seem to have withstood subsequent consideration well enough to serve as bases for this undertaking:

(1) that productivity analysis serves a variety of purposes and hence requires a corresponding variety of appropriately designed measures;

(2) that the productivity of any activity system should refer not to any single input–output ratio, but to an integrated network of such measures;

(3) that the effects of productivity adjustments depend not only on their magnitudes, but also on the sources responsible for them, on the nature of the changes in input–output relationships involved, and on managerial choices among alternative means of harnessing their potential benefits; and

(4) that evaluating such effects requires supplementing physical with cost measures and then with successively broader criteria until these reflect the guiding objectives of the system under study.

Such conclusions imply that productivity adjustments may assume many forms, that apparent increases in productivity levels need not always be beneficial, that the same pattern of productivity changes may have quite different effects in dissimilar circumstances and, finally, that productivity increases are not ends in themselves but merely one means of promoting more fundamental ends. Further development is necessary to extend the original analysis beyond standardised commodity production to other economic activities, beyond a plant or firm to larger aggregates, and beyond short periods. But such elaborations of this framework first require the strengthening of its conceptual foundations.

3.1 BASIC CONCEPTS

Many of the limitations of productivity analysis are traceable to the effects of its early development in agricultural and simple manufacturing processes. The shifting of such efforts from relatively primitive production operations to highly complex activity systems, and from the context of engineering measurements of physical relationships to that of managerial appraisals of economic relationships, requires far-reaching readjustments in purposes, concepts and methods which have often been overlooked.

3.1.1 On the Nature of Productivity Adjustments

It is a striking anomaly that acceptance of productivity as an important measure of economic performance has grown simultaneously with the declining relevance of its common meanings to modern economic processes. One of these meanings derives from the agricultural concept of relative fertility and reflects differences in the output potentials of equal-sized plots of land (actual yields being expected to fluctuate in all plots with weather changes). Because such differences are attributed to the unequal natural endowments of the plots, this particular input is regarded as the active or creative agent in determining output differentials, while other inputs are viewed as essentially passive. The other common meaning of productivity derives from the engineering concept of efficiency and reflects the relationship between the actual and the potential output for any process, as may be illustrated by the percentage of the energy potential of fuels actually converted into brake horsepower or other forms of energy output by an engine.

Differences between the input creativity and the conversion efficiency concepts of productivity are important enough to warrant reviewing them in some detail. Specifically, the conversion concept shifts the focus of analysis from disparities in performance potentials among different systems to changes in the proportion of each system's potentials actually utilised; it shifts the scope of measurement from comparing total output with one input to comparing it with total input; and it shifts the basis for explaining productivity changes from the creativity of active inputs (for these would alter the system's potentials) to the effectiveness of the conversion process, which embodies engineering (and perhaps managerial) contributions to system performance. Incidentally, the latter also illustrates attendant differences in interpretive viewpoints between farm owners and process engineers concerning what is important and, therefore, to be measured. Another important difference is that the input creativity approach emphasises the non-comparability of inputs and outputs, whereas the conversion efficiency approach stresses the reduction of both to common terms (e.g. British Thermal Unit equivalents)—thus limiting fertility comparisons to systems with similar inputs and similar outputs, whereas relative efficiency levels may be compared among quite dissimilar mass and energy conversion systems (e.g. thermal, mechanical and electrical).

Despite such sharp distinctions, prevailing concepts of the nature of productivity adjustments reflect an unrationalised mixture of both approaches, thus sharing the limitations of each as well as the conflicts between them. This has come about partly because the development of economic activity systems has endowed most of them with characteristics associated with both these primitive concepts, and partly because differences among interest groups have encouraged comparably polarised approaches.

Each of these concepts of productivity adjustments is weakened by its myopic concentration on one component of a complex of relationships. By attributing increases in total output per unit of a given input to improvements in the qualitative contributions of that factor, the input creativity concept implies that there have been no changes in: (a) the nature and composition of output; (b) the volume, quality and utilisation of each of the other inputs; and (c) the nature of production processes. By attributing input–output adjustments solely to processing innovations which reduce the wastage of inputs, or increase the effectiveness with which processes harness the potential contributions of inputs, the conversion efficiency concept likewise implies no attendant changes in other conditions. Moreover, the general conclusion in each case that increases in output–input ratios are economically beneficial rests on the further assumption that factor and product prices are unchanged. In each case, therefore, the interpretation may be valid only when all of these implied conditions are complied with.

Reasonable approximations to such restrictive conditions do occur, of course. The former may be illustrated by increases in butter output due to the use of richer milk, and the latter by increases in heat produced from unchanged inputs through improved combustion conditions in the same furnace. But such cases tend to be increasingly uncommon because modern economic systems tend to generate unceasing pressures for improvements both through changing products, processes and inputs and through improving their adjustments to one another. Indeed, the original fertility concept has become inadequate even in respect to agriculture in view of the responsiveness of yields to improved seeds, more fertiliser, farm machinery and pesticides. And the original conversion efficiency concept has become inadequate even in respect to most processing innovations because of their tendency to alter the quality and relative quantities of various inputs and, often, of outputs as well.

The widespread confusion resulting from the application of such primitive concepts to modern industry may be illustrated at three levels. At the level of basic concepts, one may note that productivity adjustments are usually measured by comparing total output with one input, as in the input creativity approach; but results are interpreted as indicating changes in the efficiency of the process—although output per man-hour, for example, cannot measure variations in the productive efficiency of most industrial operations, nor in the efficiency of labour efforts alone, nor even in the sheer magnitude of labour's contributions to output (which would be more closely akin to the input creativity concept). At the level of interpreting findings, each input group's view of itself as the sole source of creative gains in productivity, despite the active involvement of other inputs in modern production adjustments, often leads to simultaneous claims by several groups for credit in accounting for observed gains in output–input ratios (and to unembarrassed reversals of the same arguments in blaming unfavourable adjustments on other factors). And at the level of appraisal, the general, but unwarranted assumption that all improvements in input–output ratios are necessarily beneficial may be traced back to these primitive conceptions that such gains can only be due to the enhanced creativity of inputs, to reduced wastage of inputs or to process improvements which more fully harness the productive potentials of inputs.

To analyse the complex domain of input–output relationships in modern industry, however, it is necessary to relax the unrealistic constraints inherent in the above approaches. This involves broadening the concept of the nature of productivity adjustments to include the effects of changes: in the quality and degree of utilisation of any or all inputs as well as in the

quantitative proportions of various inputs; and in the qualitative characteristics of each product as well as in the quantitative proportions of
different products. As a result, three new problems of measurement must
be dealt with: how to combine different product (or input) flows into
meaningful aggregates; how to deal with qualitative changes in particular
inputs or outputs through time; and how to keep input and output
measurements independent of one another.

3.1.2 On the Objectives and Requirements of Productivity Measurement

The absence of a unitary concept of efficiency which is widely applicable
means that productivity studies in modern economies cannot undertake to
measure the efficiency of a given activity system. Instead, such studies
must be designed to appraise the effects of changes in various input–output relationships on specified performance objectives of the system, thus
shifting from a descriptive to an analytical viewpoint. Inasmuch as different activity systems are likely to have different objectives, and each system
is likely to have a variety of performance criteria—as will be discussed in
greater detail later—it follows that each system may be characterised by
an array of productivity relationships at any given time and also that
identical measurements may have widely disparate meanings in different
systems. This does not mean that there is anything especially subtle about
the process of productivity measurement [18] but only that the variety of
relationships is so great that making effective choices requires defining the
particular activity sectors to be probed as well as the evaluation criteria
to be applied.

It also follows that merely juxtaposing the comparative magnitudes of
specified inputs and outputs reveals nothing more than the level of, or
changes in, the given ratio. To evaluate such quantitative findings, the
variables should be derived from an analytical framework which encompasses all of the inputs and outputs of the system and provides a theory of
how it functions.* Such a framework permits working backward from
specified performance objectives to determine which variables should be
studied, how they should be related to one another, and what measurements should be used for each in order to make most use of resulting findings. Accordingly, productivity measurements cannot provide the basis
for a theory of the determinants of effectiveness in marketing, education
[3, pp. 19–28], or research [13]; on the contrary, such theories are prere-
quisites for determining the elements and structure of input–output

---

* A widely accepted contrasting view is expressed by Solow [17] as follows:
'The economist really need not know at all what it feels like to be inside a steel
plant . . . he quantifies technological change by making measurements of output per hour, or output per unit of this or input per unit of that.'

measurements which are meaningful for evaluating the performance of these systems. In general, then, the less rigorous and detailed the analytical framework used, the less significant may be the measures contrived and the more vulnerable the interpretations attempted, as has been amply illustrated by indiscriminate reliance on output per man-hour measures over a wide range of economic activities.

The significance of given input–output ratios depends not only on the analytical relevance of the categories used, but on five additional requirements whose intuitive recognition in simple production systems has often been overlooked in other applications. Two of these concern the qualitative stability of each input and output category through time and the susceptibility to measurement of those attributes which bear directly on the evaluative criteria being employed. The former emphasises that changes in the inputs or outputs may confuse interpretation of observed adjustments in quantitative input–output relationships, as may be illustrated by changes in the productivity of smelters traceable to variations in the metal content of ores. And the second warns of the dangers of quantifying peripheral rather than core aspects of input and output flows, as may be illustrated by the common use of tonnage shipped to measure the output of steel mills, although most production efforts beyond the furnaces seek to increase the value of products by changing the shape, and incidentally reducing the weight, of the steel being processed.

The three remaining requirements are that the numerator and denominator of productivity ratios should relate to congruent sectors of activity; that they should relate to properly linked time periods; and that the contribution of the input must be absorbed into, and affect the output. In emphasising that the inputs and outputs being compared must relate to the same department, plant, firm or industry, the first requirement merely seeks to prevent such errors as comparing all of the inputs of a plant with only part of its output (e.g. relating total man-hours in an integrated steel mill to the ingot tonnage output of the furnaces). The second counsels against using input and output data for the same period unless all of the input is absorbed into the output within that period. Thus, in an operation involving a six-month production cycle, it may be more meaningful to compare output levels with the material consumption levels of six months earlier than with their current levels. The direct implication of the third requirement is that outputs should be compared with input measurements covering all of the factors which can be substituted for one another. To illustrate: it would be easy to misinterpret changes in the ratio of pig iron input to open hearth steel output if no account were taken of corresponding changes in the scrap steel inputs which may be used in place of pig iron.

Finally, the uses to be made of productivity findings may generate additional requirements bearing on the design of effective measures. For example, efforts to determine the economic significance of changes in physical input–output relationships, or the physical bases for changes in economic relationships, may require a superstructure of additional measures, as will be shown later. And if appraisal efforts are also to be directed towards the managerial objectives of improvement and control, productivity measures might be redesigned so as to maximise the separation of components which are responsive to managerial guidance from those which are not.

3.1.3 On the Role of Productivity Networks

The analytical approach to productivity measurement also requires a fuller mapping of the complex of relationships likely to influence the functioning of an activity system. (For an interesting but much simpler approach to the elements of productivity changes, see Salter [12].) In the study cited at the beginning of this chapter [5], such elaboration involved three successive stages: the first extended the analysis to cover each of the basic direct inputs other than man-hours of labour (purchased materials and fixed investment); the second included the proportions in which these direct inputs are combined in order to take account of substitutions among inputs (e.g. machines in place of labour, or a shift from some made components to bought ones); and the third permitted differentiation between the productivity of inputs when fully used and reductions in their output contributions due to partial idleness (as in the case of under-utilised equipment).

Briefly summarised, the approach which was employed began with a series of six two-factor models. For example, changes in output per man-hour could be attributed to changes both in the proportions in which man-hour inputs are combined with purchased material inputs and in the productivity of the latter (as represented by the level of such inputs relative to output). Alternatively, changes in output per man-hour could be attributed to the proportions in which man-hours are combined with actively utilised fixed investment and to the productivity of fixed investment (as represented by the ratio of productive capacity to investments in fixed assets). Similar twin models can be formulated to account for changes in the productivity of fixed investment as well as in the productivity of purchased materials and supplies.

$$\text{(A)} \qquad \frac{\text{Output}}{\text{Man-Hours}} \equiv \frac{\text{Materials Volume}}{\text{Man-Hours}} \times \frac{\text{Output}}{\text{Materials Volume}}$$

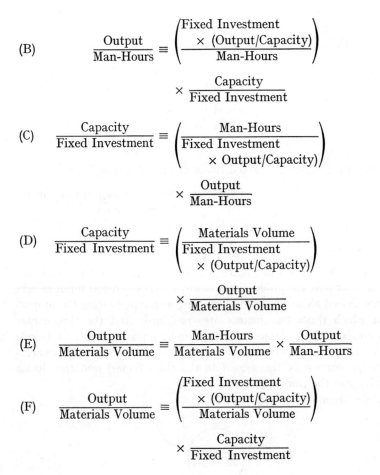

(B) $\quad \dfrac{\text{Output}}{\text{Man-Hours}} \equiv \left(\dfrac{\begin{array}{c}\text{Fixed Investment} \\ \times \text{ (Output/Capacity)}\end{array}}{\text{Man-Hours}} \right)$

$\qquad\qquad\qquad \times \dfrac{\text{Capacity}}{\text{Fixed Investment}}$

(C) $\quad \dfrac{\text{Capacity}}{\text{Fixed Investment}} \equiv \left(\dfrac{\text{Man-Hours}}{\begin{array}{c}\text{Fixed Investment} \\ \times \text{ Output/Capacity)}\end{array}} \right)$

$\qquad\qquad\qquad \times \dfrac{\text{Output}}{\text{Man-Hours}}$

(D) $\quad \dfrac{\text{Capacity}}{\text{Fixed Investment}} \equiv \left(\dfrac{\text{Materials Volume}}{\begin{array}{c}\text{Fixed Investment} \\ \times \text{ (Output/Capacity)}\end{array}} \right)$

$\qquad\qquad\qquad \times \dfrac{\text{Output}}{\text{Materials Volume}}$

(E) $\quad \dfrac{\text{Output}}{\text{Materials Volume}} \equiv \dfrac{\text{Man-Hours}}{\text{Materials Volume}} \times \dfrac{\text{Output}}{\text{Man-Hours}}$

(F) $\quad \dfrac{\text{Output}}{\text{Materials Volume}} \equiv \left(\dfrac{\begin{array}{c}\text{Fixed Investment} \\ \times \text{ (Output/Capacity)}\end{array}}{\text{Materials Volume}} \right)$

$\qquad\qquad\qquad \times \dfrac{\text{Capacity}}{\text{Fixed Investment}}$

(For further discussion, see [5, pp. 61–8]. For a more recent use of identities to explore a related area, see Siegel [16].)

These six two-factor models were then elaborated into three three-factor models. For example, changes in output per man-hour could now be attributed to changes in the ratio of labour to materials inputs, the ratio of the latter to actively utilised fixed investment, and the productivity of such investment.

(G) $\quad \dfrac{\text{Output}}{\text{Man-Hours}} \equiv \dfrac{\text{Fixed Investment} \times \text{(Output/Capacity)}}{\text{Materials Volume}}$

$\qquad\qquad\qquad \times \dfrac{\text{Materials Volume}}{\text{Man-Hours}} \times \dfrac{\text{Capacity}}{\text{Fixed Investment}}$

(H) $\dfrac{\text{Capacity}}{\text{Fixed Investment}} \equiv \dfrac{\text{Materials Volume}}{\text{Man-Hours}}$

$$\times \dfrac{\text{Man-Hours}}{\text{Fixed Investment} \times (\text{Output/Capacity})}$$

$$\times \dfrac{\text{Fixed Investment}}{\text{Materials Volume}}$$

(I) $\dfrac{\text{Output}}{\text{Materials Volume}} \equiv \dfrac{\text{Man-Hours}}{\text{Fixed Investment} \times (\text{Output/Capacity})}$

$$\times \dfrac{\text{Fixed Investment} \times (\text{Output/Capacity})}{\text{Materials Volume}}$$

$$\times \dfrac{\text{Output}}{\text{Man-Hours}}$$

All of these are shown in Figure 3.1. Thus, the two-factor models are shown to cover only the productivity of any two of the direct input factors which are circled along with the connecting arm representing the proportions in which those two factors are combined. And the three-factor models simply continue around the diagram by replacing the second circle in the two-factor model with its equivalent in the form of the next connecting arm (proportion of the second to the third factor) and the circled productivity of the third factor.

For further discussion, see [5, pp. 88–91].

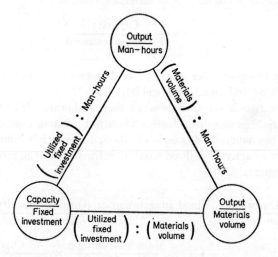

Fig. 3.1 Network of productivity relationships among direct input factors

Perhaps the most important implication of this approach is that productivity can no longer be regarded as one-dimensional, with adjustments limited to increases or decreases in some homogeneous attribute. On the contrary, changes in productivity may now be viewed as involving alternative combinations of increases and decreases in each of the six components constituting the network of productivity relationships. Indeed, it is not possible to change any one of these components without affecting one or more of the other components of this integrated system. Another implication of major significance is that any given initial impact on the network of productivity relationships may be absorbed through a variety of adjustments in the other components, thus presenting options for managerial choice. And it should be emphasised in this connection that different patterns of adjustment in the productivity network may have quite dissimilar effects on costs and on other determinants of managerial performance, as will be discussed later.

Two additional proposals were developed for broadening the perspectives of productivity analysis. One provided a means of encompassing the role of salaried inputs by regarding them not as a separable contribution to productivity adjustments, but rather as an indirect means of making more advantageous adjustments in the productivity network involving the three direct input factors [5, pp. 155–64, 176–7]. The second suggested consideration of the relative dominance of given production systems by different factors, indicating the major differences to be expected among labour-dominated, machine-dominated and material-dominated systems in respect both to the most likely sources of major changes in productivity relationships and to the effects of given adjustments, e.g. in output per man-hour. (See [5, pp. 188–96] and for a discussion of the wider significance of these ideas, see [8, pp. 143–155].)

But this still leaves productivity measures crystallised at the level of relationships between aggregates—between the total volume of each input and total output (or capacity)—implying that productivity analysis has no concern with what happens inside the black box into which inputs are absorbed and out of which products flow. Effective management, however, requires penetration beneath aggregate productivity relationships to the behaviour of the components which comprise them—entering into what was designated in the earlier study as 'point-efficiency' or interior sectoral studies. By helping to promote the more effective allocation of resources *within* firms, such techniques would provide a means of reinforcing the effects of market competition which tend to improve resource allocations only as *among* firms. Thus, aggregate output might be decomposed into the output of each product line and separate networks of input–output measures developed for each. Alternatively, the entire production process might be divided into successive operations or departments with input–output relationships developed for each. And subdividing each stage by product, or subdividing each product by stage of production, would yield input–output relationships for still smaller components of the system.

Such approaches would provide progressively more explicit guides to detecting the loci of all significant changes in input–output relationships and to probing attendant causes and effects over wider sectors of associated operations. Thus, adjustments in aggregate inputs or outputs could be traced to their roots and the effects of localised innovations in mechanisation, labour tasks or processing techniques traced upward to aggregate relationships, as will be illustrated later. In addition, productivity measures might be developed whose coverage of activities would conform with established organisational groupings, thus integrating such measures into the structure of administrative controls.

It should be recognised, however, that such elaborations require formulation of the system's analytical framework in greater detail so as to guide more refined probing of component relationships within each activity sector. Moreover, an array of appropriately differentiated input and output measures must be devised to accord with the progressive transformation of work in process through sequential operations.

3.1.4 Relevant Evaluative Criteria

Fundamental problems of measurement also arise from the variety of specialised interest groups with distinctive criteria for evaluating input–output adjustments. In the earlier study, this was dealt with initially by differentiating among three categories of analytical foci (output-centred, input-centred and point-efficiency studies), by defining five groups with interests in such analyses (resource suppliers, resource purchasers or hirers, resource users, product marketers and product buyers), and by then reviewing which analytical foci and which particular measures were most relevant to each group (Figure 3.2). (As an illustration of reliance on certain similar concepts, see [7a, pp. 145–6].)

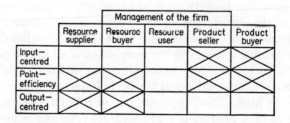

Fig. 3.2   Foci of interest in productivity analysis

For example, the suppliers of productive inputs are obviously interested in productivity ratios which relate their particular inputs to the output of prospective users. Specifically, suppliers of coal, electricity or cotton are concerned with changes in the physical amounts of these inputs required by the user per unit of his output, and reductions in such unit input requirements are usually regarded as disadvantageous by these suppliers. Providers of investment funds, sellers of machinery and labour unions likewise share this emphasis on resource-oriented aspects of productivity adjustments. However, manufacturers and other users of such inputs are more deeply interested in the cost than in the quantity of such inputs per unit of output. Moreover, such users are more interested in the aggregate cost of all inputs per unit of output than in separate costs for each input, because the user seeks to find more advantageous combinations of all inputs. In evaluating his overall operation, on the other hand, including marketing as well as procurement and production, the manufacturer is more interested in maximising the value than the volume of his product relative to input costs. And the consumer is more interested in the service values yielded by each product relative to its price than in the sheer physical volume of total output relative to input quantities and costs.

Examples of the multiplication of potential criteria include welfare considerations and the need to choose among the many specific alternatives within each of the broad categories of physical and financial resource flows. Labour inputs, for instance, may be measured in terms of numbers employed, man-hours worked, energy expended, skills applied, hazards borne, wages paid, etc. Outputs may likewise be measured in terms of physical quantities (e.g. number, weight or volume), of financial worth (e.g. product value, sales income or value added), of serviceability to buyers (e.g. years of wear, economy of operation or saving of effort) and even of contributions to the general welfare (e.g. improvements in safety, health or national security). Each of these criteria may be of dominant significance for some purpose, but none can be of dominant significance for all. And since these different aspects of contributions and of returns need not be correlated with one another, even one fixed pair of inputs and outputs may yield a variety of productivity relationships.

Thus a complex network of input–output relationships may be recognised, each of which involves interactions with others but nevertheless remains more important than others to particular interest groups. As a result, what may be regarded as advantageous adjustments by some may be regarded as harmful or unimportant by others.

Fundamentally, the need to integrate productivity measures at various levels of aggregation arises from the fact that component sectors of performance cannot be appraised except in respect to the larger activity matrices from which their tasks have been derived. Thus, improvements in the input–output ratios of one production sector may or may not be desirable, depending on their net impact on the rest of the system; and, conversely, managerial efforts to improve productivity ratios for the aggregate system may lower such ratios in some sectors while raising them in others—or lower some ratios in the short run in order to raise them over longer periods.

To facilitate decision making within the individual firm, therefore, it becomes necessary to develop a framework for interrelating the criteria applicable at successively higher levels of management. In particular, this would involve beginning with physical input–output relationships in production and eventually linking these to the determinants of changes in the rate of returns on investment as presented by the managerial control ratios in Chapter 2.

3.2 EVALUATIVE MEASUREMENT AND INCREASING AGGREGATION

In exploring the effects of suggested conceptual modifications on productivity analysis at increasing levels of aggregation, attention will be given first to the analytical coherence of different types of aggregative groupings and to corresponding variations in evaluative criteria. Subsequent sections will then review the problems of fulfilling specified requirements for measuring input and output flows and the implications of the methods employed.

3.2.1 Analysis Potentials by Types of Aggregated Systems

Productivity studies suggest a need to sharpen economic analysis by differentiating between organically integrated and artificially contrived groupings, instead of continuing to apply essentially similar analytical frameworks to successively higher levels of aggregation—e.g. plants, firms, industries and regions—without regard to the coherence of such systems. This need is highlighted partly because the productivity concept is focused on interrelationships instead of representing individual variables, such as output, price, income, capital formation and other basic economic concepts. And it is further emphasised by the requirement specified earlier that productivity measurements can be meaningful only if they relate to an integrated system of resource flows and are derived from explicit and measurable evaluative criteria. Because these restrictions are not limited to productivity studies, considerations of system coherence may also prove of increasing importance to other major sectors of economic analysis.

Possible aggregation levels cover a continuum ranging from one-man operations to the entire national economy and beyond. Among them, four basic types may be singled out for examination:

(1) *Control systems*, or actual networks subject to centralised control over all resource flows;

(2) *Specialised decision systems*, or synthetic frameworks covering those segments of actual input–output networks which bear upon the decision-making evaluations of particular input suppliers or output buyers;

(3) *Group analysis systems*, or synthetic frameworks designed to analyse the position of entire clusters of competitors with essentially similar interests; and

(4) *Descriptive groupings*, or arbitrary categories lacking analytical coherence but useful as intermediate steps in computational aggregation and disaggregation.

These are shown in Figure 3.3 as diversely oriented components of a generalised segment of economic activities encompassing the flow of labour, materials and capital into several firms producing multiple products for sale to an array of buyers.

The *control system* is illustrated by any firm whose management controls the conversion of all inputs into outputs in the interests of maximising specified relationships (usually financial) between total outputs and total inputs. Among *specialised decision systems*, two kinds are illustrated: one represents evaluations by an input supplier of changes in demand for that input relative to the total output of products using it (as in the trade union model—Panel (c)); the other represents evaluations by a buyer of changes in total inputs per unit of output among all suppliers of the given product (Panel (d))—each being analytically complete from the evaluative viewpoint of only one decision-making interest.

Both *group analysis systems* and *descriptive groupings* represent multifocal aggregates, meaning that the individual firms comprising them are each subject to centralised controls and evaluative criteria, but the group as a whole is not. In *group analysis systems*, all of the components have closely similar inputs and outputs, as illustrated by competitive firms in a homogeneous industry (Panel (e)). As the residual category, *descriptive groupings* represent either incomplete or heterogeneous systems. The former are characterised by leakages into or out of the production channels linking inputs and outputs, as may be illustrated by subtotals for each region of a nationally organised industry like automobile production (Panel (f)). Heterogeneity involves significant qualitative differences among the inputs and outputs of the firms in the group, and may be illustrated by totals for

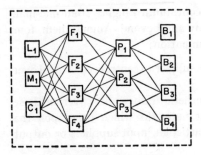

(a) General economic system

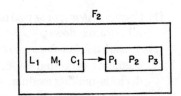

(b) Control system

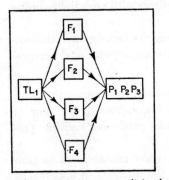

(c) Special decision system (labour)

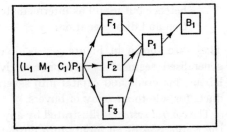

(d) Special decision system (buyer)

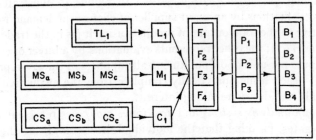

(e) Group analysis system

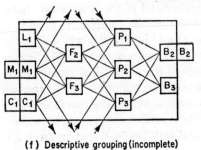

(f) Descriptive grouping (incomplete)

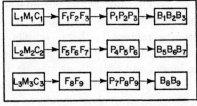

(g) Descriptive grouping (heterogeneous)

Fig. 3.3

each region covering all manufacturing activities, or by national totals for such heterogeous economic sectors as Agriculture or Transport (Panel (g)).

Multi-focal aggregations pose special evaluative problems. In descriptive groupings which are homogeneous but incomplete (e.g. automobile production in one state or county), inputs and outputs may each be readily aggregated for all firms, but comparisons between inputs and outputs tend to be invalidated by intervening leakages. In descriptive groupings which are complete but heterogeneous (e.g. total manufacturing in one state or county), qualitative differences interfere even with the aggregation of the inputs or the outputs, to say nothing of allowing meaningful comparisons between them. Because they are both complete and homogeneous, group analysis systems (e.g. all firms comprising the steel industry in the U.S.A.) allow the aggregation of inputs and of outputs and also provide the congruence in their respective coverages needed to justify comparisons between them. But the interpretation of results is subject to two conditions. First, to provide an effective analytical focus, such systems must be designed in accordance with the purposes and evaluative criteria of a specified interest group: all competing firm managements; or all suppliers of a common input; or all buyers of a common product. And, second, all findings must be recognised as no more than average relationships among aggregates for the group. This means that such relationships need not be applicable to actual decision making by a particular competitor. More important, however, it means that such findings are difficult to interpret; one cannot automatically appraise the desirability of changes in average input–output ratios when these may result from substitutions in input factors, changes in product-mix, alterations in the relative output of different firms, or adjustments in total output. Indeed, it would be fundamentally wrong to evaluate results in competitive industries by applying the evaluative criteria of its individual firms, for the latter often seek to enhance their achievements by undermining those of others.

Fig. 3.3   Basic types of aggregated systems

L_1L_2:	Various categories of labour inputs.
M_1M_2:	Various categories of material inputs.
C_1C_2:	Various categories of capital inputs.
F_1F_2:	Different firms.
P_2P_2:	Different products.
B_1B_2:	Separate buyers.
TL_1:	Trade Union for L_1.
MS_aMS_b:	Different suppliers of M_1.
CS_aCS_b:	Different suppliers of C_1.
$(L_1M_1C_1)P_1$:	All inputs for P_1.

In short, the economic analysis of relationships between inputs and outputs, incomes and outlays, or other attributes of presumably integrated systems, may be highly **vulnerable** when applied to multi-focal systems. This need not prevent all efforts to probe relationships at levels of aggregation other than those constituting control systems. But it would restrict the effective exploration of direct decision-making alternatives to activity sectors which can be recast into specialised decision systems. In such cases, each set of results would represent only one point of view; and these could never be merged to represent a combined point of view, because non-integrated systems cannot have the single focus or performance criteria which represent such a controlling viewpoint. And the only other level of analysis applicable to multi-focal systems would be restricted to homogeneous activity sectors which can be recast into group analysis systems in order to facilitate appraisal of the general framework of pressures (or input–output relationships) affecting each group with similar interests.

The far-reaching implications of this become apparent only with the realisation that in western economies most of the progressively higher levels of aggregation represent multi-focal groupings. Beyond the level of individuals and families, control systems are readily identifiable only at the level of separate enterprises (private firms, non-profit institutions and governmental agencies). There are no control systems which encompass the total economy of any geographical area (city, state or region), for these usually take the form of incomplete as well as heterogeneous descriptive groupings which serve as intermediate steps in cumulating widely dispersed resources into successively broader aggregates. Nor do control systems often reach beyond individual firms to cover entire industries, except in cases of nationalisation. Hence, with the exceptions already noted, the interpretation of average input–output relationships for regions and industries in accordance with the evaluative criteria and analytical framework of the individual firm is likely to be as unsound as projecting the concept of individual personality to regional and national levels.

On the other hand, particular regional interests might be served by synthesising specialised decision or group analysis systems to explore input–output adjustments affecting the demand for a local mineral, or for specified sectors of the local labour force, as well as others affecting the conditions of supply for certain locally consumed products. And group analysis systems might also be synthesised to evaluate adjustment patterns within reasonably homogeneous, competitive industries from the viewpoints of trade unions, of suppliers of materials and capital, of buyers of specified products, and of the managers of the individual firms comprising the industry.

3.2.2 Changing Evaluative Criteria with Increasing Aggregation

The relative importance among the various physical, financial and welfare attributes of input and output flows tends to change with the level of aggregation. Within control systems, evaluative criteria tend to be derived downward from the guiding objectives of the whole through successively smaller subdivisions; and controls over resource flows tend to be developed backwards from the intended output pattern through successively antecedent stages to the initial inputs. Hence, all input–output adjustments must be interpreted within the context of their specified restrictions.

In the elemental units of a factory (single jobs or job clusters which produce one part for a marketable product), the relationship of physical input quantities to physical output quantities tends to dominate the evaluation of changes in performance. Output in such units can be measured only in terms of the number of parts meeting the required specifications. While inputs may be measured either in physical quantities or costs, the former tend to dominate performance evaluations within the unit because the qualitative specifications for labour, materials and equipment as well as the prices and charges for such inputs are usually fixed by other parts of the organisation (e.g. procurement, engineering, industrial relations and accounting). Welfare constraints are also specified for the given unit through health and safety standards, insurance protection and other components of general company policies and trade union agreements. Thus, physical criteria are dominant only because financial and welfare conditions are fixed outside the elemental unit. Indeed, significant changes in any of these prescribed constraints would make it difficult to interpret resultant changes in physical input–output ratios, without careful evaluation of their effects within some larger framework. One may also note that reductions in the quantity of inputs required to produce the specified output quotas are likely to be strongly preferred over unsought (and, hence, possibly wasteful) increases in output from the same level of inputs.

In evaluating the integrated system of operations involved in manufacturing the given product, cost supersedes physical quantity as the dominant aspect of input flows to be compared with physical output within any given set of physical and welfare constraints. The production manager may seek to improve performance not only by decreasing the quantity of each input per unit of output, but also by altering the qualitative specifications of inputs, by adjusting factor proportions and by reducing factor prices—thus reflecting an emphasis on lowering unit costs. But the interpretation of adjustments in unit costs presents difficulties if accompanied by substantial changes in product design or other constraints.

At the level of the whole firm, financial aspects of both output and input flows become dominant, although physical and welfare aspects remain as essential constraints. Reducing costs relative to physical output is less important than raising income relative to costs, and increasing profit relative to total investment is usually even more important. Further intermediate levels of performance evaluation may then be distinguished by exploring the determinants of changes in this basic, though hardly exclusive, measure. The managerial control ratios, for example, attribute such changes to the interaction of adjustments in product price, unit costs, capacity utilisation, the productivity of fixed assets and the internal allo-

Managerial control ratios

P/IF	Rate of Profit on Total Investment
VP/PO	Product Prices
TC/PO	Total Unit Costs
PO/CAP	Capacity Utilization
CAP/IF	Productivity of Fixed Investment
IF/IT	Internal Allocation of Capital

Unit costs

M/PO	Unit Material Costs
W/PO	Unit Wage Costs
FC/PO	Unit Fixed Costs

Cost proportions

M/TC	Materials Proportion of Total Costs
W/TC	Wage Proportion of Total Costs
FC/TC	Fixed Costs Proportion of Total Costs

Factor prices

Mp	Materials Prices
W/M-Hr	Wage Rates
FC/IF ÷ PO	Fixed Charge Allocation Rate/Output (FCAR)

Factor 'productivities'

PO/M-Hr	Output/Man-Hours
PO/MV	Output/Materials Volume
CAP/IF	Capacity/Fixed Investment

Factor proportions

MV/M-Hr	Materials Volume/Labour
$MV\left(\dfrac{PO}{CAP} \times \dfrac{CAP}{IF}\right)$	Materials Volume/Actively Utilised Fixed Investment (ACFI)
$M\text{-}Hr\Big/\left(\dfrac{PO}{CAP} \times \dfrac{CAP}{IF}\right)$	Labour/Actively Utilised Fixed Investment (ACFI)

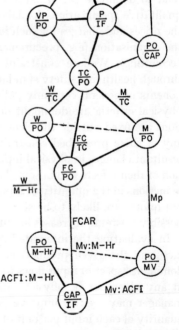

Fig. 3.4   Relationships among physical productivity ratios, unit costs and other profit determinants

cation of capital, with only the first two of these and output determining short-term changes in profits on investment—as discussed in Chapter 2.

Figure 3.4 may help to understand the analytical framework by showing how productivity relationships may be integrated with the managerial control ratios presented in Chapter 2, first through linkages with factor prices which determine each sector of unit costs and then through cost proportions which determine the effect of changes in each category of unit costs on total unit costs. Detailed discussion of this framework will be delayed, however, until after the discussion of costs.

Several principles are suggested by the discussion up to this point. First, because the variety of physical, financial and welfare aspects of input and of output flows may interact with one another, changes in any given aspect cannot be readily interpreted unless other significant aspects remain fixed. (Compare with [1, p. 90].) Second, the relative importance of these different aspects changes not only with the focus of the evaluator, but also with the framework of constraints within which variations reflect performance. Third, each successively lower subdivision within a control system requires additional constraints to facilitate reintegration. And fourth, although improvements in input–output ratios in one sector may generate benefits at more aggregative levels, these may also be offset by (and even cause) unfavourable adjustments in other components of the same aggregate. Together, these principles enphasise the dangers of measuring selected input–output relationships without defining relevant constraints, of applying identical measures to different levels of aggregation, and of projecting observed adjustments from one level to another.

With respect to the other systems discussed earlier, it may suffice to add: first, that governmental agencies and private non-profit institutions are also characterised by sequential shifts in the relative importance of physical, financial and welfare criteria, although their patterns differ from that of private firms; and second, that such evaluative criteria do not change with the synthesis of more aggregative systems around a special interest group, for these continue to reflect the objectives of the individual members.

3.2.3 Aggregation and the Measurement of Inputs

Aggregation usually involves squeezing an increasing variety of distinctive resources into relatively few categories to provide synoptic measures of changes in the total system. The need arises because each operation in a plant may require different materials, labour qualifications and equipment and facilities. But the hundreds of such distinguishable categories to be found even in modest sized plants would frustrate top management's need for a few key determinants of performance levels. On the other hand, such managerial pressures have induced widespread resort to the following gross expedients. Lacking any meaningful physical common denominator, the variety of capital goods is usually aggregated in terms of investment values. The diversity of purchased materials, fuels and other supplies similarly invites aggregation in terms of total outlays rather than physical units. The latter are still widely used, however, to add labour inputs, although total man-hours disregards wide differences in skills, and also to add salaried inputs, although total numbers employed lumps together clerks, engineers and executives. Such aggregates are patently not comparable with one another and their interpretation is likely to be less straightforward than is commonly recognised.

Three basic problems are encountered in seeking to bridge the gap between the above extremes: (a) the need to differentiate between changes in the composition of a category of inputs (e.g. labour) and changes in the level of any given pattern of such inputs; (b) the need to differentiate between changes in the physical aspects of inputs and in their factor prices; and (c) the need to differentiate between changes in the general level of that factor's prices (e.g. general wage rate levels) and changes in the structure of price differentials among such factors (e.g. wage differentials for different skills). Each is important because it affects the appropriate interpretation of aggregate input measures.

Changes in total man-hours per unit of output, for example, are usually interpreted on the assumption that the composition of such inputs was unchanged. Nor is there an effective alternative to this assumption since the aggregation procedure resorts to progressively broader measurement units, thereby ignoring the heterogeneous qualities which define specific input requirements in various sectors. This procedure is usually defended, especially over two to three year periods or less, on the ground that significant changes in the composition of inputs tend to occur only over longer periods. It is apparent, however, that the differential flexibility of various labour inputs means that fluctuations in output levels tend to alter the composition of such inputs. Moreover, the tendency for the composition of labour requirements to differ among diverse products suggests that variations in product-mix would also alter the composition of inputs. Thus, this common interpretation is open to serious question even in the short term. In the long run, the changing composition of labour (and of other inputs) is tacitly admitted, of course, yet resulting adjustments in such total inputs per unit of output continue to be interpreted as though alterations in composition were invariably inconsequential.

Changes in total cost (e.g. wages) per unit of output are usually attributed to changes in the quantity of the input (e.g. labour man-hours), assuming no change in its composition, and to changes in the general level of such factor prices (e.g. wage rates). Because the latter is usually computed by dividing total wages by total wage earners or by their man-hours, it assumes that it is unnecessary to make the additional differentiations mentioned above. But it is difficult to disentangle higher wage rates for fixed input qualities from the effect on average wage rates of changes in the nature of input requirements. For example, a plant with 1000 wage earners is likely to have more than 200 jobs with significantly differentiated skills; as well as a large group of production specialists who frequently change the manual techniques, machine speeds and tooling, and quality standards which define the personnel requirements for each job and also affect its output norms, base rates and special incentives. Under these conditions, much of an apparent increase in general wage rates may really be due to a rise in the quality of required labour inputs. And another portion may be due to disparate changes in different occupations rather than to common adjustments in all. Moreover, although both of these shortcomings tend to become increasingly serious over longer periods, little account is taken of them.

These apparent conflicts between the synoptic value of aggregate measures of inputs and the adequacy of interpretive detail may be resolved not by trying to invent statistical means of combining them, but rather by recalling the managerial purposes they serve. According to section 3.2, managerial evaluative criteria for inputs at the level of the total firm and of its major functional divisions are dominated by cost rather than physical aggregates. Hence, the overriding objective in making an unchanged product is to reduce its unit cost, whether this involves an increase or a decrease in total man-hours or any other input category per unit of output. On the other hand, either an increase or a decrease in total man-hours per unit of output might be preferable at this level depending on their respective cost effects. Thus, ambiguities are likely to affect the interpretation of aggregative measures of inputs only when these do not accord with the dominant criteria for managerial evaluations at the level being studied.

The foregoing does not deny the relevance of 'physical input–physical output' measures for performance evaluation. On the contrary, it reinforces the thesis of section 3.2 that most changes in aggregates are the passive result of changes which actually occur at the level of component operations and, therefore, that managerial penetration within the total system requires a structure of differentiated input–output measures reaching down from 'financial input–financial output' through 'financial input–physical output' to 'physical input–physical output' ratios (Figure 3.4) with corresponding price, quality and welfare constraints facilitating interpretations at each level. It should also be recalled that quite different measures may be required by interest groups other than the management of the firm or of its component units. For example, resource suppliers may be concerned with changes in a firm or industry in total physical requirements per unit of output of particular kinds of materials or labour or equipment. Such results should be interpreted as measuring changes in relative unit input requirements, however, rather than in productivity levels or cost efficiency.

3.2.4 Aggregation and the Measurement of Output

Aggregation simplifies one problem in measuring output by replacing innumerable categories of intermediate products with the relatively few final products into which all component parts are absorbed. Moreover, it is only at the aggregative levels representing finished products that management can effectively relate physical outputs to prospective value outputs as a basis for comparison with input costs, for the probable market value of work-in-process is difficult to establish.

But aggregation also poses serious problems for output measurement in cases involving product heterogeneity. Even in the simple case of a plant which makes a single product in a range of sizes and models, total output can be physically aggregated only by disregarding all qualitative differences. But such a measure defies interpretation. For example, an increase in the number of units, without any indication of changes in the ratio of small to large, or of high quality to low, need not have any meaningful relationship even to the level of aggregate production activity. Nor does it support any meaningful concept of the average unit of output, which represents the denominator in measures of input requirements (or costs) per unit of output, for such an average unit would not only represent some non-existent composite size and model, but would change from period to period and thereby undermine the value of comparisons (see Chapter 4). Similarly misleading is the use of kilowatt-hours to aggregate the output of the electrical power industry, in view of the enormous investment as well as the quantities of other inputs required to distribute electrical energy from the generator to the eventual users. And, of course, these problems are further complicated in the case of multi-product plants and firms.

In order to avoid the limitations both of meaningless aggregation and of complete disaggregation, reliance is usually placed on the compromise technique which was refined and applied widely by Fabricant [4a]. Its object is to measure the change in physical output between two periods, which is represented by the change in the total value of product not due to a change in price. Accordingly, the quantity of each product is multiplied in each period by its average price in both (as a means of removing the effect of price changes) and the fractional change in the aggregate for all products between the two periods is considered to measure the change in physical output. What does this measure? Weighting by price means that a unit of higher priced product is regarded as representing more physical output than a unit of lower priced product. Hence, this measure represents a cost-absorption concept (including profit as a necessary cost in a private economy) of physical output. (See [5, pp. 92–7].)

Some such relative value-oriented concept of physical output is certainly necessary for aggregation having relevance for the economic rather than the purely physical dimensions of production. Moreover, it surmounts the limitations of product-by-product output aggregates as the basis for managerial evaluations of operations as a whole in multi-product plants. And it allows the addition of new products and the gradual displacement of old products which is an advance over older techniques involving a fixed range of products.

But it is also important to note certain widely unrecognised elements of this method. For example, it assumes that none of the change in a product's price is attributable to modifications in its qualitative characteristics. This may lead to increasing margins of error in the large number of industries effecting frequent modifications in product design, especially over periods of several years or more. And it clearly renders such measures unsuitable for assessing results of innovations which affect products as well as inputs. Another feature of this method is that it regards the relative physical output magnitudes of diverse products as paralleling their respective prices regardless of relative profit margins, imperfections in factor markets and differentials in marketing efforts. Consequently, production *improvements* which reduce the costs and price of a product have the effect of *reducing* the (price) weight used in computing the contribution of each unit of the product to total plant output; and *decreases* in the effectiveness of production which induce higher costs and prices serve to *enhance* each unit's contribution to total output. The implications of this for the interpretation of productivity adjustments are obviously far-reaching. It may also be of interest to note the tendency of this method to moderate computed changes in average total costs per unit of output over successive periods. Specifically, a decrease in costs per physical unit of a given product without any change in price would tend to lower the plant's total costs while leaving its output unchanged, thus lowering average costs per unit of output. But if these cost reductions should lead to price reductions —thereby tending to lower the weights used in computing each such product unit's contribution to total output—output will begin to follow the earlier decline in costs. This not only reduces the rate of decline in total costs per unit of output, but even, in time, to restore earlier levels—as is discussed further in Chapter 9.

3+

The foregoing characteristics of this kind of output measure have not been reviewed in order to criticise them. On the contrary, it is worth emphasising that the development of this technique represented an important advance precisely because it clearly undertook to measure the economic aspect of changes in physical output and thus, by implication, recognised that resulting adjustments need not parallel either purely physical or essentially use values. At the same time, serious misinterpretations can result if the distinctive features of such measurements are overlooked.

3.2.5 Differentiating Total Input from Total Output Measures

Oddly enough, one of the most serious problems generated by this technique for measuring changes in total output involves differentiating the results from changes in total inputs. Productivity analysis requires analysis of the conceptual bases of output and of input measures. Thus questions may be asked. Do changes in product value (i.e. in total costs plus profit) at fixed product prices measure changes in total output or in total input? If the former, as suggested by Fabricant, how are changes in total inputs to be measured? Application of the same approach would suggest measuring them in terms of changes in total costs at fixed factor prices, although differing conceptions of profit might suggest their inclusion or exclusion. What, then, would changes in such total input–total output relationships signify? Changes in efficiency levels (as implied by terms like 'total factor productivity' and 'aggregative efficiency index') [9a, 14], or changes in the ratio of (deflated?) total costs to (deflated?) total revenue, i.e. some form of (deflated) profit margin, or changes in the ratio of factor price to product price indexes?

To answer these questions precisely, one should consider the common meanings of the terms forming the numerator and denominator, and also that changes in these ratios may be due to variations in the quantity or price of each specific input required per unit of unchanged product, to differential adjustments between product and factor prices, to shifts in input factor proportions and to fluctuations in the product composition of output. The resulting amalgam of interacting effects reaches far beyond the implications of any of the simple interpretations suggested above. Nor can it lend itself to any other interpretation, simple or complex, until an analytical framework is developed which is focused on the relationships among such aggregates within a system with specified objectives.

Many of the foregoing difficulties seem to stem from efforts to project the objectives, analytical concepts and measuring tools which have been found relevant to the managerial evaluation and control of unified operating units on to more complex and less coherent systems, where their applicability may be questionable. For example, in many service-producing activities, changes in the value of work done (or the total margin in the case of distributive trades) cannot be adjusted for changes in the price of the services provided because the highly individualised nature of such services often precludes meaningful price quotations. Consequently, differentiations between changes in the aggregate value and in the aggregate physical volume of services performed are open to question [2]. Nor can one readily discern the significance for productivity evaluations of changes in total inputs (i.e. total costs) relative to total output (i.e. total costs plus profit). Essentially the same problem, it will be recalled, is faced in most construction activities where the extreme variability in output characteristics has often led to using inputs as measures of output [10]. And the government and other social service sectors reinforce these problems of productivity measurement and evaluation. For example, whereas the output of private enterprise activities may be measured in terms of exchange values and hence can be aggregated in terms which accord with the fundamental motivations of the managers, there is no system of common units for measuring and aggregating the output of educational, health, legal, research and many other non-commercial institutions [11]. Here, too, some analysts have resorted to the expedient of evaluating these outputs on the basis of the aggregate cost of their inputs. But this means that inputs and outputs must always be equal despite variations in the effectiveness of performance—lacking even profits as a means of distinguishing between measures of aggregate inputs and outputs—thereby eliminating the very purpose of productivity measurements.

Even more far-reaching problems confront efforts to measure productivity levels for entire economies and to compare them with one another. First, it is apparent that the bases for aggregation applicable to private enterprise are not applicable to the remainder of the economy. Second, it is apparent that these proportions may be subject to change in many countries because of cyclic fluctuations, persistent trends towards or away from private enterprise, defence emergencies and the introduction of long range development programmes involving heavy current inputs into the infrastructure in the expectation of eventual rather than immediate gains in output. Third, it is also apparent that countries differ both in these proportions and in their adjustment patterns.

There are also important difficulties to be faced in comparing productivity levels among nations, even in respect to particular industries. For example, if output per man-hour in Nation A is double that of Nation B, this need not imply that the latter is seriously disadvantaged. Unit wage costs would be lower in B if its average wage rates were less than one-half those in A. Moreover, A may be using several times as much capital investment as B per unit of output. And from another point of view, the resulting product price in B may still be less than that which would have to be paid for importing this product from A. Clearly, the interpretation of such comparisons would depend on the criteria used and these would tend to reflect the pressures and values of each economy, including concern with unemployment, the development of industrial skills, etc.

In short, one may conclude that productivity targets cannot be properly defined until the more basic economic and other objectives of the plant, industry, interest group or nation have been formulated—and that resultant findings are meaningful only within that setting. (For a more detailed review of such a planning process, see [6, Chapter 19].) Measurements may show that X jumped higher and that Y jumped further without revealing which was more successful in meeting his objective. But it is important that performance criteria should be derived from the specific targets of the system being appraised rather than from other systems.

Finally, lest this last section be misinterpreted as casting doubt on productivity analysis in general, it should be emphasised that major areas of useful application have been discussed. Within individual activity systems, as a major example, managers of specific construction projects, wholesale and retail outlets, personal service establishments, professional service outlets and even governmental units, usually find it quite feasible to appraise input requirements, output flows and performance quality through approximations to the structure of physical, financial and welfare criteria outlined earlier for use in manufacturing plants—especially in the absence of substantial shifts in objectives and activities. Useful approximations can also be developed for the higher levels of aggregation represented by what were earlier termed special decision systems and homogeneous group analysis systems, although such results tend to serve only certain limited purposes—and again assume essentially unchanged objectives and activities. Hence, productivity measurement and evaluation are likely to be open to serious shortcomings only when applied to heterogeneous or incomplete descriptive groupings, to systems in which the strategic measures of inputs and output are not fully known, or to systems which have undergone significant alterations in objectives or activities. Such exclusions cover many areas of great importance—counselling the development of other approaches to evaluating performance. But the admitted absence of universal applicability should in no way discourage the fuller development and more effective use of productivity analysis in the large domains to which it is already reasonably well adapted; nor should it inhibit efforts to achieve more effective understanding of the critical inputs and outputs

of health, educational and other systems as the basis for adding them to
the array of those amenable to productivity analysis.

3.3 ILLUSTRATIVE APPLICATION TO IRON AND STEEL MANUFACTURING

Some indication of the kinds of relationships which may be revealed by
the above approach is provided by a summary of the results of a partial
application to the basic iron and steel industry (which encompasses blast
furnaces, steelworks and rolling mills) over a period of fifty-four years.

3.3.1 Basic Data

Because this is merely an illustrative example, changes in net fixed investment have been approximated by using the American Iron and Steel Institute's estimates of the value of property, plant and equipment less depletion, depreciation and amortisation; and productive capacity has been
approximated by the Institute's estimates of steel ingot capacity. Physical
output and man-hour estimates were prepared by the U.S. Bureau of
Labor Statistics (Figure 3.5).

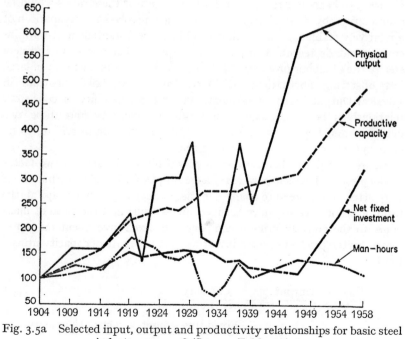

Fig. 3.5a   Selected input, output and productivity relationships for basic steel
industry, 1904–58 (Source: Table 3.1)

Figure 3.5a shows that productive capacity rose almost uninterruptedly between 1904 and 1958 to reach a peak nearly five times its 1904 level. Physical output had exceeded six times its 1904 level by the end of the period, but was characterised by sharp short-term fluctuations. Although man-hours also fluctuated considerably, the longer-term adjustment pattern was quite different, reaching a peak in 1919 and following a gradual downward trend thereafter to terminate in 1958 only 10 per cent above the level in 1904. Net fixed investment rose by half between 1904 and 1919, remained roughly unchanged over the next fourteen years and then declined to within 10 per cent of its 1904 level in 1947 before tripling over the last decade covered.

These data may now be applied to analysing the factors associated with changes in physical output per man-hour. It may be recalled that one approach suggested earlier attributed such changes to adjustments in the ratio of fixed investment to man-hours and in the ratio of physical output to fixed investment.

$$\frac{\text{Physical Output}}{\text{Man-Hours}} \equiv \frac{\text{Fixed Investment}}{\text{Man-Hours}} \times \frac{\text{Physical Output}}{\text{Fixed Investment}}$$

Figure 3.5b bears out the expectation that both of these ratios would be characterised by sharp fluctuations, since each involves the comparison of a relatively stable variable with one subject to substantial short-term increases and decreases. Thus, it would appear that the comparatively steady rise of labour productivity during the period was the result of large but offsetting fluctuations in Fixed Investment/Man-Hours and in Physical Output/Fixed Investment. As for the possibility of consistent relationships between changes in labour productivity and these two determinants, Figure 3.5b reveals none in the short term and offers no clear indications concerning the long run.

Figure 3.5c illustrates the results of shifting to the revised two-factor model presented earlier, in which changes in physical output per man-hour were attributed instead to changes in the productivity of fixed capital (the ratio of productive capacity to fixed investment) and the ratio of man-hours to the actively utilised component of fixed investment (as represented by the product of fixed investment and the rate of capacity utilisation).

$$\frac{\text{Physical Output}}{\text{Man-Hours}} \equiv \frac{\text{Capacity}}{\text{Fixed Investment}}$$
$$\times \frac{\text{Fixed Investment} \times (\text{Output/Capacity})}{\text{Man-Hours}}$$

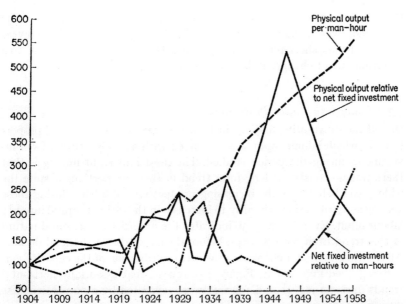

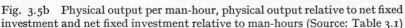

Fig. 3.5b Physical output per man-hour, physical output relative to net fixed investment and net fixed investment relative to man-hours (Source: Table 3.1)

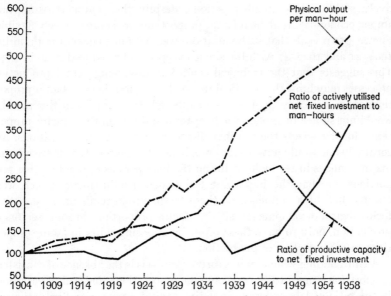

Fig. 3.5c Physical output per man-hour, productive capacity relative to net fixed investment and actively utilised net fixed investment relative to man-hours (Source: Table 3.1)

One obvious effect is that these new classifications yield far more stable series than were depicted in Figure 3.5b. But analysis still fails to reveal any consistent short-term or long-term relationship between these two determinants of changes in labour productivity.

3.3.2 Changes in Factor Proportions

One of the substantive findings in Figure 3.5c concerns the actual proportions in which labour input was combined with actively utilised fixed investment during the period studied. The most important finding is that there was no consistent long-term trend in these proportions despite the widespread belief that the increasing productivity of labour during these years was attributable primarily to increases in the ratio of capital input to labour input. Even Figure 3.5b indicates the essentially horizontal nature of this trend from 1904 to 1947, before the sharp rise of the final decade. After adjustments for changes in the rate of utilisation of the capacity embodying fixed investment, Figure 3.5c reveals that essentially horizontal trends during 1904–21 and 1927–47 were separated by a 50 per cent rise during the intervening period of six years.

Another finding of interest is that the proportions in which labour inputs were combined with actively utilised capital inputs were comparatively stable over extended periods, despite the common assumption among economists that such factor proportions are comparatively flexible. Figure 3.5c reveals that such variations were within 5 per cent both during 1904–21 and 1927–47 with the single exception of a reduced ratio in 1939. This suggests that the technical conditions governing actual production processes may limit the practical range of variations in such factor proportions more narrowly than is often supposed. However, even this premise would not suffice to explain the long-term stability in these factor proportions, for it neglects the possible effects of technological innovations. Accordingly one would have to suppose, in addition, either that there were no major changes in technology during the long periods of stable factor proportions, or that the important technological adjustments which were effected had little influence on these factor proportions, or, finally, that technological developments did alter factor proportions in some sectors of production, only to have these offset by opposing shifts in factor proportions in other sectors of production.

A third finding which invites further analysis is the absence of consistent support for either of the two common expectations concerning variations in the ratio of labour inputs to active capital inputs with fluctuations in output. One of these holds that labour inputs tend to be reduced more sharply than capital utilisation during periods of declining production because management is pressed to improve labour utilisation and unemployment threats encourage labour's co-operation in such efforts. The opposing shift in factor proportions is anticipated by those who argue that many types of capital facilities have relatively high minimum labour requirements below which they cannot be operated with acceptable efficiency, if at all. The nine years covering significant declines in the ratio of actively utilised fixed investment included five years marked by an increase in physical output (1914–19) and four years marked by output declines (1929–31) and (1937–39). The twelve years covering increases in these factor proportions—excluding 1939–54—were divided equally among periods marked by output increases (1921–23, 1927–29), unchanged output (1923–27) and decreased output (1954–58).

3.3.3 Changes in the Productivity of Fixed Capital

The most important finding in this area is the remarkably consistent upward trend in productive capacity per dollar of net fixed investment shown in Figure 3.5c from 1904 until 1947, with declines in only two two-year periods (1925–27 and 1935–37), each by less than 5 per cent. Such an outcome in a major industrial sector tends to cast some doubt on the belief, widely held by economists and businessmen, that the fixed capital cost of augmenting capacity has been rising over the long run, or that additional investments in capital goods have been yielding progressively smaller increments in productive capacity per investment dollar. Indeed, it is apparent from Table 3.1 that the tripling of capacity between 1904 and 1947 was almost wholly attributable to the increasing productivity of capital, for there was an increase of only 10 per cent in the level of net fixed investment.

Tracing these relationships in somewhat greater detail reveals the striking reversals in the roles played by the level of fixed investment and by the productivity of the assets embodying such investments in effecting observed adjustments in capacity. Four periods may be distinguished:

Period	Capacity	Fixed Investment	Capacity / Fixed Investment
1904–19	+116%	+52%	+42%
1919–31	+27%	+3%	+22%
1931–47	+15%	−29%	+64%
1947–58	+54%	+192%	−47%

In the first, the increased level of fixed investment contributed somewhat more heavily than the increased productivity of capital to the expansion of

3*

TABLE 3.1 Selected input, output and productivity relationships; basic iron and steel industry

Index numbers (1904 = 100)

Year	Output	Man-Hours	Net Fixed Investment	Capacity	Output Man-Hours	Fixed Investment Man-Hours	Output Fixed Investment	Capacity Fixed Investment	Output Capacity	Active Fixed Investment Man-Hours
	(1)	(2)	(3)	(4)	(5) $(1) \div (2)$	(6) $(3) \div (2)$	(7) $(1) \div (3)$	(8) $(4) \div (3)$	(9) $(1) \div (4)$	(10) $[(3) \times (9)] \div (2)$
1904	100	100	100	100	100	100	100	100	100	100
1909	160	128	107	—	125	84	150	—	—	—
1914	160	117	121	158	137	103	132	131	101	104
1919	232	183	152	216	127	83	153	142	107	89
1921	132	91	145	228	146	159	91	157	58	92
1923	292	164	147	233	178	90	198	158	125	112
1925	297	142	151	243	208	106	197	161	122	129
1927	297	137	155	238	217	113	192	154	125	141
1929	375	152	151	253	247	100	248	168	148	147
1931	180	79	157	274	227	199	115	174	66	132
1933	164	65	149	279	252	230	110	187	59	135
1935	241	90	133	278	269	148	181	209	87	129
1937	375	133	137	277	282	103	274	202	135	139
1939	245	102	120	290	340	117	204	241	85	104
1947	590	138	111	316	429	81	531	285	186	149
1954	626	127	236	432	494	186	257	183	145	270
1958	606	110	324	487	550	294	187	150	124	365

Sources:

(1) and (2)—1919–54, U.S. Department of Labor, *Man-Hours Per Unit of Output in the Basic Steel Industry, 1939–1955* (Washington, D.C.: U.S. Government Printing Office, Bulletin No. 1200, 1956) pp. 8–9; 1904–14 relatives based on S. Fabricant, *Employment in Manufacturing, 1899–1939* (New York: National Bureau of Economic Research, 1942) p. 316 and J. Kendrick, *Productivity Trends in the U.S.* (Princeton University Press, 1961) p. 485.

(3) and (4)—American Iron and Steel Institute, *Annual Statistical Reports* plus early 'property' estimates in a letter dated 8 18 50.

capacity. In the second period, the level of fixed investment made almost
no contribution to increasing capacity. In the third period, a sharp increase in the productivity of capital offset a reduction of more than a
quarter in the level of fixed investment to keep capacity expanding. And
in the last period, these roles were sharply reversed, with the gain in
capacity due to a tripling of fixed investment while the productivity of
fixed investment was almost halved.

Although a fuller discussion of the factors affecting the productivity of
fixed investment will be presented in Chapter 8, it may be helpful to men-
tion that this ratio is most likely to decline when there is a large scale replacement of facilities and also when major expansion is undertaken during
a period of sharp inflation. Specifically, replacement tends to leave the
numerator unchanged while increasing the denominator, as the capacity
formerly provided by largely or wholly depreciated facilities makes way for
newly purchased or constructed facilities. And adding capacity during inflation means that the relative increase in investment requirements
will be greater than the increment in capacity as compared with acquisitions during non-inflationary periods.

3.3.4 Labour Productivity, Capital Productivity and Factor Proportions

What, then, of the relationships between changes in physical output per
man-hour and in the two factors which have been suggested as its major
determinants? Figure 3.5c suggests that, instead of consistent relationships over the fifty year period, there were four periods with quite distinct
patterns:

Period	Output Man-Hours	Capacity Fixed Investment	Actively Utilised Fixed Investment Man-Hours
1904–21	+46%	+57%	−8%
1921–29	+69%	+7%	+60%
1929–47	+73%	+70%	+2%
1947–58	+28%	−47%	+144%

Between 1904 and 1921, the gain in physical output per man-hour seems
to have come not from any increase in actively utilised fixed investment
per man-hour, which actually declined, but rather from the increased
productivity of capital goods relative to the investments absorbed by
them. During the next eight years, however, these roles were reversed.
Another reversal between 1929 and 1947 restored the basic pattern of

1904–21, with the productivity of fixed capital again the major contributor to the gain in output per man-hour. And the final decade was characterised by the sharpest reversal of all, with the productivity of fixed investment declining by half while the ratio of actively utilised capital inputs to man-hours increased by almost 150 per cent.

Such findings cannot preclude the possibility that chance alone may determine which of these factors is likely to exert the greater influence on labour productivity adjustments, but neither do these findings encourage such an hypothesis. On the contrary, the virtually consistent advance in physical output per man-hour in the face of major upward and downward adjustments in both of its determinants strongly suggests that it resulted from deliberate managerial choice, along with vigorous implementing efforts, rather than from passive acceptance of fortuitous circumstances. Moreover, this judgement tends to be reinforced by the fact that management can exercise at least partial control over each of these determinants, as will be reviewed in greater detail later. Hence the need for managerial decision models which can provide guidance in evaluating alternatives at this level while also assuring the promotion of higher level organisational objectives.

4 Costs: Basic Concepts

An industrial enterprise encompasses the interaction of many specialised activities which are directed and integrated by management in the interests of the firm's guiding objectives. If costs are to serve as an effective guide to managerial decision making, they must be appraised within an analytical framework comparable in coverage and complexity to the processes to be controlled. Accordingly, the pattern of industrial costs may usefully be regarded as an intricate structure of relationships among costs at various levels of aggregation, over different periods of time, and reflecting the influence of different areas of performance. In exploring the structure of industrial costs, this chapter will focus on total costs, on cost proportions and on unit costs.

4.1 THE NATURE AND SIGNIFICANCE OF TOTAL COSTS

Total costs provide the most important basis within the structure of costs for appraising the aggregate results of a firm's operations. Moreover, it is the analysis of these same total costs that seems to offer the most promising starting point for efforts to determine why certain effects occurred and how they might have been altered. But a discussion of the potentials of the analysis of total costs requires some prior clarification of the scope and nature of such costs and of their relationship to managerial decision making.

4.1.1 Scope of Total Costs

Total costs may be variously defined. From the point of view of the economy as a whole, the total cost of the products and services provided by any firm is measured by the sum of the payments made to that firm, i.e. by its total income. While this view includes the firm's profits as a part of the cost of its goods and services, such a position may be justified by arguing that profits are a necessary part of the outlays which must be made in a private enterprise economy to induce needed productive activities.

Within the firm it is conventional, of course, to define total costs as excluding profits. This is done primarily to distinguish between the burdens and rewards for the owners. Such differentiation does not, however, imply that profits are less essential than other allocations to effective operation.

An even narrower conception of total costs is often implicit in managerial thinking. Because of their dominant interest in the activities which are directly responsive to their own control, management executives, especially those engaged in manufacturing operations, often limit their consideration of total costs to those incurred directly by the firm's own operations—thus excluding the cost of purchased supplies. Moreover, top management officials are often inclined to regard at least part of their own salaries and bonuses in the nature of a reward rather than as a part of the cost burden with which management seeks to cope.

These alternative conceptions of total costs are clearly complementary. The major differences among them are limited merely to the primary focus of emphasis in defining the categories among which the income and obligations of the firm are allocated. Hence, any study concerned with the functioning of the firm as a whole would obviously have to cover all of the component categories of allocation, without permitting an interest in the behaviour of the aggregate to subordinate interest in the accompanying behaviour of the components, and without permitting an excessive concentration on some components to lead to the neglect of others.

4.1.2 Nature of Total Costs

Clarification of the essential nature of total costs requires some further discussion of the meaning of costs as well as a brief review of the distinctive characteristics of costs which are measured at the aggregate level.

To begin with, it is necessary to conceive of costs in positive as well as in negative terms—i.e. not only as burdens which must always be reduced to a minimum, but also as measures of positive contributions to the firm's operations; not only as drains on company resources, but also as shares in the rewards earned by the firm; not only as deductions from potential profits, but also as the means of earning profits. The invidious connotation of the term 'costs' tends, of course, to discourage such a balanced view.

It may be of some help, therefore, to conceive of costs less as charges against income than as *measures* of the value of resources entering into income-producing activities. Indeed, in the interests of modifying unsound attitudes towards costs, these might even be regarded as a type of short-term investment. Such an analogy may serve both to build awareness of the constructive role of cost outlays in promoting effective operations and also to undermine the widespread, though erroneous, view that the only desirable direction in which costs can move is downward. In short, the basic objective of managerial control, whether related to investments or to costs, is to adjust each category of allocation either upward or downward until its contribution to the attainment of the firm's objectives is believed to be at a maximum under prevailing conditions.

The component of the structure of industrial costs concerned with total costs has certain distinctive characteristics. First, it is apparent that total costs represent a summation of particular outlays or allocations over the whole of some specified period and therefore do not reveal variations in their level during the period. In addition, total costs represent an aggregation of serve categories of outlay for the plant or firm as a whole, without revealing the contributions to the total of allocations within each of the operating processes and organisational units. But these analytical limitations merely serve to emphasise the constructive role of total costs as *summary* measures of performance over defined periods. Thus, total costs accumulate the results of day-to-day variations and aggregate the effects of ups and downs in the various sectors of activity to provide an integrated view of plant or firm operations, which is essential to top management's appraisal of performance.

4.1.3 Total Costs and Managerial Control

Managerial control is concerned with causes as well as effects, but results are obviously the dominant concern—and this is the need which is most directly served by total costs. It may be of interest in this connection to note that accounting, which has long been the primary source of information for analysing the effectiveness of operations, and whose purposes are directly dictated by managerial interests, has always been focused primarily on the complete and accurate measurement of total costs. And even though accounting functions have been proliferated in recent decades, the overriding concern with total costs has never been displaced.

Some of the important bases for appraising the significance of observed adjustments in total costs have already been indicated by the preceding discussion. First, because total costs measure the value of resources flowing through the firm's operations, they are the fundamental criteria for determining whether such operations have increased or decreased in value. Thus, an increase in total costs means an increase in the dollar volume of business transacted and, hence, is more likely to reflect an advance than a regression in the promotion of the enterprise's objectives. Second, since total costs measure the combined results of all operations, they offer a valuable corrective to the tendency management has to become too much engrossed in the newer and expanding sectors of operations and also to permit particularly knotty problems to obscure the significance of the wide range of more smoothly functioning activities. Third, total costs represent the accumulation of results over some extended period of time, thus providing realistic perspectives for looking at day-to-day and week-to-week developments. Fourth, because profits represent one of the basic categories in the allocation of the firm's income, the measurement of aggregate allocations also indicates the direction and extent of the changes in gross income from which net income is derived.

These bases for making use of total costs are limited to their status as measures of final results. But total costs may also be applied so as to advance management's further control objectives, which are to probe into the factors which influence results and to identify points at which management can directly effect adjustments in final results.

By way of an analytical guide to managerial decision making, total costs may be utilised in two ways. By comparing total costs for a given period with those for preceding periods, one may determine the magnitude of the changes to be explained. Next, a comparison of the relative changes in each of the total cost categories will indicate which components have increased most and least and thus help to guide further research. Of course, these uses of total cost data are little more than starting points for the detailed analysis of the factors affecting results. Yet, one can easily underestimate the practical value of beginning with a reasonably clear understanding of the magnitudes and loci of performance adjustments. Indeed, efforts to begin at the opposite extreme (i.e. by examining all of the possible effects of the numerous known adjustments in policies and operations during an extended period) would be confronted by a discouraging tangle of interacting uncertainties.

Although most categories of total cost represent the end products of processes which are subject to direct managerial control only at earlier stages, this is not true of overhead costs. Certain total costs, such as wage payments and outlays for purchased supplies, are the passive result of interactions between managerial decisions determining such costs per unit of product output (by means to be discussed later) and subsequent managerial decisions regulating the level of production. Overhead and related costs, however, are directly fixed at the level of total outlays, and it is their cost per unit of output which is the passive result of dividing these fixed totals by changing production levels. In short, it is algebraically correct to represent each category of total costs as the product of its corresponding cost per unit of output multiplied by production levels:

$$\text{Total Material Costs} = \text{Unit Material Costs} \times \text{Output}$$
$$\text{Total Wage Costs} = \text{Unit Wage Costs} \times \text{Output}$$
$$\text{Total Overhead Costs} = \text{Unit Overhead Costs} \times \text{Output}$$

But this parallelism would be misleading from the managerial point of view if it were interpreted as implying that control is exercised at the same levels in each category. Thus, total costs also provide a direct focus for managerial control in respect to such categories as depreciation charges, rent, interest burdens and salary payments. Moreover, to the extent that profit objectives are likewise established in terms of dollar totals, this constitutes another component of total costs which is directly responsive to managerial control, at least at the level of forward planning if not at the level of actual performance.

4.2 COST PROPORTIONS

It has already been emphasised that manufacturing operations represent the organic integration, rather than the mere mechanical addition, of the production factors entering into fabrication processes. This means that managerial decision making requires intensive analyses not only of the adjustments affecting each productive factor, but also of the interactions among them.

Managerial interest tends to centre around two related aspects of the interactions among adjustments in the major categories of total costs. The first concerns the relative magnitudes of the various categories of outlay. And the second is rooted in the fact that differential changes in any one of these categories automatically alters the proportion of the total outlay accounted for by the other categories. Economists are likewise concerned with these two aspects of cost interactions: the former being expressed as an interest in factor proportions; and the latter as a need to study the changing equilibria among factors which are competitive with, and to some extent capable of substitution for, one another.

The most effective tool available for the study of such cost interactions is that provided by the measurement of cost proportions, i.e. by the percentage of total costs accounted for by each of the major categories of outlay. Curiously enough, however, little use has so far been made of this tool either in managerial decision making or in economic analysis. Hence, it may be of interest to illustrate some of the rich potentials offered by their analysis.

The measurement of cost proportions help to analyse past adjustments in the structure of costs, and to guide their future course. The more important of these may be achieved by analysing the bearing of cost proportions on changes in total costs; by tracing interactions among changes in the proportions accounted for by the various cost categories; by uncovering trends in, and gauging the flexibility of, these proportions; and by determining the degree of stability of the overall pattern of cost proportions over short and over long periods.

Changes in the value of product, or in total costs, are determined not only by the relative change in each cost category, but also by the proportion of total costs accounted for by each.

$$\left(\Delta \frac{\text{Total Costs}}{\text{Output}}\right)_{1-2} \equiv \left[\left(\Delta \frac{\text{Material Costs}}{\text{Output}}\right)_{1-2}\left(\frac{\text{Material Costs}}{\text{Total Costs}}\right)_1\right]$$
$$+ \left[\left(\Delta \frac{\text{Wage Costs}}{\text{Output}}\right)_{1-2}\left(\frac{\text{Wage Costs}}{\text{Total Costs}}\right)_1\right] + \cdots$$

where subscripts 1 and 2 represent the beginning and the end of the period being studied. Thus a 20 per cent change in a category accounting for one-tenth of total costs will have less effect on the total outlay than a 10 per cent change in the cost category accounting for one-third of the total outlay. Or, stated differently, one cannot estimate the immediate effects on total cost of a 10 per cent increase in wages, or in some other cost category, until its proportion of the total costs has also been determined. In short, cost proportions may be regarded as defining the length of the lever arms by which the relative change in each category is multiplied in determining its effect on the change in total costs.

In seeking to explain adjustments in total costs during some past period, therefore, the determination of cost proportions helps to distinguish between the influence of relative changes in the various cost categories *during* the period and the influence of the relative magnitude of these categories *at the beginning* of the period mentioned. This distinction is important because the cost proportions at the beginning of the period were the cumulative outcome of earlier developments and, therefore, could not be modified by managerial efforts during the period. On the other hand, the relative changes in the various cost categories during the period may be attributable to adjustments in markets and company operations taking place during the period as well as to the continuation of previous developments.

Similarly, in the managerial planning of cost adjustment objectives, a knowledge of current cost proportions serves both to indicate the categories in which cost adjustments will have the greatest effect on total costs and also to aid in estimating the combined effect on total costs of the planned percentage adjustments in each category. The first of these obviously helps management to decide in which sectors cost reduction efforts should be concentrated. The second permits determining whether the proposed adjustments in each category would add up to the planned change in total costs.

Measures of cost proportions are also helpful in a second area of managerial concern—tracing the effects of changes in given cost categories on the other categories. Such efforts may take various forms. For example, the analysis of adjustments in cost proportions over an extended period may reveal regularities in association among changes in the major cost categories—perhaps between adjustments in material costs and in wages, or between wages and salaries, or between overhead and wages. Alternatively, cost proportions may be used to appraise the impact on the internal composition of costs of major changes in manufacturing processes, of advances in mechanisation, of changes in the scale of operations and of other important innovations whose primary impact came during some readily specified period. To give one more illustration, exploration along these lines might reveal consistent patterns of adjustment in cost proportions during recessions, during periods of recovery and during other periods characterised by special economic conditions.

Such findings would obviously strengthen the forecasting efforts which underlie budgeting. They would also facilitate the more thorough analysis of the prospective effects of planned or anticipated innovations by concentrating attention not only on the narrowly localised effects of such innovations, but also on their wider ramifications. Thus, a programme to improve labour methods would be evaluated not only in terms of expected reductions in wage outlays, but also in terms of the possible increases in equipment and supervisory costs which might be entailed. Moreover, by indicating which cost categories have tended most frequently to offset economies in materials or wages, these cost proportion determinations may help to safeguard the benefits of further advances by guiding managerial efforts to minimise the most likely of such offsetting adjustments.

A third application of cost proportion measurements involves determination of the trend and degree of flexibility which characterises the proportions accounted for by each of the major cost categories. It will be recalled that the cost proportions which prevail at the end of any period may be regarded as the result of the interaction between the cost proportions prevailing at the beginning of the period and the relative changes in each cost category during the period. Thus, any discernible trend in the cost proportions recorded at the end of successive periods reflects the cumulative effect of the cost adjustments experienced within each of these periods. Finding of such trends may help to counterbalance the tendency of management to concentrate on factors immediately affecting costs by emphasising the need to give greater consideration to the longer term pressures reflected by such trends. In addition, such trends may serve to indicate the probable course of future cost adjustments—recognition of which may guide management either to devise more effective means of adapting policies to such prospects, or to undertake major efforts to modify such trends.

Analysis of the degree of flexibility in the various proportions of total costs will reveal the practical limitations within which adjustment goals should be set during short periods. Moreover, a comparison of short-term flexibility with the long-term trend of the proportion accounted for by a given cost category should help to indicate the relative influence of long-term and of short-term factors in determining adjustments in the category —thus suggesting which of these should be the primary focus of managerial control efforts.

In analysing changes in a particular proportion, it should be emphasised that observed adjustments may be due not only to changes in this given category, but also to changes in other categories—since the sum of these proportions must always add up to 100 per cent. For example, an increase in the proportion of total costs accounted for by wage payments may be due to increases in wage rates, or in wage earner employment, or in other determinants of total wage payments. But this increased ratio of wage payments to total costs may also result from a decrease in outlays for purchased materials or for other factors of production, without any accompanying change in total wage payments. Similarly, an observed increase in total wage outlays may leave the ratio of wages to total costs unchanged, if the sum of all other costs increased at the same rate as wages. Thus, the fact that adjustments in cost proportions are the result of cost interactions means that great care must be taken to find the causes of observed changes.

Finally, the overall pattern of cost proportions offers a fourth promising focus of analysis. Determination of the stability or flexibility of the pattern of cost proportions may reveal the relative strength of the forces tending to affect all cost categories similarly and of the forces tending to affect them differentially. The extent of such overall stability will also indicate the extent to which management may expect to alter the level of total costs through general increases in efficiency, as compared with efforts to achieve such goals by modifying the proportions in which the various input factors are combined. Then, too, the stability of cost proportions may also be interpreted as indicating the extent to which innovations in production and marketing tend to affect the proportions in which the total income from operations is divided among the factors of production.

Although each of the foregoing applications of cost proportion measurements would appear to be of interest to economic analysis as well as to management officials, attention may be called briefly to some of the special benefits for general economic analysis. The consideration of factor proportions is close to the heart of the general theory of production. Yet theoretical analysis has hardly advanced beyond formulating the hypothesis that at any given time there must be some optimum combination of factor proportions—and then deliberately selecting data so as to support this result. Extended empirical analysis, however, may be expected to enrich such theoretical efforts both by elaborating the relevant framework of concepts and by producing actual results which may be used to test speculative hypotheses and to generate new hypotheses.

Specifically, such research may lead to the modification of the basic concepts of factor proportions to allow for the consideration of economic values as well as of physical quantities. Moreover, actual industrial studies may reveal the width of the margins within which different factors may be substituted for one another within relatively short periods. Trends in cost proportions may provide bases for the development of theories concerning long-term re-allocations of productive resources. Comparison of the long-term patterns of adjustments in cost proportions for a large number of industries may shed new light on the changes which may be characteristic of successive stages in the growth patterns of industries (see Chapter 9). And exploration of the cost aspects of factor proportions may yield increasingly effective means of integrating the theories of production and distribution —by supplementing the usual emphasis on tracing the effects on distribution of changes in factor proportions with a parallel emphasis on the extent to which distribution pressures may lead to the modification of factor proportions.

4.3 UNIT COSTS

The importance attributed to unit costs in managerial decision making and in economic theory is apparent from the fact that this level of costs has dominated analytical consideration almost to the exclusion of all other elements of the structure of costs. To understand the reasons for this preoccupation, it is necessary to review the purposes which unit costs are expected to serve.

4.3.1 *The Cost Aspects of Unit Costs*
Conceived in the simplest possible terms, unit costs might be regarded as the sum of outlays involved in producing a single unit of product. Thus, in an establishment devoted to making relatively simple products one at a time, unit costs could be determined by merely adding together the actual cost of each of the resources used to manufacture each unit of product. Such patterns of production may once have accounted for a major segment of industrial activity, but this is no longer true.

Modern large-scale production involves the subdivision of manufacturing activity into numerous parts. Each is continuously engaged in a network of processing and fabricating operations yielding many units of one or more types of components which are eventually assembled into categories of marketable products. The fundamental principle of such continuously functioning specialised operations is that inevitable variations in production rates on each job and in the exact dimensions and quality characteristics of each product component may be harmonised through the establishment of permissible zones of variability, which are designed to ensure the effective integration of all activities and product components conforming to these boundaries. This approach involves a fundamental shift from a direct concern with each unit of each resource used directly in making each individual unit of each product component to a direct concern with the *average* amount of each resource used directly in making the *average* unit of each product component. Under such conditions, there is a shift from the measurement of the actual cost of each direct input used in turning out each unit of product in each operation to the measurement of the average cost of each direct input in the average unit of each product.

How are these average direct unit costs determined? Theoretically, they might be determined by measuring the actual direct costs for every single unit of product in a given operation and then averaging these. This is not the procedure in common use, however. Instead, what is done is to measure the total costs of each direct resource used in an operation during a given period of time and then dividing these totals by the number of units produced during that period. Even at the level of single operations, average direct unit costs really represent a relationship between total costs and total output rather than an average of the actual costs of each unit of output.

But changes in manufacturing operations have also generated other important modifications in the development of a meaningful concept of unit costs. For example, the increasing specialisation of functions associated with large-scale production has involved a considerable elaboration of the contributory activities of so-called indirect inputs, such as planning, control, product development, methods improvement, training and supervisory activities. These, too, must be considered as part of the total manufacturing cost. In this case, however, the obvious impracticability of attempting to measure the amount of each of these costs directly applied in making each unit of product leaves no feasible alternative to estimating their contribution to unit costs by some means essentially involving the division of such total costs by total output. And much the same process is usually involved in establishing the average cost of each machine per unit of product.

Up to this point, the discussion has sought to establish two points concerning the nature of unit costs in modern manufacturing. First, that they represent statistical averages rather than determinations of the actual cost of producing each unit of product, and second, that unit costs actually represent a relationship between total costs during a given period and the volume of output during that same period. The reference above to technical, managerial and machine costs, however, introduces still another modification of the unit cost concept. Specifically, such outlays involve undertakings whose contributions to production may be unevenly distributed in time. Thus, technical development and methods improvement convey variable benefits, often involving considerable delays before the emergence of major advances. And the productive contributions of capital facilities and equipment may likewise vary in accordance with changing levels of productive activity, to say nothing of the risks associated with maintenance requirements and obsolescence. Accordingly, the inclusion of these salary and overhead costs within the framework of total unit costs involves not only the need for a statistical average of the relationship of total actual costs to total output during a given period, but also involves attributing to the period certain additional costs based upon an estimate of the probable relationship average between such costs and output over longer periods of time.

4.3.2 The Product Aspect of Unit Costs

Does the resulting composite of statistical averages yield a figure representing the average cost of producing an average unit of product in a given plant during a specified period? This introduces the troublesome question of what is meant by an average unit of product. In plants producing a single product, without variations in sizes, models and other characteristics, the definition of the average unit of product offers no difficulties. But where a plant produces a variety of products, what is the product basis for defining average unit costs? The most common means of dealing with this problem is to organise cost accounting procedures so as to yield an average unit cost for each product category—this involves additional estimates concerning the allocation of the costs of jointly used facilities among the various product lines. But even this fails to provide a basis for appraising adjustments in the average level of unit costs of the plant considered as an organic whole. And much the same shortcoming is evident at the level of the firm, especially in cases involving multi-plant operations.

In order to determine the significance of these shortcomings, it is necessary to review the purposes of measuring and analysing adjustments in average unit costs. One of these, concerned with the appraisal of production cost pressures on pricing policy, may be reasonably well served by average unit costs on a product-by-product basis, since price quotations must be established on the same basis. But a number of other important objectives, including the evaluation of past operations of the total plant and the planning of future operations, are less adequately served by such product-centred cost data.

From the standpoint of the top management of a firm, such appraisal and planning must be based on an integrated consideration of all resources within its control—and this same comprehensive approach must be employed within the sphere of production activities as a whole, as well as at the level of individual plants. The object, of course, is to maximise returns on all resources allocated to production, both on a short- and a long-term basis. Hence, product-by-product results must be combined somehow so as to provide means of assessing aggregate performance.

Viewed more closely, it is apparent that manufacturing operations are established on a plant basis. Resources are committed on that basis and returns must, therefore, be appraised on that same basis. From the standpoint of managerial decision making, such measures of aggregate performance serve two important purposes. First, they yield results which are not only more comprehensive than individual product-by-product measures, but which may differ significantly from such component findings, and second, they provide a means of gauging the effects of pressures and policies tending to affect plant operations as a whole, as differentiated from developments affecting particular product lines.

The aggregate results of plant operations may differ significantly from those reported on an individual product basis, because product lines usually differ in importance and also because their cost characteristics may be dissimilar. As an illustration one might examine the simple case of a plant producing three products, which were individually found to have experienced a 5 per cent increase, a 5 per cent decrease and a 10 per cent decrease in total unit costs. What happened to the average unit cost of production in the plant? Obviously, it might have increased, decreased or remained unchanged, depending on the proportion of total costs accounted for by each of the product lines. An even more fundamental insight is provided by a consideration of the effects of differences in the cost characteristics of the various product lines. One illustration of this is provided by the simple case in which each of the product lines is found to have experienced no change in total unit costs. Does it follow that total costs per unit of output for the plant as a whole likewise remained unchanged? Not necessarily. If the total unit cost of Product A was less than that of the other products, and if Product A's proportion of total output rose, then average unit costs for the plant would have declined according to prevailing methods of calculating such adjustments, e.g. unit cost per ton of steel shipments. And if the preceding example had concerned differences in unit wage costs rather than total unit costs, the same conclusion would obviously have followed.

The immediate purpose of these illustrations was to demonstrate that aggregate results at the plant level might differ significantly from those developed on a product-by-product basis. But the more fundamental object was to emphasise that efforts to maximise the aggregate performance of the plant requires a shift in orientation from seeking to maximise the performance of each product line considered separately in favour of seeking to maximise the contribution of each product line to the performance of the plant as a whole. Thus, for example, a programme designed to reduce unit wage costs for the plant as a whole might be more effectively promoted by reducing unit wage costs in the product lines accounting for the major proportion of total wage costs in the plant than by dispersing such efforts in the interests of seeking to effect some reduction in the unit wage cost of each product line. Similarly, total unit costs for the plant as a whole might be reduced more effectively by concentrated efforts to effect substantial reductions in the dominant product lines than by pressing for modest reductions in all product lines.

But the foregoing discussion covers only one aspect of the value of plant-wide measures of performance from the standpoint of managerial efforts to evaluate past results and to plan an effective strategy for improving them in the future. Such measures are also valuable as a means of appraising the effects of policies and pressures tending to impinge on plant operations as a whole. Such plant-wide factors are of two kinds; those involving common pressures and policies affecting all productive operations and those involving the allocation of resources as among product lines. Examples of the former would include the locational advantages and disadvantages of the plant site, the effectiveness of plant-wide production planning and controls and the soundness of managerial policies relating to labour relations, plant maintenance and inventories. The other sector of managerial decisions mentioned tends to affect operations as a whole because the competition among product lines for the best labour, equipment and supervision, for greater allocations of methods improvement and technical services, and for new resources means that the result achieved by individual product lines tend to interact with one another. Accordingly, plant-wide measures of performance may serve two additional purposes. They may throw some light on the extent to which individual product line results are traceable to common developments affecting all product lines, instead of attributing such results solely to unique factors affecting each product line, and such plant-wide results may also be used to appraise the effectiveness of plant management's performance both in allocating resources among product lines and in establishing plant-wide policies and controls.

It is obvious, of course, that this discussion is not intended to question the importance of product-centred unit cost determinations. Indeed, attention has been called to their importance as a basis for pricing policy, as a basis for revealing differences in the cost characteristics and adjustments of different product lines, as a basis for analysing detailed cost changes in individual operations, and as a basis for developing plant-wide measures of performance. But the analysis has emphasised that product-centred cost data should be supplemented by measures of plant-wide cost adjustments to provide important additional guides to the managerial evaluation of performance and to the development of programmes designed to increase the effectiveness with which all plant resources are utilised.

The development of such aggregate cost measures raises one further question relating to the interpretation of unit costs. In using the term 'average cost per unit of product', what is meant by 'unit of product' in plants and firms producing a variety of types, sizes and models of product lines? According to the original concept of unit costs, which referred to the cost of producing a discrete product, the question would have to be answered by postulating a unit of composite product. Thus, in a plant producing various sizes and models of a given product line, the product basis of average unit costs would be taken as referring not to a particular size or model, but rather to a non-existent composite product representing the weighted average of the range of sizes and models produced. For example, a refrigerator plant producing various sizes, with and without freezer compartments and other features, might well find that the average production cost per refrigerator had risen by 6·7 per cent over the preceding year, while the composite average unit had changed from a 12·54 to a 14·12 cubic foot volume with some attendant changes in motor design, insulation and colour options as well as freezer size. Clearly, this approach is of limited value for managerial purposes, because every change in the composition of output would alter the characteristics of the composite product, thus preventing unit cost comparisons from period to period, and because the concept of a composite product is meaningless from the standpoint of production as well as sales.

A more useful approach to the above question is suggested by recalling the earlier view that, under modern industrial conditions, average unit costs may be regarded as defining the relationship between total costs and total output during a given period. It is apparent, of course, that the concept of total output is no more useful for individual product pricing or for the design of sales programmes for particular products than the concept of a composite product. But the total output concept is more directly relevant to sales management's concern with differentiating between the value of sales and the volume of sales. And the concept of total output is of direct significance from the standpoint of production. Plant management is concerned with the utilisation of its total resources. From this viewpoint, production is regarded as a process involving the absorption of productive efforts and resources into marketable products. Accordingly, total output is recognised not only as directly relevant to such aspects of production management as establishing the level of input requirements, of operating activity and of capacity utilisation, but also as representing a meaningful summation of aggregate productive contributions, whatever the combination of product types absorbing such contributions.

Thus, the interpretation of changes in average unit costs as representing changes in the relationship between the level of total costs and the level of total productive contributions has direct significance for the managerial evaluation of performance. Specifically, it provides an understandable basis for appraising changes in average unit production costs at the level of individual plants, despite the common tendency towards variation in the product composition of output. Moreover, the careful refinement of such measures may also help to evaluate changes in unit production costs at the level of the firm, as well as to analyse changes in the average unit production costs of plants producing different sets of products.

5 Costs: Analytical Framework

The use of cost adjustments as guides to managerial decision making is determined partly by the nature of relevant managerial objectives and partly by managerial beliefs about the patterns of unit cost adjustment through time. The latter provides the basis for estimating prospective changes and the former provides the criteria for defining the way in which management should seek to modify expected adjustments. Together, they provide a useful framework for appraising past changes and the modification of expectations found to be seriously at odds with desired performance.

5.1 UNIT COST ADJUSTMENT OBJECTIVES

Managerial efforts to control unit costs have been concerned overwhelmingly with reducing their magnitude. Although the soundness of this objective is accepted universally, it may be useful to spell out the frequently unstated limitations within which programmes must be developed. One of these, mentioned in the discussion of managerial control ratios, specifies that decreases in unit costs are desirable only when they do not entail a more than proportionate reduction in the market value of resulting products; and, conversely, that increases in unit costs may be acceptable when they lead to more than proportionate gains in such market values. A second involves recognition of the possible justifiability of temporary increases in unit costs as a consequence of innovations which may be expected to yield significant economies in a later period. Still another limitation, which is more often unrecognised than the other two, centres around the need to differentiate between unit cost adjustments which result from extra-firm developments largely beyond management's control and those engendered by deliberate modifications within the plant. Thus, decreases in unit costs resulting from general reductions in the market level of material prices would obviously have to be interpreted differently from decreases in unit costs due to intra-plant improvements in manufacturing methods.

The objective of reducing unit costs is often interpreted as requiring un-remitting pressure to decrease each component of unit costs. Closer scru-tiny of managerial goals, however, will demonstrate that this need not follow. The basic aim is only the reduction of total unit costs. When this can be achieved by reducing each component of unit costs, the results clearly justify the process. Often, however, total unit costs have been reduced even more significantly by adopting innovations which involve increasing some unit costs in order to make compensating reductions in other unit costs. Common examples of this process include mechanisation, shifts to higher quality material inputs, and increasing technical and supervisory staffs in order to reduce direct operating costs. In any event, the objective of reducing total unit costs does not necessarily entail the reduction of each component of unit costs. On the contrary, the object is rather to maximise the contribution of each category of unit costs to re-ducing total unit costs, whether this involves increasing or decreasing the particular component. And, of course, much the same reasoning would apply to controlling the unit cost of each of the subdivisions of the manu-facturing process.

Managerial efforts to control unit costs are also concerned at times with the flexibility of such outlays. The underlying problem here is usually con-sidered to be due to a tendency for total unit costs to rise under conditions of declining output, thus restricting efforts to maintain sales by reducing product prices, and even threatening net losses when output contracts sharply. Accordingly, management might be encouraged to increase the flexibility of costs by substituting variable costs for fixed costs. While there are ways of doing this, it is worth examining their prospective effects before recommending them.

Three of these effects would seem to be most important. First, if total unit costs are expected to rise with declining production—presumably because total overhead is spread over fewer units of product—then such total unit costs might also be expected to decrease with expanding output, thereby offering unit cost advantages on the upswing which would tend to offset the disadvantages borne during the downswing. Second, the net effect of these adjustments in unit costs on total sales would depend on the extent to which the given product markets respond to attendant price adjustments, i.e., on the price elasticity of demand. If decreasing prices during a recession fail to engender significant gains in output, for example, the effect of relatively inflexible costs may be less serious than seemed to be the case. Third, the means by which fixed costs may be replaced by variable costs frequently involve an increase in the average level of total unit costs over the course of a production cycle. Specifically, resort to lower levels of mechanisation and to the reduction of technical and supervisory personnel may well decrease total overhead costs, but they may also decrease the contributions to productive efficiency derived from such equipment and specialised services. As a result, unit costs may decline more than was previously the case during periods of shrinking output, but they are also likely to rise sufficiently higher than previously during periods of increasing output to bring the average over the entire cycle to a higher level than before the change. In short, increasing the flexibility of unit costs tends to be accompanied by significant burdens as well as benefits, thus counselling careful evaluation of the net effects over the entire course of production cycles before determining the optimum level of flexibility.

5.2 INTERRELATIONSHIPS AMONG UNIT COST ADJUSTMENTS AND PRICE

The most common approach in seeking to account for adjustments in various categories of costs has been to identify the factors presumed to have a direct bearing on each category, to trace the apparent effects of such factors on the category involved, and then to explore the influences responsible for variations in these determining factors in the hope of developing guides to their more effective control. It should be recognised, however, that this independent approach to the adjustments in each category implies that such adjustments are due to pressures and developments which are essentially unique to that category and, hence, that each category tends to follow a course through time which has little relationship to the adjustment patterns experienced by the other unit outlays. But there may be similarities as well as dissimiliarities among unit outlay adjustments. And such broadened perspectives would also suggest that the changes in each category may represent the result of forces tending to affect two or more categories, as well as of pressures tending to affect each category by itself.

The latter of the two viewpoints is clearly preferable on logical grounds, because it includes the particularistic approach without excluding broader interrelationships. It is also preferable on practical grounds, because it minimises the danger inherent in the particularistic approach of over-estimating the effects of the unique factors affecting each unit outlay category, while ignoring the possibly influential effects of more pervasive developments. The most important advantage of the broader viewpoint, however, is that it accords with management's need to develop a more effectively integrated view of the interrelationships among unit cost adjustments—a fundamental requirement for the design of cost control programmes which encompass all costs simultaneously instead of representing essentially separate programmes for controlling each category of outlays.

5.2.1 Interrelationships Among Unit Costs

Interrelationships among adjustments in unit outlays are of importance to management because both the volume and the value of output represent the joint product of all inputs; because the various inputs are partly competitive with, and partly capable of being substituted for, one another; and because all inputs are subject to some forces which affect operations as a whole, as well as more specialised pressures. Accordingly, there are three aspects of such interrelationships which are most likely to be relevant to managerial decision making. One involves the similarities reflected by concurrent adjustments in each category of unit outlays. A second concerns the pattern of interactions among such adjustments. And a third involves the combined effect of unit cost adjustments on average product value per unit, or average selling price.

In analysing the interrelationships among unit outlay adjustments, one might begin by determining the extent and loci of similarities in adjustment patterns through time. Findings of consistent similarities among two or more categories might then be interpreted as suggesting that the broader forces affecting all of the categories together were more influential than the particular factors causing different adjustments in each. And, conversely, even findings of dissimilarity might mean only that the particular factors were dominant rather than that the broader pressures were non-existent.

Long familiarity with the particularistic approach to the analysis of unit cost adjustments has resulted in widespread recognition of the factors tending to concentrate their effects primarily on unit wage costs, or on unit materials cost, or on the other categories of unit outlay.* For example, changes in unit wage costs are commonly attributed to changes in wage rates and labour productivity which are traced, in turn, to employment levels, trade union strength, changes in the composition of required skills and similar labour-focused factors. But what is the nature of the forces which have broadly similar effects on two or more of the categories?

At this exploratory stage, it may suffice merely to distinguish between two groups of such broader forces. The first, concerned with broader forces operating within the framework of the given plant, firm or industry, would include changes in output levels, changes in the product composition of output, changes in basic production processes and the effects of certain

* For an interesting alternative classification of unit costs, see[1, p. 121].

general managerial policies. The second, concerned with broader forces operating over wider sectors of the economy, would include changes in general business conditions, inflationary and deflationary tides in the general price level, and the effects of war and other far-reaching economic developments. And the relative influence of these internal and successively broader external pressures might be estimated by comparing the patterns of similarity within the plant or firm with those in the industry and, finally, with those in other industries likely to be affected by the same general economic pressures.

Attention turns next to possible means of accounting for any observed differences among concurrent adjustments in unit outlays. As was indicated earlier, such differences may be due not only to the effects of the particular pressures on each category, but also to interactions among unit outlay adjustments. Three forms of interaction may prove reasonably common: one involving temporary interactions among particular adjustments; another involving persistent patterns of interaction among particular variables; and a third involving persistent patterns of interaction among several or all unit outlay adjustments.

The first occurs when significant changes in a particular category of unit costs are generated by changes in operations which entail some re-allocation of functions among the inputs, thereby leading to concurrent adjustments in other cost categories as well. For example, a reduction in unit wage costs as a result of mechanisation might well be accompanied by an increase in machine costs. Similarly, a reduction in unit material costs as the result of shifting to a lower grade of materials, or to less highly processed materials, might be accompanied by increases in unit wage as well as other costs. Such interactions would depend on the nature of the innovation, however, and would not justify the assumption that all changes in unit material costs would necessarily elicit directly responsive adjust ments in unit wage costs. In general, the analytical questions to be considered in this connection concern the extent to which such patterns of interaction may be common enough to warn management of the loci and extent of the offsetting adjustments likely to attend particular innovations. And the importance of such considerations is apparent from the fact that major improvements rarely yield the full measure of the economies anticipated at their inception, partly because of the failure of such expectations to take full account of the resulting re-allocation of functions and of associated costs.

The second form of interaction, involving persistent relationships between the differential adjustments in particular categories of unit outlays, would presuppose the existence of some general causal relationship. This would be most likely to occur in respect to categories whose adjustments are partly or wholly determined by changes in other categories. The most obvious example would be the change in profits per unit, which is determined by the relationship between the change in average selling price and the change in total unit costs. In this connection, however, consideration should also be given to the possibility that one or two categories of unit cost may have a greater or more consistent effect on adjustments in profits per unit than other categories.

The third form of interactions, involving persistent relationships among the differential adjustments in several categories of unit outlay, might be regarded as reflecting certain inherent adjustment characteristics of these categories. For example, changes in the level of operations may be attended by consistent patterns of relative flexibility among the various unit outlay categories.

It has already been noted that the differences among concurrent adjustments in unit outlays which are not attributable to interactions may be regarded as the result of pressures which bear uniquely on each category. But these pressures may be further subdivided into two groups, one comprising pressures limited to the given plant, firm or industry, and the other representing broader pressures which tend to exert similar effects on the adjustments in a given category of unit outlays experienced in a number of industries. For example, even when unit wage costs adjustments are widely at variance with concurrent adjustments in the other categories of unit cost in the given industry, they may yet be closely similar to concurrent unit wage cost adjustments in other industries. Such comparisons would then indicate the extent to which the deviation of particular unit cost categories might be ascribed to broadly pervasive pressures rather than the influence of comparatively specific developments within the given plant, firm or industry.

This suggests a general approach to the analysis of concurrent adjustment in unit outlays which differs from the commonly accepted particularistic approach in three respects: by including similarities as well as dissimilarities in such adjustments; by considering the possibility that dissimilarities may be due to interactions among the adjustments as well as to the effects of specialised pressures on each category; and by considering the possibility that both similarities and dissimilarities among intra-plant or intra-firm adjustments may be due to industry-wide and even broader economic pressures as well as to special developments and problems which are limited to the plant or firm. Application of this approach requires simultaneous examination of adjustments in all unit outlays for each period as a basis for determining the extent and loci of similarities and dissimilarities within the given plant, firm or industry. And resulting adjustment patterns would then be compared with

4+

associated sectors of industry as a guide to estimating the relative influence of internal and of external pressures on observed results.

5.2.2 Unit Costs and the Average Price of Products

Changes in average product value per unit of output may be measured by dividing index numbers of total product value by index numbers of total physical output for identical years, when both index series have the same base year. It is apparent, therefore, that the resulting series measures the relationship between concurrent changes in total product value and in the total volume of output. But the total value of products may be regarded either as the sum of all costs plus profits or as the sum of each product's output multiplied by its selling price. Accordingly, changes in average product value per unit of output may be interpreted either as the net result of adjustments in each of the unit cost categories plus profits per unit of output, or of changes in the weighted average selling price of all products manufactured. Both aspects are of major significance for managerial purposes.

The weighted average price of all products provides a valuable supplement to information about individual product prices. For example, it is frequently desirable for control purposes to determine the extent to which changes in the value of sales are attributable to changes in the level of product prices rather than to changes in the volume of production. But this is difficult to do in establishments producing a variety of products, especially when product prices have undergone differential adjustments and when these products account for differing proportions of total output. Yet this very need is directly served by determination of the weighted average selling price.* In addition, the weighted average selling price also provides a measure of average gross sales income per unit of output which may be compared directly with average total costs per unit of output to provide a second useful basis for evaluating current operations as a whole. This is particularly useful in establishments which do not have separate production facilities for each product, but rather use common facilities for various products. Under such conditions, a direct comparison of income and outlay flows for the plant or firm as a whole may provide a valuable practical check on the soundness of the cost–price relationships established for individual products as well as on the soundness of maintaining particular combinations of product output.

Viewed as the sum of average unit costs plus average profit per unit,

---

* For example, see the product price index carried in the General Electric Company's annual report for 1959, directly under net sales billed, to help differentiate between the effects of increased volume and increased prices [2, p. 30].

the average product value represents an important basis for evaluating the significance of adjustments in the individual components of unit outlays. This relationship is often viewed one-sidedly as implying that adjustments in average product value per unit are the result of changes in actual unit costs and in planned levels of profit per unit. Accordingly, the relevant analytical questions tend to concern the effects on this resultant of changes in average unit material costs, or in average unit wage costs, or in various combinations of changes in unit outlays.

On the other hand, costs may also be viewed as representing the distribution of returns from production, in which case the analytical questions would centre around determining the effect of changes in average selling price on the various categories of unit outlay. This viewpoint may be challenged on the grounds that only profits represent a variable share of returns, all other costs having been assumed prior to actual sale. But such a distinction is unrealistic in view of labour's determined efforts to share in increased returns and in view of the widespread tendency of the upper echelons of salaried personnel to do likewise. Indeed, recognition of the production process as involving continuous flows of income and outlays cannot but emphasise the circular relationship between costs and prices, thus invalidating efforts to establish an irreversible causal sequence. As will be shown later, this relationship may be probed more deeply by applying a measure designed to determine the relative contributions of the change in each category of costs (as well as in unit profits) to the concurrent change in average product price—or, reversing the implied causality, it may be regarded as measuring the proportional allocation of the change in average product price among the unit cost (and profit) categories.

5.3 ANALYTICAL MODEL OF COST STRUCTURE

The concept of a structure of costs implies that total costs, cost proportions and unit costs comprise a coherent network of relationships whose fuller understanding may provide useful guides for managerial planning and control and may also provide interesting foci for economic analysis. Accordingly, it may be helpful to summarise the analytical components of the preceding discussion so as to highlight this underlying framework.

As a first step, one may regard total product value as determined either by the sum of all costs plus profits or by the product of output levels and average product prices. And this dual approach may also be applied to total costs and to aggregate outlays within each of its component categories, as shown below:

Total Material Costs (M)   = Unit Material Costs (M/PO)
                              × Physical Output (PO)

Total Wage Costs (W)   = Unit Wage Costs (W/PO)
                              = Physical Output (PO)

Total Other Costs (O)   = Unit Other Costs (O/PO)
                              × Physical Output (PO)

Total Costs (TC)   = Total Unit Costs (TC/PO)
                              × Physical Output (PO)

Total Profits (P)   = Unit Profits (P/PO)
                              × Physical Output (PO)

Total Value of Product (VP) = Average Product Price (VP/PO)
                              × Physical Output (PO)

In turn, relative changes in total costs during any given period would be determined by the relative change in each of its component costs weighted by its respective share of total cost at the beginning of the period. And relative changes in total unit costs would similarly be determined by changes during the period in each of the unit cost categories weighted by its respective share of total unit costs at the beginning of the period.

$$(\Delta TC)_{1-2} = \left[(\Delta M)_{1-2}\left(\frac{M}{TC}\right)_1\right] + \left[(\Delta W)_{1-2}\left(\frac{W}{TC}\right)_1\right] + \left[(\Delta O)_{1-2}\left(\frac{O}{TC}\right)_1\right]$$

$$\left(\Delta\frac{TC}{PO}\right)_{1-2} = \left[\left(\Delta\frac{M}{PO}\right)_{1-2}\left(\frac{M}{TC}\right)_1\right] + \left[\left(\Delta\frac{W}{PO}\right)_{1-2}\left(\frac{W}{TC}\right)_1\right]$$
$$+ \left[\left(\Delta\frac{O}{PO}\right)_{1-2}\left(\frac{O}{TC}\right)_1\right]$$

where subscripts 1 and 2 denote the beginning and end of the given period.

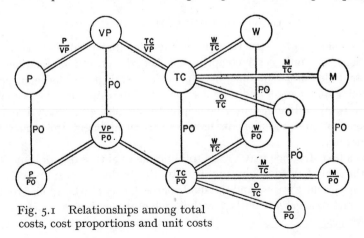

Fig. 5.1   Relationships among total costs, cost proportions and unit costs

These relationships are illustrated in Figure 5.1 (in which the lower right portion concerned with total unit costs and its components ties into the middle portion of Figure 3.4).

These relationships may also be used to calculate the relative contributions of changes in each of the unit cost categories during a period to the corresponding change in total unit costs (or in average product prices). As indicated in the earlier discussion, this involves weighting the change in each unit cost during the period by its share of total costs (or value of product) at the beginning of the period and then dividing each of these weighted contributions (CW) by the sum of all CW's. The general technique as devised by Mills [4, pp. 115–17] may be summarised as follows:

$$(\Delta M/PO)_{1-2} \times (M/TC)_1 = CW_m \qquad (\Delta M/PO)_{1-2} \times (M/VP)_1 = CW_m$$
$$(\Delta W/PO)_{1-2} \times (W/TC)_1 = CW_w \qquad (\Delta W/PO)_{1-2} \times (W/VP)_1 = CW_w$$
$$\underline{(\Delta O/PO)_{1-2} \times (O/TC_1) = CW_o} \qquad (\Delta O/PO)_{1-2} \times (O/VP)_1 = CW_o$$
$$\qquad\qquad\qquad\qquad\qquad\qquad\qquad (\Delta P/PO)_{1-2} \times (P/VP)_1 = CW_p$$
$$(\Delta TC/PO)_{1-2} \times 1{\cdot}00 \quad = \Sigma CW \qquad \underline{}$$
$$\qquad\qquad\qquad\qquad\qquad\qquad\quad (\Delta VP/PO)_{1-2} \times 1{\cdot}00 \quad = \Sigma CW$$

The net sum of CW's (subtracting negative from positive values) equals the change in TC/PO (or VP/PO). The gross sum of CW's (ignoring signs) measures the total upward and downward pressures exerted on TC/PO (or VP/PO). Comparison of each unit cost's CW with the gross sum measures its relative contribution.

The results may also be interpreted, of course, in a distributive perspective indicating, for example, the relative distribution among productive factors of the change in total payments derived from price changes.

Analysis of the structure of costs may be extended by noting that the unit cost of each input factor is determined by the product of its price and the quantity employed per unit of output. Thus, unit material costs are the product of the prices paid for materials and the quantities used per unit of output. Unit wage costs are the product of average hourly earnings and man-hours required per unit of output. And other costs may be treated similarly. For example, depreciation charges per unit of output may be regarded as determined by the rate of such charges relative to fixed investment (analogous to the factor price) and the level of fixed investment actively utilised in producing the specified output (measured by adjusting the productivity of fixed investment for the rate of capacity utilisation).

$$\frac{\text{Fixed Charges}}{\text{Output}} = \left(\frac{\text{Fixed Charges}}{\text{Fixed Investment}}\right)$$
$$\div \left[\left(\frac{\text{Capacity}}{\text{Fixed Investment}} \times \frac{\text{Output}}{\text{Capacity}}\right)\right]$$

At this point it will be recognised that the structure of cost relationships has joined on to the network of productivity relationships, as shown in Figure 5.2 (and earlier in Figure 3.4).

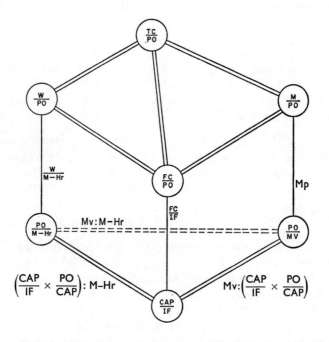

Fig. 5.2   Relationships between unit costs, factor prices and productivity network

One additional extension which may be considered at this point is the possible influence of changes in the general price level (GPL) on factor prices and, through them, on unit costs. As a result, the framework presented as the first step in this discussion may be expanded as follows to incorporate some of the points made subsequently:

$$M = M/PO \times PO = Mp \times \frac{Mq}{PO} \times PO = \frac{Mp}{GPL} \times GPL \times \frac{Mq}{PO} \times PO$$

$$W = W/PO \times PO = W/M\text{-}Hr \times \frac{M\text{-}Hr}{PO} \times PO$$

$$= \frac{W/M\text{-}Hr}{GPL} \times GPL \times \frac{M\text{-}Hr}{PO} \times PO$$

$$S = S/PO \times PO = S/SE \times \frac{SE}{PO} \times PO = \frac{S/SE}{GPL} \times GPL \times \frac{SE}{PO} \times PO$$

$$FC = FC/PO \times PO = \frac{FC}{IF} \times \left(\frac{IF}{CAP} \times \frac{CAP}{PO}\right) \times PO$$

$$= \frac{FC/IF}{GPL} \times GPL \times \frac{IF}{PO} \times PO$$

where Mq = quantity of materials input; S = salaries and SE = salaried employees.

This suggests at least initial approaches to the possibiltiy mentioned earlier of exploring the common as well as the dissimilar forces affecting the various components of the structure of costs. In noting that all cost categories are influenced by common changes in output levels and in the general price level, I am not arguing that the given changes in output or in the general price level need have identical effects on the various cost categories. Rather, two points are emphasised. The first is that previous over-concentration on the particular forces tending to affect one or another cost category might well be redressed by a more intensive search for, and evaluation of, such common factors as the general price level. For a detailed review of the factors affecting individual factor proportions and unit input quantities, see [3, pp. 107–166]. The second is that previous over-commitment to a universal conception of the effect of output variations on the major categories of unit cost might similarly be redressed by more intensive empirical examination of possible differences in such effects among industries—and even more intensive review of the assumptions leading to such expectations in theoretical models (see Chapter 7).

Finally, it is apparent, of course, that each of the total and unit cost categories used so far is itself an aggregate of many components. Material costs usually include hundreds and even thousands of categories of purchased materials and supplies at various levels of fabrication. Wage costs cover payrolls for dozens of skill and wage rate classes. Salary costs include payments to clerks, technical staff and supervisors as well as senior executives. Other costs include selling expenses, depreciation charges, etc. Hence, the preceding structure of costs may be elaborated further in two steps which parallel the earlier treatment of the total unit cost of each category of input factors: the first indicating that changes in total unit material costs, for example, represent the weighted average of changes in each of its components categories; and the second indicating that the unit cost of each of these component materials is determined by the product of its price and the quantity used per unit of output.

$$\left(\Delta \frac{M}{PO}\right)_{T1-2} = \left[\left(\Delta \frac{M_A}{PO}\right)_{1-2}\left(\frac{M_A}{M_T}\right)_1\right] + \left[\left(\Delta \frac{M_B}{PO}\right)_{1-2}\left(\frac{M_B}{M_T}\right)_1\right] + \cdots$$

Where M_A, M_B etc. are component materials; M_T represents total material costs

$$\frac{M_A}{PO} = (M_A \text{ price})\left(\frac{M_A\text{vol.}}{PO}\right)$$

What follows is an illustration of the structure of costs in order to suggest means of approaching the analytical foci which have been presented above. It will provide some actual findings for an industrial sector which is important enough and for a long enough time to offer useful guidance in the formulation of at least tentative hypotheses concerning cost behaviour as viewed in a larger framework than has dominated most previous inquiries.

6 Empirical Exploration of the Structure of Costs

Manufacturing costs obviously play an important role in the functioning of an economy. They are a major determinant of production and pricing policies. They constitute an initiating point in the process of income distribution. They are directly influenced by, and may well influence, secular economic forces as well as short-term fluctuations. Thus technological advances, the depletion of natural resources, and changes in the scale of production probably exert much of their pressure on the farther reaches of the economy through their immediate impact on production costs in manufacturing. Costs are likewise deeply imbedded within the network of interactions involved in recurrent changes in price levels, investment requirements and employment. In addition, costs provide a means of measuring changes in the allocation of resources among industries as well as in the porportions in which each industry combines major productive resources.

Sound thinking about industrial cost–price relationships has been seriously handicapped by the secrecy which necessarily veils individual company data and by the striking scarcity of research dealing with manufacturing costs at more broadly aggregate levels. As a result, businessmen and economists have been forced, in grappling with immediate problems of policy, to bridge over these factual voids with a series of assumptions. Thus, recognition of the critical importance of labour-management relations, of the extraordinary progress in technology during recent decades, and of other major currents in industrial development led to widespread acceptance of a variety of such beliefs as the following:

(1) that manufacturing wage costs account for the greater part of the selling price of products in most manufacturing industries;

(2) that the increasing efficiency of production processes and the more thorough utilisation of by-products have led to a progressive and substantial reduction in the ratio of cost of materials to the selling price of manufactured goods;

(3) that sharply increased production per man-hour, attributable largely to more extensive mechanisation and more effective management controls, has steadily reduced the relative importance of wage costs in total product costs;

(4) that the proportion of total selling price accounted for by salaries, overhead, and profits has risen significantly as a result of the combined effects of a higher ratio of managerial and technical personnel to wage earners, of the increased overhead costs attendant on heavier mechanisation, and of the maintenance or expansion of profits presumed to have supplied the necessary incentive to further investment in technological improvements;

(5) that increasing efficiency all along the line has generated a long-term trend toward lower prices for manufactured goods;

(6) that, because of frequent fluctuations in raw material prices, wage rates, profit margins, and levels of production, the internal composition of manufacturing costs is subject to continuous and substantial variation;

(7) that variations in production levels have a marked and inverse effect on total unit cost levels.

Working assumptions such as these have exerted a heavy influence on union policies, on the direction of cost reduction efforts by business firms, on the development of industrial price policies, on government measures for dealing with inflationary and deflationary tides, on public reactions to legislative proposals affecting price, wage and profit levels, and on the economists' view of the impact of advancing industrialisation on the growth and stability of the community's material welfare.

How well do such seemingly logical assumptions hold under the test of facts? By providing the factual basis for a fuller and more accurate understanding of past experience and recent trends in production-cost–price relationships, more intensive research in this area may well contribute to the emergence of sounder guides to the formulation of public and private policies relating to industrial development.

It should be emphasised, however, that the following analysis is presented at this point in order to illustrate how the structure of costs of an industry (or company) may be explored systematically as well as to provide some initial results of such efforts. For this purpose, attention will be restricted to the experience of the iron and steel industry of the United States over the forty year period 1899–1939. The basic data on value and cost elements are from the Census of Manufactures, available for every fifth year from 1899 to 1919 and for odd-numbered years thereafter to 1939.

6.1 CHANGES IN TOTAL COSTS

The group of industries engaged in the manufacture of iron and steel and their products may be divided into three major components: first, blast furnace establishments; second, steelworks and rolling mills; and third, 'all other' iron and steel products which embrace the residual production (outside steelworks and rolling mills) of wire and wirework, forgeings, structural and ornamental products, tin cans and tinware, hardware, plumbers' supplies, steam fittings and other heating apparatus and the products of fifteen additional industries defined in the Census of Manufactures as engaged primarily in turning out iron and steel products. The series used here were constructed so as to retain the largest possible degree of comparability in the face of changing census classifications during the years covered.*

The comparative size of these components within all iron and steel manufacturing and changes in their relative positions may be indicated by their relative contributions to the total, either in terms of physical output or in terms of the value added in the course of processing purchased materials and supplies into goods available for sale. Between 1899 and 1937, the relative contribution of blast furnace production to the estimated physical output of all iron and steel manufacturing declined from 10·5 to 4·6 per cent; that of steel works and rolling mills rose slightly from 48·8 to 49·7 per cent; and that of 'all other' iron and steel products increased from 40·7 to 45·7 per cent [1, p. 271]. Similar adjustments, though differing somewhat in magnitudes, are reflected by census data on value added for the same years: the contribution of blast furnaces declining from 17·6 to 4·4 per cent; that of steelworks and rolling mills rising from 48·2 to 51·4 per cent; and that of 'all other' increasing from 34·2 to 44·2 per cent.

While the total value of the products manufactured by the iron and steel group rose from $1103 million in 1899 to $5790 million in 1939, this period of expansion was marked not only by abrupt variations in the rate of growth but by repeated and sharp declines as well (Fig. 6.1). A comparison of adjustments in the value of product for total iron and steel manufacturing with those for major components reveals that, while the timing of ups and downs was reasonably similar for the total and its several parts, no such uniformity prevailed in either the amplitude of their fluctuations or their

* In addition to those listed above, the group entitled 'Iron and Steel and Their Products, excluding Machinery' includes the following industries: bolts, nuts and washers; galvanising and other coating; nails and spikes; steel springs, excluding wire; wrought pipe, welded and heavy riveted; cast iron pipe; metal doors, shutters, and window sash and frames; firearms; safes and vaults; screw machine products; stoves and ranges, excluding electrical; cutlery; files; saws; and tools, excluding edge tools, machine tools, files and saws. This classification is identical with that published by Fabricant [1, pp. 625–6].

average rates of expansion during the period as a whole. Thus, it may be
noted that between the years 1899 and 1939 the value of blast furnace products rose by 166 per cent; of steelworks and rolling mill products, by 378
per cent; and of 'all other' iron and steel products, by 697 per cent. Blast
furnace product value reached a peak in 1923 of almost five times its 1899

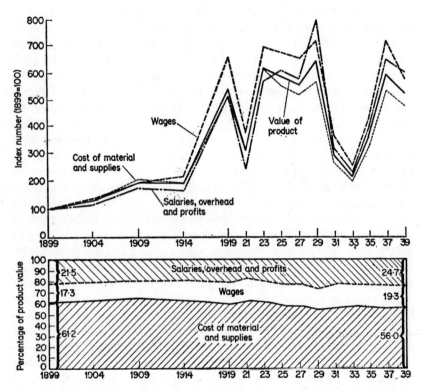

Fig. 6.1   Changes in total costs and in internal composition of costs for all
iron and steel manufacturing, 1899–1939. (Taken from Tables 6.1 and 6.2.)

level, while the other two major categories of output reached peaks in
1929, the value of steelworks and rolling mill products reaching 5·6 times
the 1899 level and that for 'all other' products swelling to almost ten times
the level of thirty years earlier (Figure 6.2).

6.2 CHANGES IN THE INTERNAL COMPOSITION OF COSTS

Some reflection of long-term trends as well as of shorter-term fluctuations in the internal composition of costs may be provided by examination

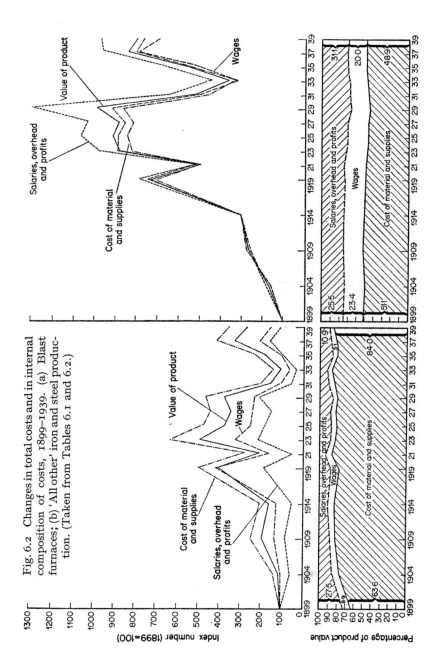

Fig. 6.2 Changes in total costs and in internal composition of costs, 1899–1939. (a) Blast furnaces; (b) 'All other' iron and steel production. (Taken from Tables 6.1 and 6.2.)

of the comparative changes in the following census subdivisions of value
of products:

(1) cost of materials, fuel, purchased electric energy and containers;
(2) wages;
(3) all the remainder of value of product, consisting mainly of salaries,
overhead and profits. (See footnote to Table 6.1.)

The first classification is referred to hereafter as cost of materials; the
third, as salaries, overhead and profits or, more briefly, as SOP. This latter
classification, of course, is an obviously heterogeneous one dominated by
overhead costs and profits. It has been argued, however, that this aggregate may be more meaningful for certain purposes than estimates of its
components inasmuch as such internal allocations are heavily responsive to
managerial preferences, especially in the short run [2, p. 9].

Figure 6.1 may be used not only to demonstrate that each of these cost
categories experience frequent and substantial increases and decreases,
usually similar to the course of adjustments in the value of product, but
also to show the range of dispersion among such cost components in
selected periods as well as the emergence of consistent patterns or sharp
reversals in their relative magnitudes. An even more significant measure
of changes in the internal composition of manufacturing costs is provided
by variations in the proportion of the total value of product accounted for
by each of its major components. As these ratios are traced through the
forty years of economic turbulence between 1899 and 1939, encompassing
the enormous impacts of the First World War, the sharp recession of 1921,
the extraordinary prosperity and boom of the 1920s, the catastrophic
depression of the early thirties, and the subsequent recovery, as well as
the several-fold expansion of the iron and steel industries and the revo-
lutionary advances effected in their technology, the results present a
picture of quite remarkable stability. It would be to misread the lower
panel of Figure 6.1 to imply that it reveals no changes of significance. What
is striking, however, is that such changes have emerged so slowly and have
been of such limited proportions as to contrast sharply with most indices
of economic changes during the period. Indeed, removal of the dates on the
horizontal scale would leave one hard put to it to approximate the loci
of even such extreme phenomena as wars, booms and depressions.

This pronounced stability in the internal composition of costs has proved
to be characteristic of most of the other industry groups and individual
industries that have been studied so far. (See Figures 9.1 to 9.7.) Thus, for
manufacturing as a whole, these relationships reveal a pattern of stability
even greater than that found by Simon Kuznets to characterise the proportional division of the national income among the major categories of

TABLE 6.1 Indexes of value of product and costs for All Iron and Steel manufacturing and major components, 1899–1939*

Index Numbers (1899 = 100)

Year	All Iron and Steel				Blast furnace products				Steelworks and rolling mill products				'All other' iron and steel products			
	Value of product	Cost of materials	Wages	Salaries overhead and profit	Value of product	Cost of materials	Wages	Salaries overhead and profit	Value of product	Cost of materials	Wages	Salaries overhead and profit	Value of product	Cost of materials	Wages	Salaries overhead and profit
1899	100.0	100.0	100.0	100.0	100.0	100.0	100.0	100.0	100.0	100.0	100.0	100.0	100.0	100.0	100.0	100.0
1904	127.8	128.4	138.3	117.7	112.1	136.0	102.2	59.9	112.9	112.9	119.7	106.1	168.7	161.7	175.1	176.7
1909	196.9	206.4	191.7	174.1	189.3	243.8	133.0	81.3	165.1	168.2	159.5	158.7	265.8	271.7	254.4	264.4
1914	193.6	194.7	220.7	168.5	153.6	201.2	123.2	53.3	153.8	151.1	183.9	134.3	300.5	300.5	300.4	300.7
1919	533.1	507.5	649.5	512.3	398.6	489.7	413.0	183.1	473.7	429.9	623.3	491.1	744.6	721.2	750.5	786.2
1921	311.2	315.1	380.8	244.0	203.0	274.6	158.9	51.6	248.1	257.2	317.7	145.7	512.0	498.3	531.9	521.2
1923	615.8	612.2	691.0	565.4	487.2	629.4	318.4	213.2	528.2	523.0	623.5	453.9	879.3	825.9	888.4	979.4
1925	583.5	551.1	671.4	605.4	370.1	469.5	244.9	180.6	493.3	463.5	601.2	499.1	911.4	845.1	887.1	1,066.3
1927	555.5	521.2	652.6	575.0	342.8	440.8	239.5	149.6	465.5	432.3	587.8	470.0	882.5	818.1	856.8	1,034.9
1929	643.4	568.7	720.8	793.8	373.0	464.1	227.0	209.7	563.6	487.1	673.5	743.0	989.7	867.4	920.6	1,297.8
1931	294.9	265.4	367.8	320.2	150.5	197.0	104.3	57.9	234.9	212.8	330.8	223.6	514.6	458.8	491.7	647.3
1933	220.5	204.8	259.3	234.1	103.3	139.9	62.7	31.9	191.5	177.1	253.0	185.6	359.4	331.7	320.5	450.7
1935	364.6	333.8	430.4	399.4	181.2	228.7	102.2	97.0	323.4	284.1	429.8	366.5	573.9	551.7	518.2	669.3
1937	591.6	534.1	719.9	652.0	325.2	414.4	205.4	157.7	557.7	468.4	762.3	692.2	843.5	805.3	794.0	965.3
1939	525.0	480.3	585.9	603.2	266.3	351.6	153.0	106.0	478.1	413.0	597.9	605.1	797.4	763.3	682.8	970.6

* Value of product is selling price at the plant. The classification called briefly 'Cost of Materials' is that defined in the Census of Manufactures to include cost of materials, supplies, containers for products, fuel, and purchased electric energy. That of 'Wages' is made up in general of the pay, whether on time rates or piece rates, of those who perform manual work in manufacturing establishments. All the remainder of value of product, briefly called SOP in later tables and in the text, is predominantly salaries, overhead and profits but of course includes other items of lesser significance. Refer to Sixteenth Census of the United States, 1940, Manufactures, 1939, Volume I, pp. 4–6.

TABLE 6.2 Changes in ratio of cost elements to value of product for All Iron and Steel manufacturing and major components, 1899–1939

Year	All Iron and Steel			Blast furnace products			Steelworks and rolling mill products			'All other' iron and steel products		
	Materials cost to VP	Wages to VP	S O P to VP	Materials cost to VP	Wages to VP	S O P to VP	Materials cost to VP	Wages to VP	S O P to VP	Materials cost to VP	Wages to VP	S O P to VP
	%	%	%	%	%	%	%	%	%	%	%	%
1899	61·2	17·3	21·5	63·6	8·9	27·5	65·5	17·1	17·4	51·1	23·4	25·5
1904	61·5	18·7	19·8	77·2	8·1	14·7	65·4	18·2	16·4	49·0	24·3	26·7
1909	64·2	16·8	19·0	81·9	6·3	11·8	66·7	16·6	16·7	52·2	22·4	25·4
1914	61·6	19·7	18·7	83·3	7·2	9·5	64·3	20·5	15·2	51·1	23·4	25·5
1919	58·3	21·1	20·6	78·1	9·3	12·6	59·4	22·5	18·1	49·5	23·6	26·9
1921	62·0	21·2	16·8	86·0	7·0	7·0	67·9	21·9	10·2	49·7	24·3	26·0
1923	60·9	19·4	19·7	82·2	5·8	12·0	64·8	20·2	15·0	48·0	23·6	28·4
1925	57·8	19·9	22·3	80·7	5·9	13·4	61·5	20·9	17·6	47·4	22·7	29·9
1927	57·4	20·3	22·3	81·8	6·2	12·0	60·8	21·6	17·6	47·4	22·7	29·9
1929	54·1	19·4	26·5	79·1	5·5	15·4	56·6	20·5	22·9	44·8	21·7	33·5
1931	55·1	21·6	23·3	83·2	6·2	10·6	59·3	24·1	16·6	45·6	22·3	32·1
1933	56·9	20·3	22·8	86·1	5·4	8·5	60·5	22·6	16·9	47·2	20·8	32·0
1935	56·1	20·4	23·5	80·3	5·0	14·7	57·5	22·8	19·7	49·1	21·1	29·8
1937	55·3	21·0	23·7	81·0	5·7	13·3	55·0	23·4	21·6	48·8	22·0	29·2
1939	56·0	19·3	24·7	84·0	5·1	10·9	56·6	21·4	22·0	48·9	20·0	31·1

recipients. Exploration of the factors contributing to such major sources of stability in the economy represents only one of the further undertakings for which studies of this kind may provide useful data.

Special interest also attaches to the relative magnitudes of these three cost components. In 1899, the cost of materials and purchased supplies accounted for 61·2 per cent of their value of product, wages for 17·3 per cent, and salaries, overhead, and profits for the remaining 21·5 per cent of the total. Fluctuations in such ratios are readily discernible in the lower panel of Figure 6.1, but these were so small as to leave comparatively un-altered the relative ordering of the magnitudes of the three components. Accounting for 54–64 per cent of the value of product, the cost of materials and supplies consistently exceeded the combined weight of wages and SOP. The share going to wages varied only within the narrow limits of of 17–22 per cent. SOP accounted for 17 to 26 per cent of product value, exceeding the wage ratio in every census year except 1914, 1919 and 1921. One need hardly emphasise that this scale of relative magnitudes is significantly at variance with prevailing conceptions held by many business and labour union executives, to say nothing of the public at large.

In this connection, one may recall the widespread reference to iron and steel manufacturing as an outstanding example of dominance by capital facilities costs, whereas such costs obviously average well under 20 per cent if selling expenses and profits are deducted from SOP—closely comparable with the *average* for all manufacturing industries combined (see Figure 9.7).

The marked diversity among the major industry groupings engaged in the manufacture of iron and steel products, which was noted earlier in respect to changes in the value of product, is also apparent in the composition of their costs. During the greater part of the period 1899 to 1939, wages accounted for only 5–7 per cent of the value of blast furnance products, while the comparable ratio for the 'all other' group was between three and four times as great. Other noteworthy differences between the lower panels of Figure 6.2 include the ratios of SOP to value of product and the ratio of cost of materials to product value.

Perhaps the most striking feature of Figure 6.2, however, is not the difference between components of total iron and steel production illustrated by the left- and right-hand panels, but rather the contrast between the sharp fluctuations depicted in both upper panels and the comparative stability evident in both lower panels. In short, whereas the changes in the total value of product and in total material, wage, and SOP costs represent the result of quite dissimilar trends and variations among the several industrial groups engaged in manufacturing iron and steel products, the stability in the ratios of cost components to product value for all iron and steel products seems attributable to a pervasive stability in such relationships within each of the constituent industrial groups. This contrast between the pronounced variability of total costs and the relative stability in the internal composition of costs is also emphasised in Figure 6.3. By

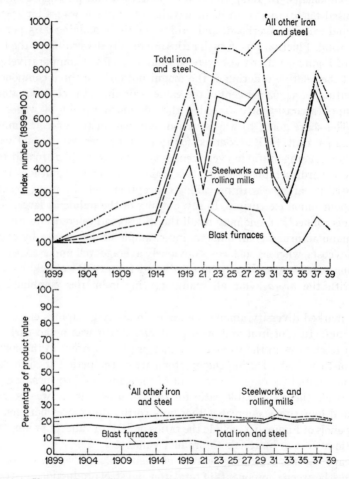

Fig. 6.3   Changes in total wages and in the ratio of wages to value of product for all iron and steel manufacturing and major components, 1899–1939. (From Tables 6.1 and 6.2.)

focusing the comparison on one category of costs—wages—one can see even more clearly how sharp the differences among related industry groupings may be in the magnitude, trend and variability of a category of total costs and, on the other hand, how pervasive may be the tendency toward stability in the ratio of this cost component to the value of product within each industry grouping. Also, notice the tendency, borne out in the analysis of most industry groupings and individual industries studied so far, for wages to account for some relatively minor proportion of product value, usually 25 per cent or less. (See Chapter 9 for similar findings related to a number of manufacturing industries.)

6.3 CHANGES IN COSTS PER UNIT OF OUTPUT

As was noted earlier, variations in the value of product may be traced to the combined effect of changes in the physical volume of output and changes in the average selling price per unit of output. Similarly, fluctuations in the total cost of materials and supplies, in all wages paid, or in aggregate SOP may be considered to be the product of adjustments in the physical volume of production and in the magnitude of these respective cost elements per unit of output. Since rigorous analysis along these lines requires the closest possible comparability between indices of costs and production, the cost series used have been prepared in exact accordance with the industrial classifications employed by Fabricant in his comprehensive estimates of the physical volume of production in manufacturing industries [1, pp. 608–36].

6.3.1 Unit Value and Costs—All Iron and Steel Manufacturing

Study of the relationship between value of product and physical volume of production permits determination both of the course of fluctuations in average selling price per unit of output and of the relative contributions of changes in physical output and in average unit selling price to observed shifts in total product value. As estimated by Fabricant and presented in Figure 6.4, the physical volume of all iron and steel products manufactured rose steadily during the first half of the period being studied, almost tripling between 1899 and 1919. After declining by one-fifth between 1919 and 1921, the physical output resumed its upward course, almost doubling during the next two years, adding a slight gain during 1923–27, and finally rising to a peak in 1929 more than four and a half times the 1899 level. The last decade saw even more violent fluctuations, with physical output declining by 55 per cent during the four years ending in 1933, almost doubling during the next four years, and finally initiating a renewed downward trend which, however, was arrested before long by the onset of war.

Division of the index numbers of product value by the index numbers of the physical volume of production for identical years (both series having 1899 as base year) yields an index number series which represents the average value of product per unit of physical output or average selling price. According to these computations, the average selling price per unit of all iron and steel products manufactured declined by 15 per cent between 1899 and 1914, turned sharply upward during the next five years to reach a level almost twice that of 1899, and then followed a generally downward course until 1933, when it approximated the 1899 level. Average selling price rose by about one-third during the four years terminating in 1937

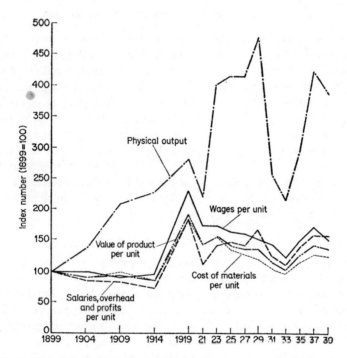

Fig. 6.4   Changes in physical output and in unit costs and selling price for all iron and steel manufacturing, 1899–1939. (From Table 6.3.)

before easing off slightly between 1937 and 1939, to wind up at a level just 34·4 per cent above that prevailing forty years earlier (Figure 6.5).

The relative contributions of adjustments in the volume of physical production and in average selling price per unit to observed variations in product value are depicted for selected periods of general economic significance in Figure 6.5. Thus, it may be observed that the rise of 93·6 per cent in the value of all iron and steel products between 1899 and 1914 was due to the combined effect of a rise of 128·6 per cent in the physical volume of output and a reduction of 15·3 per cent in average unit selling price. Contrary to prevalent opinion, the rise of 175 per cent in product value during the First World War period was due primarily not to an expansion of physical production but rather to price inflation. Physical production increased by only 23 per cent, while unit selling price rose by

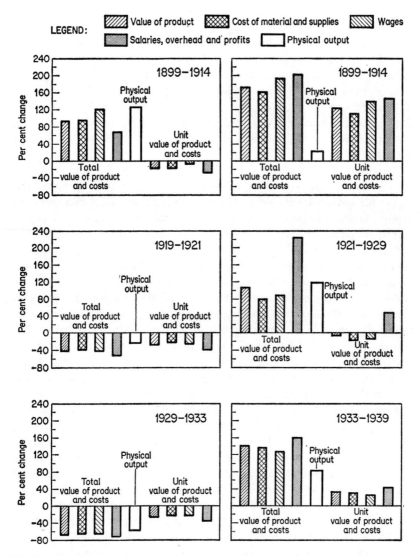

Fig. 6.5 Percentage changes in total costs, physical output, and unit costs for All Iron and Steel manufacturing for selected periods during 1899–1939. (From Table 6.4.)

five times as much. The decline in product value between 1919 and 1921, a period usually characterised as dominated by a price-oriented recession, is found to have been caused by almost equal percentage reductions in physical output and price.

Changes between 1921 and 1929 closely resembled those recorded between 1899 and 1914, with a doubling of product value traceable to an even greater expansion in physical output, combined with a small reduction in unit selling price. During the severe depression of 1929 to 1933, unit selling price declined by less than a quarter while physical production contracted by more than half. The sharp recovery in product value between 1933 and 1939 resulted from an increase of about one-third in unit selling price and of four-fifths in physical output. From 1899 to 1939, the net increase of 425 per cent in product value was accounted for by an increase of 34·4 per cent in unit selling price and an increase of 290·5 per cent in physical output.

Variations in unit costs also may be determined by dividing indices of the aggregate of such costs by indices of the physical volume of production. Figure 6.4 shows that the general course of unit costs for all iron and steel manufacturing was downward between 1899 and 1914, wages per unit of output declining by only 3·5 per cent while material costs per unit and SOP per unit declined by 14·8 and 26·3 per cent, respectively. During the next five years, each category of unit costs rose to a peak never again surpassed in any census year until 1939; unit material costs rose by 112 per cent, unit wage costs by 139 per cent, and SOP per unit by 147 per cent. Similarity in the direction of change of these unit cost categories was continued during 1919–21, but despite the popular characterisation of that period as dominated by sharp contraction of material prices, material costs per unit of production declined by only 20 per cent, as unit wages decreased by 25 per cent and as SOP per unit was reduced by 39 per cent.

Both the unit material costs and the unit wage costs declined between 1921 and 1929, diverging from the generally upward trend of SOP per unit: thus, while the latter increased by half, unit wage cost declined by 13 per cent and unit material cost by 17 per cent. Sharp as was the contrast in most respects between the boom of the late twenties and the contraction of the early thirties, little trace of this abrupt reversal is apparent in the course of unit material and unit wage cost adjustments—both of them declining by 20 per cent between 1929 and 1933, or by somewhat more than the reductions effected during 1921–29. In respect to SOP per unit, the depression resulted in a reduction of one-third, bringing its level in 1933 back to that which prevailed in 1921. Between 1933 and 1939, unit wage costs rose by 24 per cent, unit material costs by 29 per cent, and SOP per unit by 41 per cent. Finally, comparison of 1899 with 1939 reveals

TABLE 6.3   Indices of physical output and of unit costs and selling price for All Iron and Steel manufacturing and for selected major components, 1899–1939*

Index numbers (1899 = 100)

Year	All Iron and Steel					Blast furnace products					Steelworks and rolling mill products				
	Physical output	Val. of prod. per unit	Materials cost per unit	Wages per unit	S O P per unit	Physical output	Val. of prod. per unit	Materials cost per unit	Wages per unit	S O P per unit	Physical output	Val. of prod. per unit	Materials cost per unit	Wages per unit	S O P per unit
1899	100·0	100·0	100·0	100·0	100·0	100·0	100·0	100·0	100·0	100·0	100·0	100·0	100·0	100·0	100·0
1904	138·1	92·5	93·0	100·1	85·2	118·8	94·4	114·5	86·0	50·4	120·8	93·5	93·5	99·1	87·8
1909	209·5	94·0	98·5	91·5	83·1	181·2	104·5	134·5	73·4	44·9	179·2	92·1	93·9	89·0	88·6
1914	228·6	84·7	85·2	96·5	73·7	165·6	92·8	121·5	74·4	32·2	183·3	83·9	82·4	100·3	73·3
1919	281·0	189·7	180·6	231·1	182·3	218·8	182·2	223·8	188·8	83·7	262·5	180·5	163·8	237·4	187·1
1921	219·0	142·1	143·9	173·9	111·4	121·9	166·5	225·3	130·4	42·3	158·3	156·7	162·5	200·7	92·0
1923	400·0	154·0	153·0	172·8	141·4	290·6	167·7	216·6	109·6	73·4	337·5	156·5	155·0	184·7	134·5
1925	414·3	140·8	133·0	162·1	146·1	262·5	141·0	178·9	93·3	68·8	341·7	144·4	135·6	175·9	146·1
1927	414·3	135·0	126·1	159·2	140·6	262·5	130·6	167·9	91·2	57·0	337·5	137·9	128·1	174·2	139·3
1929	476·2	135·1	119·4	151·4	166·7	312·5	119·4	148·5	72·6	67·1	416·7	135·3	116·9	161·6	178·3
1931	257·1	114·8	103·3	143·2	124·7	137·5	109·5	143·3	75·9	42·1	195·8	120·0	108·7	168·9	114·2
1933	214·3	102·9	95·6	121·0	109·2	100·0	103·3	139·9	62·7	31·9	179·2	106·9	98·8	141·2	103·6
1935	290·5	125·5	114·9	148·2	137·5	159·4	113·7	143·5	64·1	60·9	266·7	121·3	106·5	161·2	137·4
1937	423·8	140·7	126·7	171·8	155·3	275·0	118·3	150·7	74·7	57·3	404·2	138·0	115·9	183·6	171·3
1939	390·5	134·4	123·0	150·0	154·5	237·5	112·1	148·0	64·4	44·6	358·3	133·4	115·3	166·9	168·9

* Index numbers of physical output based on estimates given by Solomon Fabricant in *Employment in Manufacturing, 1899–1939*, National Bureau of Economic Research, New York, 1942, pp. 314, 315, 317. Indices of values of product, cost of materials, etc., as given in Table 1 were divided by the corresponding indices of physical output to derive indices of values of product per unit, cost of materials per unit, etc.

TABLE 6.4 Percentage changes in total costs, physical output and unit costs for All Iron and Steel manufacturing and major components for selected periods during 1899–1939*

| Period | Total costs | | | | Unit costs | | | | |
	Value of product %	Cost of materials %	Wages %	S O P %	Physical output %	Value of product per unit %	Materials cost per unit %	Wages per unit %	S O P per unit %
All Iron and Steel									
1899–1914	+ 93.6	+ 94.7	+120.7	+ 68.5	+128.6	− 15.3	− 14.8	− 3.5	− 26.3
1914–19	+175.4	+160.7	+194.3	+204.0	+ 22.9	+124.0	+112.0	+139.5	+147.4
1919–21	− 41.6	− 37.9	− 41.4	− 52.4	− 22.1	− 25.1	− 20.3	− 24.8	− 38.9
1921–29	+106.7	+ 80.5	+ 89.3	+225.3	+117.4	− 4.9	− 17.0	− 12.9	+ 49.6
1929–33	− 65.7	− 64.0	− 64.0	− 70.5	− 55.0	− 23.8	− 19.9	− 20.1	− 34.5
1933–39	+138.1	+134.5	+126.0	+157.7	+ 82.2	+ 30.6	+ 28.7	+ 24.0	+ 41.5
1899–1939	+425.0	+380.3	+485.9	+503.2	+290.5	+ 34.4	+ 23.0	+ 50.0	+ 54.5
Blast furnace products									
1899–1914	+ 53.6	+101.2	+ 23.2	− 46.7	+ 65.6	− 7.2	+ 21.5	− 25.6	− 67.8
1914–19	+159.5	+143.4	+235.2	+243.5	+ 32.1	+ 96.3	+ 84.2	+153.8	+159.9
1919–21	− 49.1	− 43.9	− 61.5	− 71.8	− 44.3	− 8.6	+ 0.7	− 30.9	− 49.5
1921–29	+ 83.7	+ 69.0	+ 42.9	+306.4	+156.4	− 28.3	− 34.1	− 44.3	+ 58.6
1929–33	− 72.3	− 69.9	− 72.4	− 84.8	− 68.0	− 13.5	− 5.8	− 13.6	− 52.5
1933–39	+157.8	+151.3	+144.0	+232.3	+137.5	+ 8.5	+ 5.8	+ 2.7	+ 39.8
1899–1939	+166.3	+251.6	+ 53.0	+ 6.0	+137.5	+ 12.1	+ 48.0	− 35.6	+ 55.4
Steelworks and rolling mill products									
1899–1914	+ 53.8	+ 51.1	+ 83.9	+ 34.3	+ 83.3	− 16.1	− 17.6	+ 0.3	− 26.7
1914–19	+208.0	+184.5	+238.9	+265.7	+ 43.2	+115.1	+ 98.8	+136.7	+155.3
1919–21	− 47.6	− 40.2	− 49.0	− 70.3	− 39.7	− 13.2	− 0.8	− 15.5	− 50.8
1921–29	+127.2	+ 89.4	+112.0	+410.0	+163.2	− 13.7	− 28.1	− 19.5	+ 93.8
1929–33	− 66.0	− 63.6	− 62.4	− 75.0	− 57.0	− 21.0	− 15.5	− 12.6	− 41.9
1933–39	+149.7	+133.2	+136.3	+226.0	+ 99.9	+ 24.8	+ 16.7	+ 18.2	+ 63.0
1899–1939	+378.1	+313.0	+497.9	+505.1	+258.3	+ 33.4	+ 15.3	+ 66.9	+ 68.9

* Based on data in Table 6.1 and Table 6.3.

that between these years the unit cost of materials had risen 23 per cent, unit wage costs by 50 per cent, and SOP per unit by 54 per cent.

Because the periods for which cumulative changes were shown in Figure 6.5 are unequal, a better indication of the pressures on management for policy adjustments may be provided by measures of the average annual rate of changes in unit costs. Such computations reveal that the average annual rates of decline in unit costs between 1919 and 1921 ranged between 11 and 22 per cent as compared with a range of only 5 to 10 per cent between 1929 and 1933. The periods marked by the most rapid rates of increase were 1914–19, when the average annual rates ranged between 16 and 20 per cent, and 1933–39, when the comparable range was 4–6 per cent. Reductions during 1899–1914 were effected at average annual rates of less than 3 per cent, while the mixed adjustments registered during 1921–29 were at average annual rates of 2–5 per cent. Also worthy of note is the fact that rates of change in SOP per unit were invariably greater than those experienced by unit wage and material costs, usually by a very substantial margin.

6.3.2 Unit Value and Costs—Blast Furnace Products and Steel Mill Products

Changes in the physical volume of steelworks and rolling mill production during 1899–1939 offer a reasonably close parallel, though generally pitched on a somewhat lower level, to those described for iron and steel manufacturing as a whole. The physical volume of blast furnace production, on the other hand, presents a significantly different pattern, rising by smaller amounts, declining more sharply, and generally exhibiting more frequent fluctuations. Thus, between 1899 and 1939, the net gain in volume of production was 138 per cent for blast furnaces, 258 per cent for steelworks and rolling mills and 290 per cent for all iron and steel manufacturing. Variations in the average selling price of steelworks and rolling mill products were almost identical with those in the average price of all iron and steel products, while blast furnace product prices followed a quite divergent pattern.

The close similarities between all iron and steel manufacturing and steelworks and rolling mill output, and their difference from blast furnace production, are also apparent in respect to variations in unit costs. In unit cost of materials, the distinctive features of blast furnace experience were: a rise of 21 per cent between 1899 and 1914, while the others were declining by 15–18 per cent; a reduction of 34 per cent during 1921–29, surpassing reductions of 17–28 per cent in the others; and a notably greater stability during all of the remaining periods than either steelworks and rolling mills or all iron and steel manufacturing. For the entire period under study, the unit cost of materials rose for each industrial category: by 15·6 per cent for steel mill products, by 23·6 per cent for all iron and steel products, and by 48·3 per cent for blast furnace products.

Differences in the course of unit wage cost adjustments between 1899 and 1939 are reflected by the fact that steelworks and rolling mills recorded an increase of 67 per cent and all iron and steel manufacturing an increase of 50 per cent, while blast furnace output was marked by a reduction of no less than 36 per cent in this element of unit costs. SOP per unit experienced a greater amplitude of fluctuations during the period studied than the other unit cost elements and also recorded a wider range of net changes between 1899 and 1939 for the three industrial groups being compared—with increases of 53 per cent for all iron and steel products and 68 per cent for steel mill products contrasting sharply with a decline of 56 per cent for blast furnace products.

6.4 RELATIVE EFFECTS OF COST ADJUSTMENTS ON PRICE

The relative contribution of each cost factor to the change in average selling price (i.e., in total costs, including profits, per unit) in any period may be determined by weighting the change in its unit cost during the period by its proportionate share of total costs at the beginning of the period—as was reviewed in Chapter 5.3. Thus, for example, it has already been noted that the average selling price of all iron and steel products manufactured rose by 34·4 per cent between 1899 and 1939. To determine the relative contributions to this price increase of the various cost factors, one need only multiply the increase in unit material costs, 23·0 per cent, by the proportion of total costs accounted for by materials in 1899 (i.e. the ratio of material cost to value of product), 0·612, to get a weighted contribution of 14·08 per cent of the actual increase in selling price of 34·4 per cent; multiply the increase in unit wage costs of 50·0 per cent by its proportionate share of product value in 1899, 0·173, to get a weighted contribution of 8·65 per cent; and multiply the increase in SOP per unit of 54·5 per cent by its share of product value in 1899, 0·215, to secure a weighted contribution of 11·72 per cent. The sum of the weighted contributions, of course, equals the observed gain of 34·4 per cent.

Hence, the ratio of each weighted percentage change in unit costs to the percentage change in average price indicates its relative contribution to the price change. Thus, increases in material costs accounted for 40·9 per cent of the gain in the average price of all iron and steel products, increases in wage costs accounted for 25·1 per cent of the price increase, and increases in SOP accounted for the remaining 34 per cent of the price rise. Both because it evaluates various cost pressures in terms of their effect on price (generally the focus of market competition), and because it considers not only the degree of change in each cost factor per unit but also its relative importance among all cost elements, this analytical tool may be of considerable practical value in helping to guide managerial efforts to reduce costs.

Application of this procedure to the several periods of economic significance between 1899 and 1939, shown in Figure 6.6, reveals something of

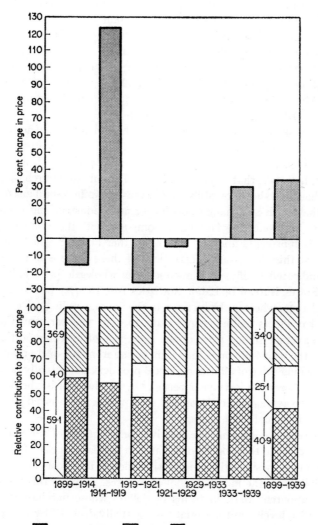

Fig. 6.6 Changes in selling price and in the relative contributions of cost elements to price changes for All Iron and Steel manufacturing and major components for selected periods during 1899–1939. (From Table 6.5.)

the wide variability in relative contributions to observed price adjustments with which industrial management must contend. Thus, in these periods, proportionate contributions to changes in the average price of all iron and steel manufacturing varied within the following ranges: materials, 45·2–59·1 per cent; wages, 4·0–22·2 per cent; and SOP, 22·2–38·6 per cent. There were materially greater ranges of variation in both blast furnace production and steel mill production. In accounting for variations in blast furnace product prices during the same periods, the relative contribution of cost factors varied within the following ranges: wages, 1·8–29·7 per cent; materials, 5·7–80·3 per cent; and SOP, 11·2–64·6 per cent. The relative contributions to observed variations in steel mill product prices covered a comparably wide range: wages, 0·3–26·5 per cent; materials, 3·7–71 per cent; SOP, 20·5–69·8 per cent (Table 6·5).

The foregoing analysis has been carried through in units of actual dollars because these tend to be of greater interest to persons concerned primarily with the immediacies of industrial production and pricing policies. It should be noted, however, that conversion into dollars of fixed purchasing power may, as has been shown by Mills, [3, pp. 118–120] offer useful insights bearing on the relative exchange position of any industry, and even of the returns to its productive factors, as compared with the economy at large. While this represents another area of further analysis which cannot be explored at this time, some illustrations of these changes in relationships can be indicated briefly. For instance, the wholesale price index of the United States Bureau of Labor Statistics rose by 47·7 per cent between 1899 and 1939, whereas the increase in the average selling price of all iron and steel products manufactured came to only 34·4 per cent. Compared with the average selling price of the aggregate of all commodities represented in the wholesale price index (including iron and steel products), the average selling price of all iron and steel products had actually declined by 9·0 per cent over the forty year period. Or, in other words, the purchasing power of the average unit of iron and steel production was 9·0 per cent less in 1939 than it had been in 1899.

One may also determine the relative contributions of the various production factors to this observed decline in the relative price of all iron and steel products, by similarly dividing the index of unit costs as expressed in actual dollars by the index of wholesale prices. Through this procedure it becomes apparent that, in terms of dollars whose purchasing power is fixed at 1899 levels, unit material costs actually declined by 16·7 per cent, while unit wage costs and SOP per unit actually increased by 1·6 and 4·6 per cent, respectively. In short, all the reduction in the relative price of iron and steel products was contributed by the reduction in the returns per unit of iron and steel output received by the suppliers of the materials entering into such production; while both wages and SOP increased in purchasing power per unit of iron and steel production. In the case of blast furnace production, on the other hand, all of the 24·1 per cent reduction in relative price was contributed by reductions in the purchasing power of

TABLE 6.5 Changes in selling price and in the relative contributions of cost elements to price changes for All Iron and Steel manufacturing and major components for selected periods during 1899–1939

(From Tables 6.2 and 6.4)

Period	Change in selling price %	Relative contributions to changes in selling price		
		Materials %	Wages %	SOP %
All Iron and Steel				
1899–1914	− 15·3	59·1	4·0	36·9
1914–19	+124·0	55·6	22·2	22·2
1919–21	− 25·1	47·2	20·9	31·9
1921–29	− 4·9	48·8	12·6	38·6
1929–33	− 23·8	45·2	16·4	38·4
1933–39	+ 30·6	53·3	15·9	30·8
1899–1939	+ 34·4	40·9	25·1	34·0
Blast furnace products				
1899–1914	− 7·2	39·5	6·6	53·9
1914–19	+ 96·3	72·8	11·5	15·7
1919–21	− 8·6	5·7	29·7	64·6
1921–29	− 28·3	80·3	8·5	11·2
1929–33	− 13·5	34·2	5·6	60·2
1933–39	+ 8·5	58·5	1·8	39·7
1899–1939	+ 12·1	62·4	6·5	31·1
Steelworks and rolling mill products				
1899–1914	− 16·1	71·0	0·3	28·7
1914–19	+115·1	55·2	24·3	20·5
1919–21	− 13·2	3·7	26·5	69·8
1921–29	− 13·7	57·9	13·0	29·1
1929–33	− 21·0	41·9	12·3	45·8
1933–39	+ 24·8	40·6	16·5	42·9
1899–1939	+ 33·4	30·0	34·2	35·8

wage and SOP recipients per unit of blast furnace output, while the recipients of payments for material costs actually increased their purchasing power per unit of blast furnace production. It is hoped that these instances will help to suggest the significance of more comprehensive analysis along these lines for furthering our understanding of changes in the division of the nation's total output of goods and services among those contributing to the aggregate productive effort.

6.5 PRODUCTION CHANGES AND UNIT COSTS

In penetrating somewhat further into the complex of causes responsible for changes in unit costs, attention will be turned first to the relationship which is so prominent in the thinking of industrial executives concerned with production and cost policies, namely, that between changes in the level of production and accompanying changes in unit costs. Economic theory has tended to emphasise both that variations in production have a very marked effect on unit costs and also that the relationship between production adjustments and unit cost changes is an inverse one below practical capacity, i.e. that increases in production tend to reduce unit costs and vice versa. As generalisations for major industries, however, neither of these widely accepted hypotheses or beliefs is given much support by the data analysed so far.

In the case of all iron and steel manufacturing, adjustments in production and in unit costs were in the same direction more frequently than in the expected opposite directions. For example, of the fourteen intercensal periods between 1899 and 1939, it may be seen that changes in physical output were in a direction opposite to changes in total costs per unit (i.e. in average selling price) in only five: 1899–1904, 1909–14, and the three two-year periods between 1923 and 1929. Of course, it may be argued with good reason that the inclusion of profits in selling price would offset somewhat the tendency toward an inverse relationship between production variations and resultant fluctuations in total costs per unit.

That this cannot be the main reason why the expected inverse relationship does not materialise, however, is apparent from the infrequency with which such inverse relationships are to be noted even when unit material costs and unit wage costs are compared with changes in production levels. Thus, adjustments in unit material costs were opposite in direction to production changes in only six of the fourteen intercensal periods, and inverse relationships between production and unit wage adjustments emerged in only five of these periods. Indeed, even a comparison of production changes with those in SOP per unit, which might have been expected to yield results substantially divergent from those found in the unit wage and unit material cost comparisons, because of the inclusion of profits in SOP, shows inverse relationships in four of the intercensal periods or in only one period less than in the case of wages. A similarly low frequency of inverse relationships between production and unit cost adjustments is found in blast furnace and steel mill operations.

Analysis of the magnitude of production adjustments relative to the magnitude of corresponding unit cost adjustments also fails to reveal any particularly meaningful relationships. As may be seen on Figure 6.4, small changes in physical output were sometimes accompanied by large changes in unit costs and at other times by small ones. Large changes in physical output produced an equally broad range of unit cost reactions. Between 1899 and 1914, an increase in the physical output of all iron and steel manufacturing of 128·6 per cent was accompanied by decreases in unit costs of between 3·5 and 26·3 per cent. In the very next intercensal period, 1914 to 1919, an increase in physical output of only 23 per cent was accompanied by unit cost increases varying between 112·1 and 147·2 per cent. The other periods exhibit disproportions between physical output and unit cost adjustments which lie between the extremes already referred to.

An interesting point, which is shown in Figure 6.4, is that all unit cost elements moved in the same direction as adjustments in physical output in half of the intercensal periods studied: 1914–19, 1919–21, and each of the five two-year periods between 1929 and 1939. Because of the powerful price tides associated with these periods, this indicates that the direct effect of changes in physical output on unit costs may be obscured in such comparisons by significant changes in the general price level. For example, a sharp inflationary upsurge in the general price level might generate much greater pressures toward raising unit costs than the counterpressures toward lowering unit costs which might be exerted simultaneously by rising production levels. Much of the effect of changes in the general price level upon unit costs can be removed by expressing the latter in terms of dollars adjusted for the former instead of in current dollars (a conversion effected by dividing the index number series for each unit cost element, as depicted in Figure 6.4, by the Bureau of Labor Statistics' index of wholesale prices, with 1899 as the base year of each series).

Translation of each of the unit cost series into dollars adjusted for changes in the general price level alters the unit cost curves shown in Figure 6.4 in several respects: it lowers the absolute level of these curves, because the general price level was consistently above its 1899 level during the period under study; it modifies the shape of these curves by removing the effects of changes in the wholesale price level, which exhibited a marked upward trend until after the First World War and then followed a generally downward course; and it reduces the amplitude of fluctuations in these curves by removing the influence on the level of unit costs of the substantial fluctuations experienced in the general price level. So far as the relationship between adjustments in production and in unit costs is concerned, the translation of unit costs into dollars adjusted for price level changes tends to increase the number of intercensal periods when an inverse relationship between these two may be detected, by revealing such relationships in periods when their existence tended to be obscured by sharp price movements paralleling the direction of production changes, as in 1914–19, in 1929–31 and in 1937–39. Thus, for all iron and steel manufacturing, the number of intercensal periods in which an inverse relationship is found between production and unit cost adjustments increased as follows: from five periods to seven in the comparison between physical output and total costs per unit; from five periods to seven in the comparison with unit wage costs; and from six periods to ten in the comparison with unit material costs. Only in the comparison with changes in SOP per unit was there no change in the frequency of inverse relationships.

This indicates that changes in the general price level do exert a significant influence on the relationship between production adjustments and accompanying changes in unit costs. Nevertheless, even after the removal of this factor, the expected inverse relationship between adjustments in production levels and in unit costs manifested itself in no more than one-half of the intercensal periods studied—except in comparisons between physical output and unit material costs. Moreover, by reducing the amplitude of their fluctuations, the translation of unit costs into dollars adjusted for changes in the general price level also tends to contract the magnitude of the adjustments in unit costs corresponding to the observed changes in physical output. And such variations in magnitude as remain after the expression of unit costs in terms of adjusted dollars fail to reveal any obvious relationship to changes in the magnitude of production levels.

Accordingly, more comprehensive analytical frameworks would seem necessary for a more effective exploration of the nature of relationships between adjustments in production and in the level of unit costs for iron and steel manufacturing as well as for other industries. Their development will be discussed in the next chapter.

6.6 FOUNDATIONS OF A MYTHOLOGY OF INDUSTRIAL COST BEHAVIOUR

Before concluding, it may be of interest to examine some of the reasons for continued widespread acceptance of such working assumptions about industrial cost behaviour as the seven mentioned in the introduction to this chapter, despite their conflict with several decades of actual experience in one of the basic sectors of American industry. Unlike many other traditional beliefs or mythologies, these are not impossible to test, nor do they seem to provide sources of spiritual reassurance. Rather, their survival seems to be reinforced by the narrow viewpoints associated with increasing specialisation, and the consequent receptivity to static analyses for which academics are frequently derided but whose appeal in the face of complex interactions is no less powerful to 'practical' decision makers. In particular, most of the tendencies underlying these assumptions actually did exist and were indeed important, but their expected effects were offset in varying degrees by other pressures which were neglected.

Thus, there is ample evidence to support the claim that increasingly effective use was made of materials and of labour inputs, the second and third assumptions, see Figure 9.6. But their effects on the ratio of material and of labour costs, respectively, to product value were modified by accompanying changes in materials prices and wage rates, in the quality of materials and labour skills required, in the costs of all other inputs, in the complexity of products manufactured and in the effects of market pressures on the need to share production economies with consumers through lower prices. Similarly, while one can readily demonstrate the correctness of the fourth assumption, that fixed investment increased, as did technical and managerial staffs, the deduction that these tended to raise the ratio of fixed to total costs ignores the possibility that attendant offsetting contributions to greater output and to lower costs might be of comparable proportions. And although, in accordance with the fifth assumption, most analysts recognise substantial advances in the productive efficiency of most manufacturing industries, the resulting effects on their product prices would again obviously depend on changes in factor prices and on the complexity of resulting products. However, such comparisons of absolute price levels through time also raise even more basic questions derived from the concept of prices as representing relative exchange values at any given time—as will be discussed further in Chapter 9.

Again, no one can seriously question that factor prices, output levels and profit margins are subject to frequent changes, as stated in the sixth assumption. But their effects on the composition of costs clearly depends, as has already been noted, on the extent to which these differ in the timing and magnitude of their adjustments, i.e. in their relative sensitivity to common forces tending to affect them similarly as against forces tending to affect each differently. The bases for the seventh assumption will be examined at length in the next chapter, although previous discussion has already indicated that, as in the case of each of the other working assumptions which have been discussed, basic discrepancies between the outcomes which they postulate and those given by our empirical studies are overwhelmingly attributable to the omission of major parts of the analytical framework which has been developed in the preceding chapters concerned with managerial control ratios, the network of productivity relationships and the structure of costs.

The first working assumption has been left to the last because it seems to involve considerations beyond those dealt with previously. The seemingly extraordinary exaggeration of the role of wage costs in total manufacturing costs reflected in this assumption—after all, wages average well under 20 per cent of the value of product in all manufacturing (see Figure 9.5)—may be traced to three different approaches. The first is the common tendency of production executives to regard the cost of materials as given—partly because of the feeling that the market is too large to be responsive to their efforts and partly because procurement represents somebody else's responsibility—and to regard overhead as likewise given (due to past investments and fixed charge rates established by accountants). This leaves wage costs as the major single target of cost control efforts. In contrast to this narrow view is the over-expansive perspective of top management people who argue that 'in the last analysis, all costs are really labour costs', meaning that their purchased materials and capital facilities costs are heavily affected by labour costs in the supplying industries. It is apparent, however, that this claim is off the immediate point, which concerns the role of labour costs in the given industry, not in those supplying its inputs. Moreover, the implication that material costs, which include the cumulation of labour costs at all previous stages of production, tend to become an increasing proportion of total costs as goods move from the extractive industries through successive stages of further processing and fabrication is not generally true in manufacturing. A third approach to explaining the patent over-statement of the role of wage costs is essentially behavioural: labour, especially when represented by a trade union, is regarded as a common adversary by management at large and represents a convenient common scapegoat for shortcomings in corporate performance for which blame might otherwise have to be allocated among different senior executives and their respective organisational units. Thus, one can understand the variety of factors tending to reinforce the psychological emphasis on wage costs even when analysis shows it to be out of line with its economic weight.

7 Short-Run Costs:
Theory and Empirical Findings

One of the most intriguing phenomena in economics has been the prolonged confrontation between a deductive theory of short-term cost behaviour which lacks substantial empirical support and a contrasting series of empirical findings which lack any persuasive theoretical rationale. The former holds that total unit costs tend to trace a U-shaped function with increments in plant output, decreasing up to some point near practical capacity and then rising sharply, whereas most empirical studies have reported flat total unit cost functions over the range of actual output variations. Surveys of the literature* suggest that this anomaly has been maintained partly because most work continues to be polarised between theoretical speculation or empirical research to the comparative neglect of the zones of interaction between them. And another difficulty may be the unrepresentativeness of the narrow economic sectors in which most empirical studies have been concentrated.

Without common objectives, concepts and limiting conditions, there can, of course, be no effective basis for comparing theoretical expectations with empirical findings and no significance can be attached to differences between them. Accordingly, section 7.1 will seek to strengthen the basis for empirical generalisations by supplementing published findings covering different industries, using different measures and relating to different periods with a new set of actual cost adjustment patterns in a large number of industries during identical periods and using identical measures. Section 7.2 will then explore the range of theoretical models which may be developed as the framework yielding U-shaped curves is subjected to successive modifications involving closer conformity with the determinants of empirical cost behaviour.

* Standard early references include [7] and [19]. The most useful current references are Johnston [16] and Walter's extensive bibliography [22]. One of the few observable effects of this controversy seems to be a tendency for recent textbooks to present flatter cost functions than were common before 1945 without, however, altering the theoretical discussion to account for this modification.

7.1 SOME NEW EMPIRICAL FINDINGS

In order to provide a reasonable array of empirical findings under similar conditions, cost adjustment patterns will be examined in twenty individual manufacturing industries,* in all Iron and Steel Manufacturing combined and in All Manufacturing Combined—the latter indicating the weighted average of changes in the aggregate for comparison with findings for the particular industries used. In order to cover a giant swing in activity levels, and thus meet the criticism that many empirical findings encompass only moderate variations in output, the period 1929 to 1937 was chosen. (For a summary of this range, see [14, p. 370]; and for a criticism of its narrowness, see [18, p. 267].) The cost data are from the U.S.A. Censuses of Manufactures for 1929 and the following two-year periods and the output data are from Fabricant [8]. These are combined to yield index numbers of average costs per unit of output after first adjusting each census industry category to conform exactly with that used by Fabricant. Attention will be given first to actual unit costs and then to deflated unit costs.

7.1.1 Actual Unit Cost Functions

Figure 7.1 presents the relationship between adjustments through time in output and in average unit costs in the form of unit material, unit wage and unit salary cost functions† for each of the twenty-two manufacturing

* The industries used and their identifying numbers in later charts and tables are as follows: (1) All Manufacturing Combined; (2) Blast Furnaces; (3) Steel Works and Rolling Mills; (4) All Iron and Steel Combined; (5) Cement; (6) Coke Oven Products; (7) Rubber Tyres and Tubes; (8) Petroleum Refining; (9) Canned Fruits and Vegetables; (10) Paper Products; (11) Pulp; (12) Cotton Goods; (13) Woollen and Worsted Goods; (14) Leather Shoes; (15) Glass; (16) Paints and Varnish; (17) Meat Packing; (18) Lumber Mill Products; (19) Flour Milling; (20) Bread and Cakes; (21) Woollen Carpets and Rugs; (22) Men's Clothing. These may be grouped in accordance with their dependence on crop, livestock, forest and mineral inputs, or in accordance with their servicing of food, clothing, construction and other consumer needs, or in accordance with whether they are primary or secondary processors of raw materials, etc.

† Although it might be questioned on certain technical grounds, this specialised use of the term 'cost function' is suggested both by its frequent use in previous studies and by the awkwardness of repeated references to: 'the relationship between adjustments through time in output and in [specified categories of] average unit costs'. Nor do the individual 'unit cost–output' points in the following charts result from infinitesimal samples of only momentary relevance. Specifically, each such point represents the weighted average of the array of all cost–output adjustments which occurred during the designated year, thus tending to reflect substantial experiential bases for estimating such average relationships. These data are also based on complete enumerations rather than samples of the plants constituting the industry. And, incidentally, the characteristics of the period 1929–37 were such as probably tended to minimise the likelihood of widespread introductions either of major technological innovations or of major additions to capacity.

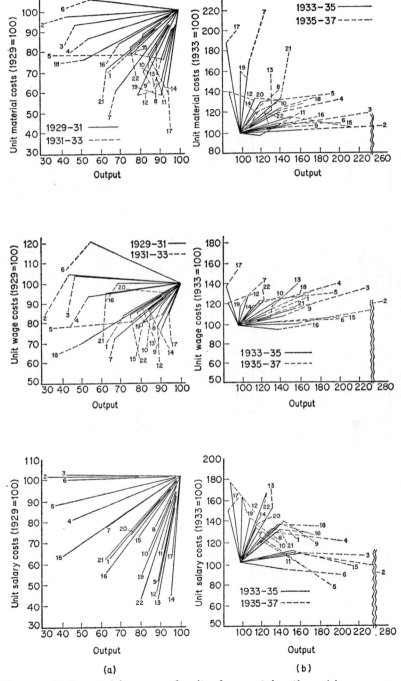

Fig. 7.1 Unit material, wage and unit salary cost functions. (a) 1929–1933; (b) 1933–1937

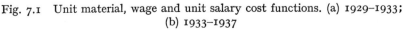

TABLE 7.1 Direction of adjustments in output and unit costs, 1929–37
Twenty individual manufacturing industries, All Iron and Steel Combined, and All Manufacturing Combined

Changes		Unit material costs						Unit wage costs						Unit salary costs			
Output	Unit cost	29–31	31–33	29–33	33–35	35–37	33–37	29–31	31–33	29–33	33–35	35–37	33–37	29–33	33–35	35–37	33–37
+	+	0	1	0	19	16	21	0	0	0	19	20	21	0	19	3	17
+	−	0	5	0	1	4	0	0	6	0	1	2	0	0	1	17	4
−	+	1	2	1	2	2	1	4	1	1	2	0	1	2	2	1	1
−	−	21	13	21	0	0	0	18	15	21	0	0	0	20	0	1	0
−	=	0	1	0	0	0	0	0	0	0	0	0	0	0	0	0	0
Total series		22	22	22	22	22	22	22	22	22	22	22	22	22	22	22	22

TABLE 7.2 Ratio of changes in unit costs to output, 1929–33 and 1933–37
Frequencies indicated by code number of each industry

	−	−	+	+	+	+	+	+	+	
	>1·25	<·25	0<·25	·25<·4	·4<·75	·75<1·25	1·25<2·00	2·00<3·00	≥3·00	Total series
Unit materials 1929–33		6	2	3, 4, 5	16, 18	1, 15, 20, 21	8, 9, 10, 12	7, 19, 22	11, 13, 14, 17	22
Unit materials 1933–37	17		2, 3, 6, 9, 15, 16	4, 11	1, 5, 18	8, 10, 14, 20, 22	13, 21	12	7, 19	22
Unit wages 1929–33		6	2, 3, 16, 20	4, 5	18, 21	1, 7, 19	8, 10, 12, 15, 22	9, 13	11, 14, 17	22
Unit wages 1933–37	17		2, 3, 6, 15, 16	4, 5, 8, 9, 11, 21	1, 10, 13, 14, 18, 20		7, 22	12	19	22
Unit salaries 1929–33		2, 3	6, 5	4	7, 18	1, 16, 20, 21	8, 15	10, 19, 22	9, 11, 12, 13, 14, 17	22
Unit salaries 1933–37	17	2, 5, 6, 15	3, 11	4, 9, 16	1, 8, 10, 18, 21	7	14, 20	13, 22	12, 19	22

series both during the general downswing between 1929 and 1933 and during the general upswing between 1933 and 1937. Major findings may be summarised briefly as follows:

(a) **Each category of unit cost functions displayed a broad range of slopes among industries but was dominated by large positively inclined slopes.**
In each category of cost functions, more series had slopes representing changes in unit costs exceeding 75 per cent of the change in output than had slopes of 25–75 per cent, and the latter were more numerous than those with slopes of less than 25 per cent (see Tables 7.1 and 7.2, pp. 123–4).

(b) **In each category of unit functions, most industries experienced sharp changes in slope between successive two-year periods and resulting adjustment paths covered a wide range of shapes.**
The actual two-link cost functions representing the two-year components of each four-year period may be grouped into many or few categories, of course, depending on the narrowness of each. But even a crude system of four slopes (horizontal, decrease and two rates of increase) for each link yields fifteen different two-link patterns. Of 110 cases (twenty-two series for each of two two-year periods in respect to unit material costs and also unit wage costs as well as one four-year period for unit salary costs), essentially similar slopes in both two-year periods account for eighteen; significantly changing slopes in the same direction account for forty-one; significant reversals in direction account for forty-four; and no change in one two-year period combined with an increase or decrease in the other accounts for the remaining seven (Table 7.3, p. 126).

(c) **In each category of unit cost functions, most industries had adjustment paths which differed significantly in slope and shape between the two (basically recession and recovery) halves of the period.**
Similar slopes occurred in both halves of the period in only five of the twenty-two series for unit material cost functions, in seven for unit wage cost functions, and in five for unit salary cost functions. Between 1933 and 1937, slopes were larger for three to four series in each cost category; and slopes were reversed in sign from the earlier period in two unit material, two unit wage and five unit salary cost functions (Table 7.2). With respect to the shapes of their adjustment paths in the two halves of the period, analysis reveals twenty-one four-link combinations of the fifteen two-link patterns noted earlier. Those representing similar shapes in both halves account for only six of the twenty-two series in respect to unit material and also in respect to unit wage cost functions, whereas combinations representing oppositely shaped adjustment patterns in the two halves account for

TABLE 7.3 Patterns of two-link unit cost functions, 1929–33 and 1933–37. Frequencies indicated by code number of each industry

		Unit materials		Unit wages		Unit salaries
		1929–33	1933–37	1929–33	1933–37	1933–37
A	/	1, 2, 9	2, 3, 9, 16	9, 18	1, 3, 6, 8, 11, 15, 18, 20	
B	_/	8, 18	14, 21	19	2, 9, 21	7
C	\/	19, 20		20	16	
D	/⌐	3, 4, 7, 10, 15, 16, 21	1, 4, 5, 7, 8, 10, 18	1, 4, 7, 8, 10, 15, 21	4, 5, 7, 10, 14, 19	20
E	/\	6		6		2, 5
F	/‾		15, 19, 20	2, 3		1, 4, 8, 9, 10, 14, 16, 19, 21
G	<	11, 13, 14, 17, 22	17	11, 12, 13, 14, 17, 22	12, 17	17
H	∠	12				
I	>		13, 22		13, 22	13
J	∖		12			12
K	_/	5	11	5		
L	/‾		6	16		3, 18
M	\					6
N	/\					11, 15
O	/|					22
Total series		22	22	22	22	22

ten unit material and six unit wage cost functions (Table 7.4). Finally, very few industries had unit material or unit wage cost functions which were similar both in slope and shape in the two halves of the period: two in respect to unit materials; and four in respect to unit wage costs. Figure 7.2 illustrates the wide range of patterns relating to unit material costs.

TABLE 7.4   Patterns of four-link unit cost functions, 1929–37. Frequencies indicated by code number of each industry

Pattern	Unit materials	Unit wages	Pattern	Unit materials	Unit wages
Same:			Mixed:		
AA	2, 9	18	AB		9
DD	4, 7, 10	4, 7, 10	AD	1, 3, 16	1, 8 15
GG	17	12, 17	CA		20
Opposite:			EA		6
BD	8, 18, 21	19, 21	FA		3
CF	19, 20		GA		11
FB		2	DE	15	
GB	14		EL	6	
GI	13, 22	13, 22	GD		14
HJ	12		GK	11	
KD	5	5	LC		16

5*

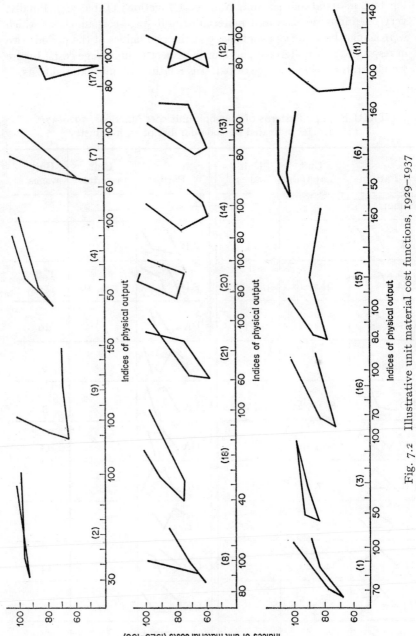

Fig. 7.2 Illustrative unit material cost functions, 1929–1937

(d) **Most industries were characterised by significant differences among the adjustment patterns of their three unit cost functions in each half of the period.**

Of the twenty-two series, twenty had positive slopes for unit material and unit wage cost functions in both halves of the period and sixteen also had positive slopes in both halves for unit salary cost functions. As regards

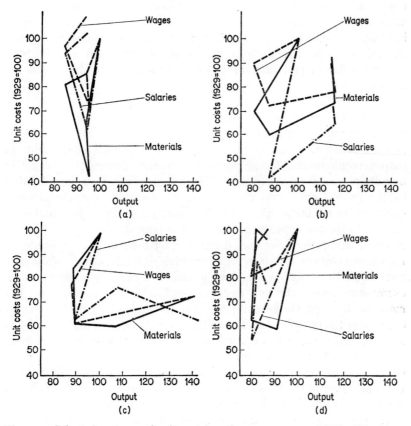

Fig. 7.3 Selected patterns of unit cost functions, 1929–1937. (a) Meat Packing; (b) Woollen and Worsted Goods; (c) Pulp; (d) Flour Milling

the magnitude of their slopes, however, only six of the twenty-two had all three unit cost functions in the same average slope category in 1929–33, with a like number in the second half (Table 7.2). As regards the shape of their two-link adjustment patterns in each half, fourteen series had the same shapes for both unit material and unit wage cost functions in the first half, and nine displayed such similarities in the second half, although only two of the latter also had similarly shaped unit salary cost functions during 1933–37. Finally, there were only four series in which all three cost functions had the same average slopes in the first half and in which unit material and unit wage cost functions also had similar shapes (industries (4), (11), (14) and (17)); while three series displayed comparable similarities in the second half (industries (3), (4) and (17)). Thus, the combined pattern of all three unit cost functions over both halves of the period was different for virtually every one of the twenty-two series. In order to illustrate these, Figure 7.3 includes Meat Packing (similar slopes and shapes), Pulp (similar slopes, different shapes), Woollen and Worsted Goods (similar shapes, different slopes), and Flour Milling (different slopes and shapes).

7.1.2 Deflated Unit Cost Functions

Changes in the general price level represent an average of changes in many product prices and each of these is affected by specific adjustments in output requirements, factor prices and market demand as well as by broadly pervasive price pressures. Hence, costs which have been deflated by the general price level do not represent real costs (i.e. the physical quantities of the inputs absorbed), but merely the change in actual costs relative to the accompanying change in the general price level since some specified base period. Nor does deflation alter the relative magnitudes of the various costs at any time, for all are divided by the same general price level index. But deflation does alter the slope of cost changes through time: decreasing it when the unit cost changes in the same direction as, but more rapidly than, the general price level; increasing it when the unit cost changes in the opposite direction to the general price level; and reversing the sign of the slope when the unit cost changes in the same direction as, but more slowly than, the general price level. Therefore, the consistency of the effect of such deflation on unit cost adjustment patterns depends on the consistency of the relationship between the directions and magnitudes of the changes in each unit cost and in the general price level.

The present section will first summarise the relationships found between changes in each of the three unit costs and the accompanying changes in the general price level (as represented by the All–Commodity Wholesale Price Index of the United States Bureau of Labor Statistics). Attention will then turn to the effects as shown in Figure 7.4 of deflating the earlier unit cost functions for changes in the general price level—which declined from an assigned index value of 100 in 1929 to 76·6 in 1931 and 69·1 in 1933 before rising to 84·0 in 1935 and 90·6 in 1937. The major findings may be summarised briefly as follows:

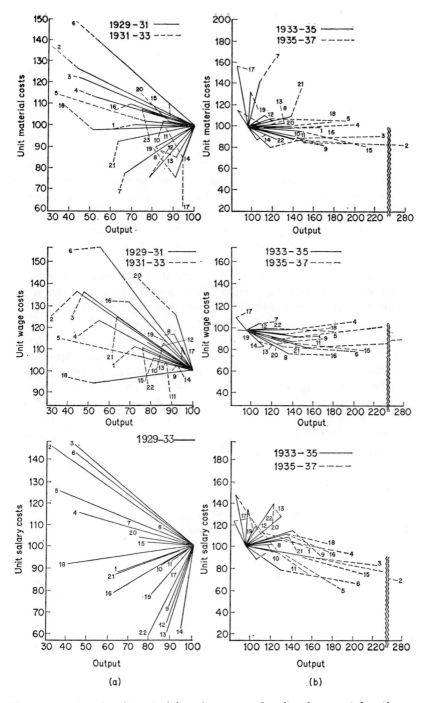

Fig. 7.4 Deflated unit material, unit wage and unit salary cost functions.
(a) 1929–1933; (b) 1933–1937

(e) **Although unit costs tended to move in the same direction as the general price level in most cases, the relationship between their relative magnitudes differed widely among industries in each of the three unit cost categories and this relationship also varied for most industries through time.**

Unit material and unit wage costs moved in the same direction as the general price level in seventy-eight and eighty-two cases, respectively (of the eighty-eight represented by four two-year periods for each of the twenty-two industry series) and unit salary costs were also dominated by this pattern between 1929 and 1933 as well as between 1933 and 1935, before recording a reversed pattern of eighteen decreases between 1935 and 1937 when the general price level rose. But the relative magnitudes of concomitant changes in unit costs and in the general price level covered a wide range within each cost category, with unit material costs changing by more than the general price level in forty-two of the eighty-eight cases and by less than the general price level in thirty-five, while the comparable figures for unit wage costs were thirty-six and forty-six, respectively. Moreover, such relationships differed markedly within each cost category from one two-year period to another. As for consistency, only twelve of the twenty-two series had net changes in unit material cost which either exceeded the concomitant net changes in the general price level in both halves of the period (five cases) or fell short of them in both halves (seven cases). In the case of unit wage costs, two series displayed greater adjustments than the general price level in both halves and eleven displayed smaller adjustments in both halves; and in the case of unit salary costs, the comparable frequencies were seven and eight, respectively. On the other hand only three of the twenty-two series showed consistent relationships for each of the four two-year periods between the relative magnitudes of unit material cost and general price level changes (one consistently larger adjustments and two consistently smaller); and these same frequencies were also found in respect to unit wage costs (Table 7.5, p. 133).

(f) **Deflation increased the ratio of negative to positive slopes in each of the three categories of unit cost functions.**

Deflation served to rotate the entire distribution of undeflated unit cost functions in a clockwise direction to the extent of the change in the general price level, shifting many slopes from a positive to a negative inclination. Accordingly, deflated unit material costs moved in the same direction as output in only twenty-four of the forty-four cases represented by the net changes in each half of the period for the twenty-two series, as compared with forty-two out of forty-four in the undeflated series; the comparable frequency for deflated unit wage costs was only twelve out of forty-four as against forty-two out of forty-four in the undeflated series; and the

TABLE 7.5 Concomitant changes in actual unit costs, the general price level and deflated unit costs, 1929–37
Twenty individual manufacturing industries, All Iron and Steel Combined and All Manufacturing Combined

Pattern	Actual unit cost	General price level	Deflated unit cost	Materials 29–31	31–33	29–33	33–35	35–37	33–37	Wages 29–31	31–33	29–33	33–35	35–37	33–37	Salaries 29–33	33–35	35–37	33–37
A	+	+	+				9	12	12				6	10	6		16	3	8
B	+ ∧	+	−				12	6	10				15	12	16		5	1	10
C	− ∨	+	−				1	4					1				1	18	4
A	−	−	−	9	12	13				2	18	7				13			
B	− ∧	−	+	11	6	8				16	3	14				7			
C	+ ∨	−	+	1	3	1				4	1	1				2			
D	−	−	=	1															
E	=	−	+		1														
Total series				22	22	22	22	22	22	22	22	22	22	22	22	22	22	22	22

TABLE 7.6 Direction of concomitant adjustments in output and deflated unit costs, 1929–37

Output	Deflated unit cost	Materials 29–31	31–33	29–33	33–35	35–37	33–37	Wages 29–31	31–33	29–33	33–35	35–37	33–37	Salaries 29–33	33–35	35–37	33–37
+ +	+	0	1	0	7	10	11	0	0	0	4	9	5	0	14	2	7
+ +	−	0	3	0	13	10	10	0	4	0	16	11	16	0	6	18	14
− −	+	13	9	9	2	2	1	20	4	15	2	1	1	9	2	1	1
− −	=	9	9	13	0	0	0	2	14	7	0	1	0	13	0	1	0
Total series		22	22	22	22	22	22	22	22	22	22	22	22	22	22	22	22

comparable figure for unit salary costs was twenty out of forty-four as against thirty-seven out of forty-four in the undeflated series. Aggregate findings for all four two-year periods show that deflated unit material costs moved in the same direction as output in thirty-six of the eighty-eight cases as compared with seventy out of eighty-eight in the undeflated series, and that deflated unit wage costs moved in the same direction as output in thirty of the eighty-eight cases as compared with seventy-two in the undeflated series (Table 7.6, p. 133, which should be compared with Table 7.1).

(g) **Deflation reduced the consistency of the relationship between the directions of concomitant changes in unit costs and in output over time, as indicated by the slopes of their cost functions.**

Twenty of the twenty-two undeflated unit material cost functions had either positive or negative slopes in both halves of the period as compared with twelve out of twenty-two in the deflated series; comparable frequencies for unit wage cost functions were twenty out of twenty-two in the undeflated series and sixteen out of twenty-two in the deflated series; and comparable frequencies for unit salary costs were seventeen out of twenty-two in the undeflated series and fourteen out of twenty-two in the deflated series. Even sharper was the decline in the number of series having either positive slopes in all four periods or consistently negative slopes: eleven undeflated unit material cost functions to five among the deflated and from ten undeflated unit wage cost functions to three among the deflated (Table 7.7, p. 135, which should be compared with Table 7.2).

(h) **Deflation tended more often to increase than to decrease differences between the two halves of the period in respect to the slope and pattern of unit cost functions.**

The number of series having slopes which fell into the same category in both halves declined from five among the undeflated unit material cost functions to two among the deflated; from seven among the undeflated unit wage cost functions to six among the deflated; and from five among the undeflated unit salary cost functions to two among the deflated. On the other hand, comparison of the actual slopes for each half reveals that the larger was more than three times the smaller in fifteen of the deflated unit material cost functions as compared with nine in the undeflated series; and that the comparable frequencies for unit salary cost functions were twelve and nine, respectively, while unit wage cost functions had equal frequencies of ten each in the deflated and the undeflated series (Table 7.7, to be compared with Table 7.2).

TABLE 7.7 Ratio of changes in deflated unit costs to output, 1929–33 and 1933–37
Frequencies indicated by code number of each industry

	Period	− >1·25	− ·75<1·25	− ·4<·75	− ·25<·4	− ·01<·25	+ ·01<·25	+ ·25<·4	+ ·4<·75	+ ·75<1·25	+ >1·25	Total series
Deflated unit materials	1929–33		6	2, 15, 20	3, 4	5, 16, 18	1	9, 10, 22	19, 21	7, 8, 11, 12, 13	14, 17	22
	1933–37	17			9, 14, 22	1, 2, 3, 6, 11, 15, 16	4, 5, 8, 10, 12, 18, 20		13, 21		7, 19	22
Deflated unit wages	1929–33	20	6, 8, 12, 16, 19	3, 17	2, 4, 13	1, 5, 10, 21	7, 9, 15, 18	14, 22		11		22
	1933–37	17		14, 19	8, 13, 16, 20	1, 2, 5, 6, 9, 10, 11, 12, 15, 21	3, 4, 18, 22	7				22
Deflated unit salaries	1929–33		3, 6	2, 8	4, 5, 7	15, 20	18	1, 21	10, 11, 16	19	9, 12, 13, 14, 17, 22	22
	1933–37	17		5, 11	6, 10	1, 2, 3, 4, 7, 8, 9, 15, 16, 21	18	14, 20		12, 13, 22	19	22

TABLE 7.8 Patterns of two-link deflated unit cost functions, 1929–33 and 1933–37

Frequencies indicated by code number of each industry (patterns defined in Table 7.3)

Pattern	Deflated unit materials		Deflated unit wages		Deflated unit salaries
	1929–33	1933–37	1929–33	1933–37	1933–37
A	12		7	22	
B		18, 21		4	
C	8, 19		18	3, 18	
D	7, 21	7		7	
E	15, 16		1, 2, 3, 4, 6, 8, 21	5	2, 4, 5, 8 9, 10, 21
F	10	5, 19	15		14, 18, 19 20, 22
G	13, 17			17	
H					
I		13			13
J	11, 14, 22	12, 17	11, 12, 13, 14, 17, 22		12, 17
K		8			
L	9				
M	2, 3, 4, 6		5	13	
N		20	9, 10		1, 16
O					
P	5	2, 6, 9		6, 8, 14, 15, 19, 21	3, 6
Q	1	4		12	
R	20	3, 10, 11, 14 22		1, 2, 9	7
S					
T		15	19, 20		15
U	18	1, 16		10, 11, 16, 20	
V			16		11
Total series	22	22	22	22	22

(i) **Deflation also increased the variety of two-link and four-link adjustment patterns displayed by unit cost functions.**

The variety of two-link adjustment patterns experienced in the two halves of the period increased from twelve for the undeflated unit materials cost functions to nineteen for the deflated series, and from ten for the undeflated unit wage cost functions to sixteen for the deflated series. The variety of four-link adjustment patterns among the twenty-two series rose from thirteen and fifteen, respectively, among the undeflated unit material and unit wage cost functions to twenty and nineteen, respectively, among the deflated functions for each of these cost categories. On the other hand, deflation obviously did not alter the relationships among the three unit cost functions of each industry inasmuch as all were adjusted for the same changes in the general price level (Table 7.8, p. 136, compared with Tables 7.2 and 7.4).

7.1.3 Cost Proportions

In order to determine their effects on total unit costs, relative changes in each category of unit costs must be weighed by their respective proportions of total costs. Analysis of the cost proportions of the twenty-two

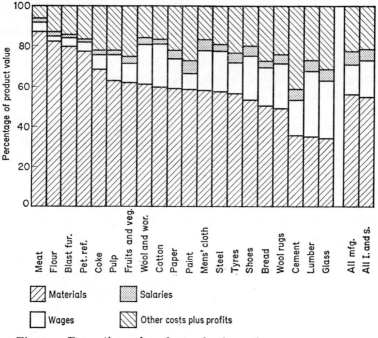

Fig. 7.5 Proportions of product value by major components, 1929

industry series during the period studied, as shown in Figure 7.5, leads to the following finding:

(j) **Cost proportions varied widely among these series, and material and wage costs combined far overshadowed all other costs plus profits in most of these series.**

In 1929, material costs ranged between 34 and 87 per cent of the total product value; wage costs ranged between 3 and 33 per cent of total product value; salary costs exceeded 5 per cent of the total product value in only one industry; and the residual, encompassing all other costs as well as profits, ranged between 7 and 41 per cent. Moreover, both the range and structure of these distributions were essentially the same in 1937 as in 1929. For evidence of stable cost proportions in individual industries over much longer periods, see Figures 9.1 to 9.7. Material and wage costs accounted for at least two-thirds of total product value in twenty of the twenty-two series and exceeded 75 per cent in half, including such capital intensive industries as Blast Furnaces and Petroleum Refineries.

7.1.4 Implications of Major Empirical Findings

First, industries differed widely in respect to the slopes and shapes of their unit materials, unit wage and unit salary cost functions as well as in respect to the proportion of total costs accounted for by each of these components. Such findings suggest that industries probably differ even more widely in the shapes of their total unit cost functions, including U-shaped and flat curves as well as a wide variety of other—posing the possible need for a comparably differentiated array of theoretical models.*

Second, unit cost functions were found to differ significantly in shape and slope between successive periods of recession and recovery—and even between successive increases or decreases in output—in almost every industry and in each category of costs. So it may be necessary to reconsider the relevance, even within relatively short periods, of the assumption that unit costs move up and down along the same track, and also to identify in relevant theoretical models the sources and uniformity of such displacements.

---

* These empirical findings also fail to support any of the three apparent bases for expecting universally flat total unit functions: that each unit variable and each unit fixed cost function is flat, thereby leaving total unit costs unaffected by differences in cost proportions; that although some unit cost functions need not be flat, those which are flat invariably account for the overwhelming proportion of total costs; or, that although unit cost functions may cover a variety of shapes, these are invariably combined in any industry so as to offset one another's deviations from the horizontal.

Third, although unit costs moved in the same direction as the general price level in most cases, the relationships between such concurrent adjustments were so inconsistent that deflation tended to increase rather than decrease the heterogeneity of unit cost functions.

Fourth, a number of findings suggest the desirability of further disaggregation in defining the components entering into the determination of total unit cost functions. For example, observed differences between unit material and unit wage cost functions may warrant separate consideration of each in place of the usual assumption of uniformity in the behaviour of variable costs. Similarly, explanation of the unexpected patterns of unit salary cost functions may require more refined probing of its components, and comparable differentiations may be found among the adjustment patterns of other constituents of fixed costs. And such disaggregation is also encouraged by the finding that disparities among such elementary components are bound to be intensified in their effects on total unit cost functions by observed substantial differences in cost proportions among industries.

Finally, it should be emphasised that the preceding findings serve less to contradict than to supplement preceding empirical studies of cost adjustments in manufacturing industries by covering a wider series of industries and an unusual range of output adjustments during the very same period.* Such results may serve several purposes. Most directly, they offer sounder guides to managerial estimates of probable adjustments in the average total unit costs of major industries. Viewed in broader perspective, they provide somewhat more comprehensive foundations for exploring the behaviour of industrial costs during business cycles and relating it to industrial price patterns, which are presumably more responsive to the average cost of all producers than to the theoretical costs of one hypothetical producer. (See [21] and [2] for a comparison of these approaches.)

7.2 DEVELOPING THEORETICAL MODELS APPLICABLE TO EMPIRICAL FINDINGS

7.2.1 Foundations of U-Shaped Total Unit Cost Functions

This review seeks to map the less apparent as well as the familiar restrictions of the common approach before subjecting each to change.

* Cf. Hultgren [15]. This study covered more industries and longer periods but was restricted to unit labour costs. Although its primary focus was on average adjustment patterns over repeated cycles, it is interesting to note that his findings for unit labour costs during 1929–33 support those presented above (pp. 35, 45–7) and so does his finding that average adjustment patterns differed substantially between the downswing and recovery phases of cycles (p. 41).

We turn our attention first to the narrowly restrictive field within which the prevailing theory of cost behaviour in individual firms has been developed and confined. Our purpose is not to test such expectations through comparison with the preceding findings—which represent a very different analytical environment—but, rather, to explore the range of theoretical models which may be developed as the framework yielding U-shaped cost curves is subjected to successive modifications involving closer conformity with the determinants of empirical cost behaviour.

U-shaped cost functions define the immediate changes in the total costs per unit of output of a given plant likely to result from changes in its output. Such expectations are rooted in two sets of simplifying assumptions: the methodological, which define the restrictive conditions within which cost behaviour is to be explored; and the substantive, which specify the supposed characteristics of the component costs in order to determine the behaviour of resulting total unit costs.

The most important methodological premises are that the analysis and resulting expectations will apply only: (a) to alternatives at a moment of time; (b) to a single plant whose output is small compared with its industry; (c) when there is no significant change in the total output of the rest of the industry, nor in the total demand for its inputs by all industries; (d) if the plant produces a single product or has a fixed product-mix; and (e) if individual managements cannot alter the outcome in accordance with their preferences. The first three of these prevent significant changes in the price of the output or in the rates of payment for input factors by freezing the total supply and demand for each. The fourth eliminates the possibility that changes in the composition of output would alter a plant's total unit cost functions because of differences among the input requirements and costs of individual products. And the last premise prevents the differences in cost functions among plants which might result if managerial preferences differed and if cost functions could be reshaped accordingly.

The U-shaped function is also based on three substantive assumptions: (a) that overhead costs per unit of output vary reciprocally with changes in output; (b) that variable costs per unit of output follow a shallow dish-shaped curve with increases in output up to 'practical capacity' and then rise sharply beyond it [13]; and (c) that overhead costs are substantial as compared with variable costs [3]. It is the latter which ensures a sufficient influence by the sharply declining unit overhead costs to yield significantly declining total unit costs up to a point approaching practical capacity [5].

Such premises and assumptions must yield a U-shaped cost function, but provide no basis for projecting this form beyond the sharply restricted scope of the analysis.

7.2.2 *Alternative Cost Adjustment Tendencies at a Moment of Time*

The need to achieve greater relevance to empirical findings, to serve managerial decision making more directly and to integrate cost theory more effectively into the larger structure of economic theory demands a broadening of the scope of cost models. In exploring such possibilities, attention will be given first to the effects of alternative substantive assumptions and then to the effects of relaxing the methodological premises.

(a) **Alternative substantive assumptions**

Overhead costs per unit of output vary inversely with output only if total overhead is fixed and if it is prorated at fixed rates per unit of time. The first condition is fulfilled at any moment of time, but this still allows for alternative methods of proration yielding differently shaped unit overhead cost functions. For example, allocating depreciation charges in accordance with the rate of capacity utilisation, or through a fixed burden per machine hour or per unit of output,* would leave unit overhead costs relatively unaffected by output variations. Thus, unit overhead cost functions might assume a variety of shapes between a rectangular hyperbola and a horizontal line, depending on the combination of allocation methods applied to the components of total overhead costs in given sectors of industry.

With fixed prices for input factors also ensured by the methodological premises, the expectation of a shallow dish-shaped function for total variable costs per unit of output must assume that this is the shape of the production functions representing labour and materials requirements per unit of output. There is no evidence, however, that this assumption conforms to most industrial experience [16, pp. 7–8]. Indeed, it might be equally justifiable to assume production functions which are upward sloping, or flat, or tilted downwards—and industrial practices readily illustrate such alternatives. (See [10] for a further discussion of these points, and [15, p. 17] and Figure 9.7 for a variety of empirical adjustment patterns.) To assure applicability to various industries, therefore, it may be necessary to develop a variety of unit variable cost functions, allowing for differences between labour and material cost functions in the same plant and also allowing each to assume various shapes for different plants and industries.

---

* 'The most common basis for charging burden is direct labour cost. If, for example, the machine shop carried a burden rate of 175 per cent of direct labour cost, this would mean that for every dollar of direct labour cost charged in the machine shop there would also be charged $1.75 of burden' [11]. In the steel industry, some companies use different rates of overhead allocation for different levels of capacity utilisation. For other evidences of the widespread use of fixed mark-ups over variable costs to allocate overhead, see [12].

As for the third substantive premise, it is obvious that overhead and variable cost proportions cannot be deduced—they can only be determined empirically. More important, even the most casual knowledge of the patterns of industrial specialisation suggest that such proportions are likely to vary widely among industries, with comparably different effects on total unit cost functions. And the wide range of such variations has been illustrated in Figure 7.5.

In short, U-shaped cost functions cannot be established as the most justifiable theoretical expectation. The first substantive assumption was

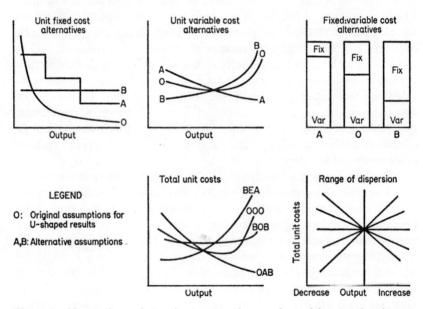

Fig. 7.6   Alternative substantive assumptions and resulting total unit cost functions at a particular time

found to be reasonable and probably of wide applicability, but not without important alternatives; the second was found to represent an arbitrary choice among multiple possibilities; and the third was found to lack any logical or factual support. Hence, even within the original methodological restrictions, theoretical expectations should encompass a broad variety of cost adjustment patterns, including U-shaped and flat curves—as may be illustrated by selections among the twenty-seven possible combinations of merely three simple alternatives relating to each of the substantive assumptions (Figure 7.6).

(b) **Alternative methodological premises**

Continued restriction of the analysis to a moment of time need not preclude alterations in the remaining methodological premises. For example, the second and third premises would seem to limit the analysis to patently unrepresentative plants and conditions. In most competitive industries, significant changes in the output of representative plants are usually associated with similar changes in the industry's output and, therefore, in its total labour and material input requirements (except when the output change is offset by the slope of the industry's average production functions)—thus tending to push factor prices and unit variable costs in the same direction [20]. Relaxation of the third premise also permits elimination of the second, for its concentration on small producers would no longer suffice to prevent changes in total input requirements and in factor prices.

Further refinement of the foregoing analysis suggests additional conclusions. First, unit cost functions may differ among material inputs (as well as between labour and material inputs) because of dissimilarities in their respective production functions, in the demand for such inputs by other industries, and in the responsiveness of such factor prices to changes in demand. Second, whenever factor prices are not equally responsive to increases and to decreases in demand, as in the case of wage rates, it may be impractical to trace the effects of variations in output along a single cost function. For example, if a sharp increase in output engenders higher wage rates, a later return to the original output level may leave unit wage costs higher than originally. Third, a plant's unit variable costs may change even when its output does not, because of the effect on its factor prices of changes in the total demand by all other users. Finally, the behaviour of total variable costs per unit of output may also differ among plants and industries because of differences in the relative magnitudes of material and wage costs.

Broadening the applicability of the analysis requires relaxing the fourth premise as well, for most plants make multiple products and experience frequent changes in product-mix. Because products may differ in respect to the kinds of inputs used, the shape of their production functions and their cost proportions, alterations in product-mix tend to change total unit cost functions for the plant. Accordingly, efforts to estimate such plant functions directly may be less effective than developing unit cost functions for each product and then applying alternative product-mix assumptions in aggregating them. Of course, differences in product-mix would be another source of inter-plant differences in cost functions.

The fifth methodological premise implies that cost functions are shaped by forces beyond the control of managements, whereas industrial experience demonstrates that the latter can remould such patterns by changing processing techniques, the degree of specialisation of labour and capital facilities, the basis for allocating overhead, the pattern of make-or-buy decisions, the level of mechanisation, and the period allowed for recovering capital goods investment. This does not mean that plants can keep altering the cost functions for each product over short periods, but rather that such functions are responsive to managerial pressures, and that management's search for competitive advantages may involve the re-shaping of cost functions as well as altering their levels. For example, some managements may be willing to bear higher total unit costs than competitors above 90 per cent of capacity utilisation in return for lower total unit costs between 70 and 90 per cent of capacity.

In summary, relaxation of these four methodological premises has further broadened the analysis and contributed to bridging the gap between the earlier empirical findings and prevailing theoretical expectations. Thus, it has been suggested that attendant factor price adjustments may help to generate positively sloping unit cost functions; and also that unit cost adjustment paths may differ in response to increasing and subsequently decreasing output because of the unequal upward and downward flexi-bility of some factor prices. Finally, acceptance of the influential role of management has posed interesting new questions concerning which choices should be made within given industrial environments among alternatively shaped cost and production functions as well as among alternative cost proportions.

7.2.3 Cost Adjustment Patterns Through Time

These modified cost expectations still cannot be tested against actual industrial costs, however, because the former are focused on prospective cost responses to output changes at a moment of time, while the latter represent accounting estimates of actual cost changes through time. In order to bridge the remaining gap, the time focus must be shifted from a moment of time to an array of progressively longer time periods, thus allowing for the variability of economic forces through time. In defining these, it should be noted that, because of the practical limitations of accounting systems and the extended duration of many procurement–production–sales cycles, annual data are often more accurate than monthly and quarterly estimates, and even longer periods may be necessary to evaluate capital adjustments [17]. The original analytical focus must also be broadened to include the cost effects of changes not only in output, but in other relevant forces as well. Although this need not prevent efforts to estimate the effect of single factors, the use of statistical techniques to neutralise the presumed impact of other forces may prove hazardous until the interactions among concomitant pressures are better understood. These two adjustments require consideration of the effects of trends, fluctuations and other adjustment patterns through time not only in the variables which have already been considered, but also in other variables which have been excluded hitherto because of their stability over short periods.

(a) Changes in unit overhead costs through time

The behaviour of total overhead cost through time depends on its major components—salaried, working capital and fixed asset costs—and each of these is affected by the level of its input requirements and by the rates of payment for them. Although the most common patterns of change in each of these determinants would have to be ascertained empirically for various industries over short, intermediate and long periods, a series of hypotheses will be hazarded to illustrate possible deviations from expectations at a moment of time.

Employment in the lower salaried echelons directly servicing production and distribution flows tends to be responsive to output variations; supervisory, technical and control staffs may vary only with major changes in output; and upper echelon employment varies least. While salary levels in each echelon tend to be stable over periods of a few months, lower echelon salaries tend to follow general wage patterns from year to year; top echelon earnings, including bonuses, tend to fluctuate with profit levels; and salaries in the intermediate echelons may be influenced by both. Working capital requirements are likely to move in the same direction as output, because of the latter's effect on total input requirements, on inventory levels and on sales financing. But attendant interest rates are likely to be dominated by broader pressures. Total fixed capital charges are likely to remain stable over periods of a few months, but to change from year to year: rising as a result of replacement or expansion during periods of increasing output; and declining because of the reduction of net investment during periods of shrinking output. Thus, total payments to salaried personnel and capital charges would tend to move in the same direction as output from year to year rather than to remain unchanged, with specific adjustment patterns tending to differ among industries in accordance with the variability of the components and with their relative proportions of the total.

In respect to longer term trends, the growth of planning, control and research functions may expand intermediate echelons, while mechanisation tends to further reduce lower echelon employment. Working capital needs may be affected by trends in the ratio of inventories to output and in the extent of sales financing. And fixed asset charges may be affected by trends in interest rates, in the ratio of capital requirements to capacity, and in the time allowed for recovering such investments (as affected by such considerations as the pace of technological innovations and tax incentives or burdens).

Finally, the relationship between total and unit overhead cost functions depends on the allocation method. If total overhead rises, allocation at equal rates per unit of output would tend to induce a parallel rise in unit overhead. Because allocation at equal rates per unit of time yields a negatively sloped hyperbola for the unit overhead cost function when total overhead is fixed, increasing total overhead would cause unit overhead to represent the interaction between this positively sloped total and the negatively sloped effect of the allocation method.

(b) Changes in unit variable costs through time

Expectations concerning unit variable cost adjustment patterns at a moment of time may be transformed into expected adjustment patterns through time by allowing for the effects of concomitant changes in production functions and input factor prices.

Direct labour inputs per man-hour have long declined by more than 3 per cent per year in many manufacturing industries and by less in others [9]. Material inputs per unit of output have also declined in many industries, though rising in some. Such trends tend to alter the level of production functions from year to year. Moreover, the technological and managerial developments underlying these changes may also affect the shape of production functions, as will be illustrated in Chapter 9. Hence, allowance for such persistent trends may require that different production functions be used for short, medium and longer time periods and that the short-term function be reconsidered annually.

Reductions in the level of production functions tend to lower the level of unit cost functions both because of the direct decrease in input requirements and because this decrease tends to reduce the demand pressure on factor prices. On the other hand, widespread evidence indicates that increases in output per man-hour often tend to engender increases in average hourly earnings, whether because of piece rates, incentives or union demands. Thus, the cost effects of changes in production functions may differ between materials and labour in the same industry as well as among industries.

Unit material and unit wage costs may also be affected by changes in factor prices due to pressures external to the industry. On the demand side, these may involve changes in the output levels or production functions of other industries using the same inputs. On the supply side, such pressures may reflect changes in the available resources, in the cost of providing them, or in the extent of competition among suppliers. Significant trends in such external forces may well overshadow the effects on factor prices of changes in the given industry's demand. As a result, increases in the latter may be accompanied by increases, decreases or no change in the relevant factor prices, although empirical analysis may provide bases for estimating the more probable responses under given conditions.

(c) Other factors affecting actual cost adjustments through time

For the present exploratory purposes, only three additional sources of cost adjustments need be brought into the analytical framework to provide reasonable relevance to actual cost behaviour in industry: product-mix; the general price level; and productive capacity.

The effects of changes in product-mix on aggregate unit cost functions at a moment of time was discussed earlier. The broadening of time perspectives, however, opens the possibility of consistent product-mix patterns through time. Some industries may have repetitive seasonal adjustments in product-mix. In many others, the ratio of high-cost to low-cost products may vary directly with aggregate output over the course of business cycles, thus reinforcing the tendencies noted earlier for average total unit costs to move in the same direction as plant output. Moreover, Burns's finding of retardation in the growth of output for many commodities [6]* suggests progressive changes in the product-mix of most plants over longer periods, as new products gradually displace those facing declining demand. And attention must also be given to the possibility of an increasing emphasis on more highly fabricated products in many industries.

Actual costs may also be affected by changes in the general price level, through their tendency to draw factor prices in the same direction. It should be noted, however, that material prices cover a wide range in the speed and magnitude of their responses to changes in the general price level and that wage rate responses may exhibit still other characteristics, e.g. in being less responsive to decreases than to increases in the general price level. In addition, resulting changes in the market price of inputs are likely to have a more immediate affect on the plant's unit material costs than on other categories because of the more frequent turnover of materials and the lesser prevalence of longer term arrangements fixing the price of such inputs, as compared with wages, salaries and capital charges. Hence, empirical research would be required to determine which relationships between changes in the general price level and in each category of unit

* Although Burns interprets his findings as applicable to individual industries, most of his series are limited to single commodities. For further discussion of this, see Chapter 11.

costs are applicable to specific industries and plants from year to year and over longer periods.

Although theoretical attention has supposedly been given to the effects on total unit costs of changes in a plant's capacity through time, the resultant long-term average cost curve has nothing to do with actual cost changes through time. Moreover, its underlying premise—that expansion takes the form of major step-like increments in the capacity of all operations separated by the substantial periods required to plan, construct and install plant additions—covers only a small sector of the possibilities illustrated by industrial experience. New plant facilities may increase capacity for selected products rather than all. Capacity is often increased as a result of improvements in the equipment on hand, in processing methods and in the utilisation of available resources as well as through the acquisition of new equipment to replace older equipment or to ease bottlenecks in production. (For a more detailed discussion of the differences between changes in plant capacity and in scale of production, see [10, pp. 115–17].) Thus, capacity may change significantly from year to year and different forms of capacity adjustment may have quite dissimilar effects on the level and shape of plant cost functions.

In general, then, consideration of possible adjustment patterns through time in overhead and variable cost elements as well as in product-mix offers additional bases for modifying theoretical expectations in the general direction of the earlier empirical findings. It follows, of course, that extension of the analysis to cover cost adjustment patterns at the level of individual industries—such as were presented in section 7.1—would also require consideration of differences in industrial structures, including variability in the number of producers, their distribution in terms of relative size, and the flexibility of product diversification patterns.

7.3 MAJOR IMPLICATIONS

The basic purpose of section 7.2 was to broaden the severely restricted theoretical framework yielding U-shaped cost functions to make it more relevant to actual cost behaviour in modern industries. Successive relaxation of the substantive assumptions and then of the methodological premises yielded a progressively richer range of alternative adjustment patterns. These encompassed all of the findings in section 7.1, thus encouraging further development of this approach to bridge-building. But attention should be given first to some of the fundamental implications of such explorations on the deductive side.

With respect to the prevailing conflict over whether the universal law of short-term cost behaviour is represented by U-shaped or flat total unit cost functions, the analysis suggests: (a) that no single pattern of cost adjustments is likely to be universally applicable; (b) that these current favourites represent only two among a wide range of possibilities even within the restrictive methodological premises which suggested the U-shaped expectation; and (c) that actual cost functions are probably more a response to managerial preferences than a reflection of the operation of immutable laws.

A second implication of these revised perspectives is that universality is more likely to be achieved by developing an analytical framework which specifies the variables and interrelationships to be considered in all cases and which can be transformed into specialised models for various industrial sectors and economic conditions by inserting the relevant parameters. Such a framework would yield widely differing cost adjustment patterns among plants, firms and industries by allowing for differences among input factors in respect to their price behaviour, among products in respect to the production functions of each input as well as their proportions of cost, and among plants and industries in respect to the product composition of output. Allowance would also be made for the possibility that the relationships between unit costs and output, or the general price level, may differ between periods of expansion and contraction, and may change through time. Resulting models might then be subject to progressive improvement by seeking out the loci of continuing discrepancies between expectations and actual findings in particular industrial settings.

A third implication is that the basic foci of cost theory should be shifted from the essentially trivial tasks of assuming the shapes of universal total unit variable and total unit fixed costs, of guessing their relative magnitudes, and then computing the weighted sum of these elements. It seems apparent, for example, that this traditional approach is too limited in scope even to serve two of its basic purposes in the structure of economic theory. First, it fails to account for the pattern of cost pressures on product prices with variations in output, because such pricing depends on aggregate supply and cost functions covering all producers of a given product rather than on the behaviour of individual plants with no claim to representativeness [4]. Second, it even fails to account for output decisions in representative plants because it is restricted both to cost bases for evaluating output alternatives and to a single product. If the industry's output tends to move in the same direction as that of the representative plant, product prices are likely to be affected as well as input factor prices and unit input requirements, thus requiring managerial evaluations of output alternatives to reach beyond cost effects alone to resultant cost–price margins, as suggested by the managerial-control ratio approach. Moreover, in multi-product plants, which predominate in most industries, output alternatives must cover changes in product-mix,* as well as in aggregate output levels, and management must reach beyond maximising cost–price margins for each product line to maximising aggregate revenue relative to aggregate costs for the plant.

Even more challenging foci for theoretical analysis might include such questions as the following:

(1) By what means and to what extent can the production functions of each category of inputs be altered? What criteria should be used by management in choosing among such alternatives? What factors might engender systematic differences in the shape of production functions among industries—or systematic changes in such shapes through time?

(2) Can coherent theories be developed to account for systematic differences in cost proportions between raw material processing industries and those progressively closer to producing final capital or consumer goods? Or to account for the extraordinary stability of cost proportions in many industries over long periods of time? (See Figures 9.1 to 9.7.) Or to determine the probable range of managerial options regarding cost proportions among competitors within given industries—and to provide bases for choosing among such alternatives?

Development of a rationale which accounts for such inter-firm and inter-industry differences as well as variations through time in these components of cost behaviour may well provide the basis for a theory of costs which can play a more illuminating role in the theory of production (including the incentives to, and effects of, technological innovations), in the theory of the firm and in the theory of industrial pricing—in turn yielding new hypotheses to be tested.

In short, this Chapter recognises the need for continued theoretical explorations of the determinants of cost behaviour [1] and for continued

---

* It may be of interest to note that collections of empirical studies [e.g., 18] seem to imply that findings of flat total unit cost functions for single product plants, multi-product plants and even entire industries are necessarily consistent and reflect the same universal pattern of short-term cost behaviour. Actually, however, these can be reconciled with one another only under highly restrictive conditions whose applicability is seldom even investigated, much less established. For example, even if flat total unit cost functions were established for each of its products, total unit costs for a multi-product plant would not follow this pattern except in the uncommon case where substantial variations in total output involve no changes in product-mix. To link flat total unit cost functions for a single product plant to similar patterns for an industry covering many products and encompassing changing relative contributions to total output from plants with unequal costs requires even more extraordinary conditions.

efforts to extend the still meagre array of empirical studies. But it also concludes that bridging the gap between cost theory and empirical findings requires the development of a common analytical framework rather than a continued monopolising concern with each as an essentially separate and self-justifying focus of analysis. There is need not only for formal affirmation of interdependence, but for deliberate efforts to integrate their respective contributions.

8 Managerial Control Ratios: Applications and Extensions

While the preceding five chapters have focused primarily on the concepts, adjustment patterns and decision-making issues relating to productivity and costs, it has also been shown that effective appraisal of these major sub-systems may be integrated into the larger analytical framework represented by the managerial control ratio approach introduced in Chapter 2. Before exploring still further possible extensions of this approach, however, it may be helpful to recall its primary objectives and to illustrate some of the applications which may prove useful.

8.1 BASIC PURPOSES REVIEWED

The aim of this approach has been to develop a unified analytical framework which identifies the major determinants of changes in the rate of profits on investment at the level of the firm as well as the structure of progressively smaller and more specialised components over which the plans and resources of the whole must be decomposed, and whose differentiated performance criteria must be re-integrated to account for aggregate results. Such a framework would enable management to trace more effectively the loci and relative importance of the complex of favourable and unfavourable adjustments producing observed outcomes. And it would also facilitate more comprehensive and realistic planning by permitting definition of the combinations of adjustments at successive levels of operation necessary to effectuate given profit objectives.

Such applications may be illustrated by reference to the first and second level ratios presented in Chapter 2:

$$\frac{\text{Profit}}{\text{Total Investment}} \equiv \frac{\text{Profit}}{\text{Output}} \times \frac{\text{Output}}{\text{Total Investment}}$$

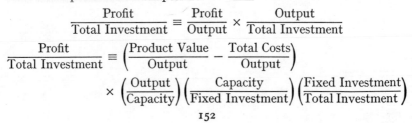

$$\frac{\text{Profit}}{\text{Total Investment}} \equiv \left(\frac{\text{Product Value}}{\text{Output}} - \frac{\text{Total Costs}}{\text{Output}}\right)$$

$$\times \left(\frac{\text{Output}}{\text{Capacity}}\right)\left(\frac{\text{Capacity}}{\text{Fixed Investment}}\right)\left(\frac{\text{Fixed Investment}}{\text{Total Investment}}\right)$$

For example, consideration of a proposal to seek a 10 per cent increase in the rate of return on total investment during the coming period would require examining the alternative combinations of relative adjustments in unit profits and in the output turnover of total investment needed to achieve such an outcome—and then determining which of these, if any, seems most readily attainable. Assessment of the attainability of such alternative combinations, however, would require similar analysis in turn of the alternative combinations of adjustments underlying them: (a) in prices and in total unit costs necessary to effect specified changes in unit profits; and (b) in capacity utilisation, in the productivity of fixed capital and in the allocation of investment between fixed and working capital necessary to effect specified changes in the output turnover of capital. And this process would then be extended further to consider possible changes in each component of total unit costs, etc.

In short, the resulting plan would take the form of a rigorously defined structure of targets covering the complex of adjustments sought for all (or major) operating units whose net interaction will determine the intended outcome. Moreover, the planning process would involve analysis not only of the likelihood of achieving alternative adjustments in each component, but also of the probable effects of each of these alternatives on adjustments in other components of the interacting system. Thus, evaluation of the possibility of achieving the desired increase of 10 per cent in Profits/Total Investment by simply raising price by 10 per cent would obviously have to consider the likelihood of at least a partially offsetting decrease in capacity utilisation, which might then give rise to an increase in total unit costs.

Conversely, the analysis of results over some past period might follow the pattern of determining the relative contributions attributable to changes in unit profits and in turnover and then tracing these findings, in turn, to concomitant changes in average prices, total unit costs, capacity utilisation, etc. Comparison of such outcomes with the previous plans for that period might then serve both to allocate penalties and rewards among responsible executives and also to improve the bases for estimating such adjustments in the future by calling attention to overlooked, under-estimated or unexpected influences.

In addition to appraising past performance and planning future adjustments, extensions of this analytical framework can help to guide evaluation of current proposals for innovation. For example, the network presented in Figure 3.4 outlines an organised procedure for analysing the prospective benefits to the firm of an innovation offering, say, an increase of 10 per cent in output per man-hour. As a first step, it suggests estimating the resulting effect on unit labour cost by considering possible concomitant effects on average wage rates. To the extent that the latter rise—either because of union demands to parallel gains in output per man-hour or because of an upgrading of required skills—the expected reduction in unit labour costs will be diminished. As a second step, it is necessary to estimate the resulting change in total unit costs. This requires consideration not only of the proportion of total costs accounted for by labour, but also of the possible impact of the innovation on other inputs. Thus, if wages account for 20 per cent of total costs and if wage rates increase only half as much as output per man-hour, the resulting 5 per cent decrease in unit labour costs alone would tend to reduce total unit costs by only 1 per cent. But if the innovation involves any increase in capital inputs, or shifts to more costly purchased materials and supplies, or expansion of technical or supervisory staff, the net change in total unit costs could be computed only after estimating the effects of each of these on its respective category of unit costs and then weighting each of the latter by its proportion of total costs. The third step would be to consider the probable effect of the innovation on profits per unit of output by supplementing the preceding estimate of the net change in total unit cost with an estimate of possible concomitant changes in the price of the product, if the innovation involves any change in product design or quality. The final step would involve examining the probable effects of any changes in the product or in its price on output, as the basis for evaluating resulting adjustments in the output turnover of investment. Only after these estimates have been made, along with estimates of the time periods over which these various direct and interacting results are likely to emerge, can they be compared with the costs and investments required to effectuate the proposed innovation.

Similar procedures may also be used, of course, to compare alternative possible innovations. In either case, it should be apparent that the analytical framework does not introduce any previously unrecognised considerations, but it does help to highlight any unintentional or deliberate neglect of clearly relevant factors—a number of which are discussed in the next chapter.

Still another application relevant to internal management purposes may be noted which may yield broader strategic guides. Systematic comparison of the firm's managerial control ratios with those of its competitors, both cross-sectionally and through time, may help to reveal the loci, magnitude and stability of disparities relative both to the more successful and the less successful. By thus penetrating beneath aggregate profit performance to the factors which not only determine such outcomes, but which are also the direct foci of policies and operations, it may be possible to strengthen efforts to concentrate on the most influential determinants of differential competitive performance.

Turning, finally, to the needs of interest groups outside the managements of individual corporations, attention should be called to the usefulness of analyses of managerial control ratios to determine the relative influence of the various ratios on profit performance in different industries over short and long periods and under conditions of expansion, recession and inflation. If findings should reveal significant differences, it would help to clarify the ways in which 'the management game' differs among economic sectors, and thus facilitate the development of more effectively differentiated criteria for the assessment by investors, lenders and economists of performance in different fields of business. And these outside groups would also be interested in the comparison of managerial control ratios among firms within each industry as further guides to allocating their resources.

8.2 NECESSARY EXTENSIONS

In order to permit such applications, the analytical framework needs to be extended in various other ways. One of these involves the coverage of inventory adjustments. A second concerns the problems of adaptation to corporate organisational structures. A third covers interactions with the surrounding environment.

8.2.1 Inclusion of Inventory Adjustments

Although the analytical framework has hitherto neglected inventory adjustments in the interest of simplicity, this shortcoming could lead to significant errors of analysis and interpretation when inventories are not accounted for on an accrual basis, especially in sectors where inventory adjustments are substantial and irregular, i.e. at business cycle turning points and in certain capital and consumer durable goods industries. Instead of assuming that all inputs are absorbed into the production of each period and that all such output is sold, a more widely applicable model would encompass Finished Goods Inventories (FGI), Work-in-Process Inventories (WPI) and Purchased Material Inventories (PMI). Thus, the following basic relationships would hold:

Finished Goods Sold = Finished Goods Produced ± Finished Goods Inventory Adjustments

$$(FGS) = (FGP) \pm (\Delta FGI)$$

Total New Production = Finished Goods Produced ± Work-in-Process Inventory Adjustments

$$(TNP) = (FGP) \pm (\Delta WPI)$$

Actual Material Cost = Material Outlays ± Purchased Material Inventory Adjustments

$$(M) \quad = \quad (Mo) \quad \pm (\Delta PMI)$$

The resulting network may be viewed as in Figure 8.1:

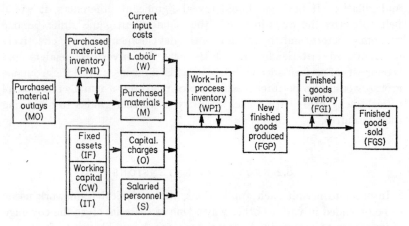

Fig. 8.1   Role of inventories in production cycles

Accordingly, the value of production in the original model would cover only the revenue from finished goods sold, whereas total costs cover all inputs absorbed into total new production, whether sold or not. This revision also poses some new problems of measurement. Specifically, the volume of physical flows can be directly measured in respect to finished goods produced and sold as well as adjustments in finished goods inventories, but not in respect to total new production (which includes adjustments in work-in process inventories whose physical output equivalence is not readily apparent). Moreover, direct measurements of total costs for the period are usually available for total new production and for adjustments in each of the three categories of inventories, but not for newly produced finished goods or finished goods sold—both of which may involve intermixture with the production efforts and costs of previous periods via inventory adjustments.

To deal with these problems, the original model, p. 152, at the beginning of this chapter, may be transformed as follows:

$$\frac{P}{IT} \equiv \left(\frac{VP_{FGS} - TC_{TNP}}{PO_{FGS}}\right)\left(\frac{PO_{FGS}}{PO_{TNP}}\right)\left(\frac{PO_{TNP}}{CAP}\right)\left(\frac{CAP}{IF}\right)\left(\frac{IF}{IT}\right)$$

where VP represents the revenue from finished goods sold and PO represents their physical quantity; where TC_{TNP} refers to the cost of total new production, including adjustments in work-in-process inventories as well as new production of finished goods; and where PO_{TNP} refers to the physical volume of total new production.

One conceptual feature of this revised model is that no direct ratio is provided to cover the total cost per unit of physical output for total new production, reflecting the fact that it includes adjustments in work-in-process inventories as well as in finished goods output. A second feature is the introduction of a new control ratio covering adjustments in the quantity of finished goods sold relative to total new production. Inasmuch as the latter represents the combined effects of adjustments in work-in-process and finished goods inventories, these may be separated by putting

$$\left(\frac{PO_{FGS}}{PO_{TNP}}\right) \equiv \left(\frac{PO_{FGP}}{PO_{TNP}}\right)\left(\frac{PO_{FGS}}{PO_{FGP}}\right)$$

All of the variables in this model can be measured directly except PO_{TNP}. This may be estimated as follows, assuming no major change during the period either in the product-mix or in the factor prices applied to work-in-process inventories and new finished goods production:

$$PO_{TNP} \equiv PO_{FGP}\left(1 \pm \frac{TC_{\Delta WPI}}{TC_{FGP}}\right) \equiv PO_{FGP}\left(1 \pm \frac{TC_{\Delta WPI}}{TC_{TNP} - TC_{\Delta WPI}}\right)$$

where $TC_{\Delta WPI}$ represents the total cost of net changes in work-in-process inventories.

Thus, changes in work-in-process inventories may be regarded as positive or negative contributions to the physical volume of new finished goods production in proportion to the ratio of changes in the cost of such inventories to changes in the total cost of new finished goods production. Finally, it should be remembered that the cost of total new production includes only the cost of materials actually entering production during that period rather than total outlays for purchased materials.

8.2.2 Adaptations to Corporate Structure

The usefulness of this analytical structure for managerial decision making would obviously be substantially enhanced if it could be effectively integrated with the organisational structure through which responsibilities are assigned and performance evaluated. At the simplest level, one might try to do this by disaggregating the successive layers of the analysis by corporate operating divisions and then by the major product lines within each, as outlined in Figure 8.2.

In order to integrate the analysis of physical resource flows with the analysis of financial resource flows, however, much work will have to be done in order to cope with various problems which have long confronted accountants even in dealing with financial flows alone, and which seem to be rooted in the fundamental nature of complex organisations.

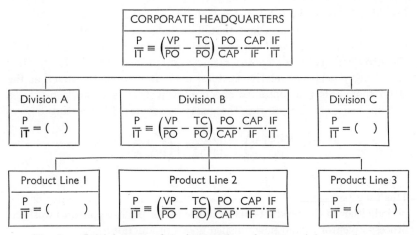

Fig. 8.2　Initial approach to integration of managerial control ratio framework with organisational structure

One of the most important of these is the fact that the criteria for evaluating the performance of firms, divisions, etc. must always be different from the criteria applicable to their respective components. This follows because the central office of such organisational units usually performs a variety of functions not assigned to its subsidiary units. Such functions may include planning, resource allocation, performance evaluation and similar staff services as well as longer range activities concerned with the development of products, markets and personnel. Because resources are withheld for such undertakings, the sum of the resources directly employed by the component units is less than the aggregate including the central office. On the other hand, the central office usually generates little or no direct income to help offset its consumption of resources. This problem is commonly resolved by distributing central office costs as an overhead to be shared among its revenue-earning components on some basis. There is ample reason for contending, however, that such expedients tend both to prevent effective evaluation of central office performance and to confuse evaluation of the comparative performance of the components. The latter shortcoming derives from loading the components with the costs of resources which were not within their control and from which their operating benefit may have been substantially greater or smaller than is reflected by such overhead assignments. Conversely, such distribution of its direct outlays as overhead burdens to its components leaves no basis for evaluating the central office's performance except in terms of the results of each of these components.

But the basic responsibility of the central office is not to maximise the performance of each component; it is to maximise the performance of the composite including the components and the central office. Progress towards such ends, whether they involve raising profitability or stimulating growth, may well be greater when performance is allowed to decline in some areas in order to enhance advances in other components, or when central office resources are used to 'subsidise' promising new undertakings by diverting resources from currently more profitable sectors. Hence, planning, control and evaluative efforts may all be enhanced by recognising such differences in responsibilities through the formulation of distinctive performance criteria and goals for the central office and for each of the component units as well as for the composite comprising the organisational entity. The performance of each could then be compared with its respective objectives and actual resource inputs, without allowing the arbitrary assignment of central office outlays to confuse evaluations of comparative performance.

A second set of problems confronting the adaptation of the managerial control ratio approach to corporate organisations is rooted in functional differences which are inherent in the processes of specialisation. For example, not all components of a large private corporation can be appraised in terms of profitability, even in ostensibly decentralised firms. At some level—whether national or regional or product-division—production must be differentiated from procurement and sales, and none of these can be evaluated in terms of its own profitability. Hence, the profitability criterion which is relevant at a level encompassing these mutually reinforcing functions must be factored into subcriteria which are meaningful for the respective activity sectors and which can be brought together again to determine their combined contributions to the profitability of the aggregate. Thus, production's goal might be specified in terms of producing stipulated levels of products in accordance with assigned design characteristics and quality standards at or below specified average levels of total unit costs, using specified wage rates, material prices and capital charges. Similarly, procurement's goal might be specified in terms of maintaining inventories of all purchased supplies adequate to support planned operating levels at or below specified average prices in relation to market prices, and meeting all assigned qualitative specifications, etc.

In short, instead of using arbitrary overhead allocations and implied revenue sharing to develop profit estimates for each unit which would be heavily influenced by these very arbitrary assumptions or decisions, it

6*

seems necessary to adjust the planning, control and evaluative criteria to accord with the actual division of responsibilities and resources involved in establishing and operating the organisation. It should be emphasised in this connection, however, that all such performance criteria for organisational components must be accompanied by clearly specified constraints representing conditions or influences which affect the given unit but which are the responsibility of other units—as was discussed in section 3.2 and illustrated in the above brief references to performance criteria for production and procurement.

As a second aspect of adaptation to corporate organisational arrangements, it is obvious that not all operating components are devoted to manufacturing. So appropriate alternatives to physical output and productive capacity must be developed in applying the managerial control ratios to other functional units. And such substitute measures of service potentials and yields would require correlative adjustments in the internal allocation of capital investment. Indeed, even in manufacturing enterprises, much fixed investment may be absorbed into distribution facilities and office buildings as well as production plants, thereby necessitating appropriately differentiated concepts of 'output' and 'capacity' for comparison with functionally differentiated kinds of fixed investment employed in specialised organisational units.

Custom-tailoring of the structure of managerial control ratios to the actual organisational structures of major corporations also requires means of coping with the simultaneous operation of undertakings with short-term goals and resource commitments as well as those with longer term goals and resource commitments. Because proportionately heavier involvements in the latter tend to affect short-term performance measures adversely, and because the latter may call for criteria which are inappropriate to the evaluation of longer range programmes, it is apparent that the requirements of effective planning, control and evaluation may counsel development of time differentiated as well as functionally differentiated evaluative criteria (see [5]).

8.2.3 *Integration into the Surrounding Environment*

Effective planning, control and performance evaluation also require differentiation between the internally controllable and the externally determined elements of observed changes in performance, or between the adjustments essentially shared with competitors and those representing advantages or disadvantages *vis-à-vis* competitors. Some initial approaches to such determinations are discernible in Figure 2.3 and were discussed in section 5.3. For example, it was suggested that changes in the output of a firm may be regarded as the product of changes in the total output of the industry and in the given firm's share of the industry's total. Then again, it was suggested that changes in product prices might be attributed to changes in the general price level and in the given product prices relative to the general price level. And the implications for performance evaluation of reductions in unit costs would obviously be very different if they were due to lower factor prices or newly purchased equipment shared by competitors rather than to internally generated economies in the utilisation of inputs. Such illustrations underline the desirability of more systematic exploration of this dimension of possible extensions of the basic analytical framework. (For further discussion of the sources of competitive advantages in productivity and costs, see [2, pp. 251–67].)

Further analysis also suggests the desirability for certain purposes of replacing this simplistic model differentiating only between inside and outside the firm with more refined conceptions. For example, Figure 9.1 includes certain links connecting the given plant or firm to its industry and, in another direction, to input factor markets. Even further elaboration may prove useful, however. Thus, in the channel leading from the given firm to the market absorbing its output, it may sometimes be helpful analytically to interpose not only a lock representing the output of others in the industry, but a further lock including readily substitutable products produced by other industries. Similarly, it seems to be worth emphasising that a given firm's links to factor markets may also be subject to differential degrees of influence by various subsectors of the economy. For example, competitors within the industry may have a greater influence on the price of materials used only in that industry than they would have on local electric power rates. And there might be greater similarity in wage rates among competititors in a highly unionised industry than in expenditures for marketing or for research and development. On the other hand, variations in the given industry's capital expenditures may have little impact on interest rates.

8.3 RELATIONSHIP BETWEEN FINANCIAL AND MANAGERIAL CONTROL RATIOS

Some of the ways in which the analysis of managerial control ratios may modify the interpretation of adjustments in the more common financial ratios are illustrated by the following empirical results of studying nine industries over a period of twenty years and also comparing the records of two companies within one of these industries [3, 4]. In particular, attention will be given first to identifying the assumptions underlying traditional interpretations of financial ratio adjustments and then to comparing them with the findings just mentioned.

For example, changes in Profit/Total Investment are commonly traced to changes in Profit/Sales, or profit margins, and in Sales/Total Investment, or the turnover of capital; and gains are considered desirable in each. Most analysts, though not all, tend to attribute gains in Profit/Sales to improvements in controlling costs, or even to greater effectiveness in utilising input factors. Since changes in Profit/Sales are affected by adjustments not only in Profit/Output, or unit profits, but also in Sales/Output, or the average price of products

$$\frac{\text{Profit}}{\text{Sales}} \equiv \frac{\text{Profit}}{\text{Output}} \div \frac{\text{Sales}}{\text{Output}}$$

such interpretations imply either that these ratios parallel one another closely, or that one is relatively unchanging or unimportant.

Figure 8.3 demonstrates that Profit/Output and Sales/Output, the two determinants of changes in Profit/Sales* follow quite dissimilar adjustment patterns in most of the industries covered and that the relationship between profit margins and unit profits differs widely among industries as well as changing through time. Thus, Profit/Sales was relatively stable in Electric Power and in Tobacco Products, but unit profits declined slightly in the first and doubled in the second. In most of the industries shown, increases in Profit/Sales during the early part of the period were due to greater increases in unit profits than in the average price of products. During the latter part of that period, however, Profit/Sales declined substantially in most of these industries because stable or rising average prices were accompanied by sharply declining unit profits. Such findings suggest that the appropriate interpretation of changes in profit margins requires information about the directions and relative magnitudes of changes in its two quite distinctive determinants.

Similarly, changes in Sales/Total Investment are usually interpreted as indicating the effectiveness with which capital resources are utilized. Again, however, this reflects either the assumption that Output/Total Investment and Sales/Output, the immediate determinants of Sales/Total

---

* For present purposes, sales are synonymous with value of products, adjustments for inventories having been discussed earlier.

Fig. 8.3 Index of the ratio of profit to value of product and the ratio of profit to physical output for selected manufacturing industries, 1938–58. (From Table 8.1.)

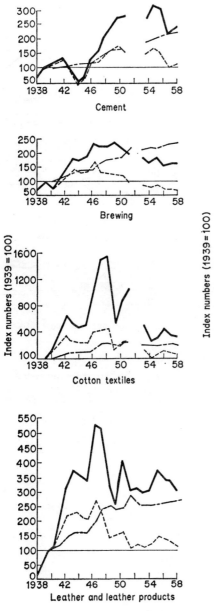

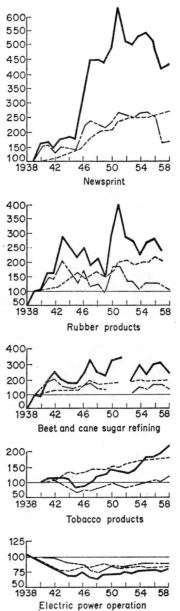

Key

—— P/PO

- - - - P/VP

—·—·— VP/PO

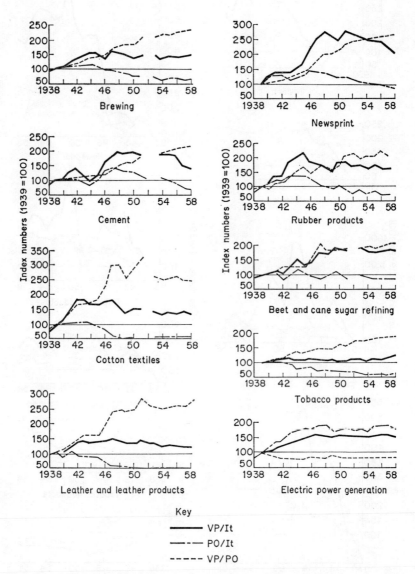

Fig. 8.4 Indexes of the ratio of value of product to total investment and the ratio of physical output to total investment for selected manufacturing industries, 1938–58. (From Table 8.1.)

Investment,* closely parallel one another, or the assumption that one of these determinants is either unchanging or unimportant. The findings in Figure 8.4 fail to support such speculations, demonstrating instead: major changes both in Output/Total Investment and Sales/Output; changing relationships between them through time in most industries; and wide differences in such relationships among industries. These suggest both the vulnerability of interpretations based on such assumptions and the increasingly effective insights provided by searching for fuller information.

8.4 HYPOTHESES CONCERNING MANAGERIAL CONTROL RATIO ADJUSTMENTS

Effective utilisation of the managerial control ratio approach to the analysis of past and prospective adjustments in the performance of industries, firms and operating components of the latter requires development of a theoretical framework identifying the most influential sources of change in each of the ratios and, where possible, indicating the most likely patterns of variation.

8.4.1 Sources and Expected Patterns of Adjustment in the Short Term

Among the primary level determinants of changes in the ratio of profits to total investment, it has already been suggested that the average price of products, average total unit costs and the rate of capacity utilisation are likely to be the most variable in the short run.

As was noted in Figure 2.3, changes in the average level of product prices (VP/PO) are determined by individual product prices and by the product composition of output. In turn, changes in individual product prices may be regarded as the product of external changes in the general price level and of changes in the ratio of the product price to the general price level— with the latter presumably reflecting the outcome of internal managerial evaluations of product improvements, unit cost adjustments and the price and income elasticities of demand for that product. And changes in the product-mix of the firm may be attributed to external changes in consumer incomes and tastes as well as internal managerial evaluations of the relative profitability of, as well as capacity limitations on, various products. Although management can probably exert greater influence on individual product prices than on product-mix in the short term—in view of the latter's dependence on consumer response—even its decisions on individual

$$* \quad \frac{\text{Sales}}{\text{Total Investment}} \equiv \frac{\text{Sales}}{\text{Output}} \times \frac{\text{Output}}{\text{Total Investment}}$$

product prices necessitate direct consideration of the other two determinants of short-term changes in the ratio of profits to total investment:
unit cost levels and the expected effects on capacity utilisation as represented by the demand elasticities referred to just above.

In general, average product prices may be expected to vary in the short-
term directly with the general price level, as well as with fluctuations in
demand and income—the latter because of the widespread tendency for
product-mix to shift towards higher priced goods when demand and incomes
rise. But such expectations might well vary among industries depending on
the influence of competitive industries or foreign suppliers, of newly
adopted technologies and of governmental pressures as well as other special
considerations. (For a detailed review of hypotheses in the economic,
accounting and related literature concerning expected adjustment patterns in each of the managerial control ratios, see [4].)

Changes in average total costs per unit of output, the second of the
primary managerial control ratios, may be traced initially to changes in
the average total unit cost of each product and to changes in the product
composition of output. Having already discussed the latter, short-term
changes in the former may be traced—as was discussed in detail in Chapter
7—to changes in average variable costs per unit of output, to changes in
average fixed costs per unit of output and to their respective shares of total
costs. In turn, changes in unit variable costs are shaped by externally
determined wage rates and materials prices as well as by the internally
determined amounts of labour and materials required per unit of output.
And changes in overhead costs per unit are determined by the level of
such total costs and by the bases used for allocating them to current
production.

Average total unit costs are also generally expected to vary directly in
the short term with the general price level and with output. As was indicated in the preceding chapter, this expectation follows from the tendency
of factor prices to move in the same direction as the general price level and
output; of these price adjustments to overshadow any concurrent changes
in direct labour and materials inputs per unit of output; and of variable
costs to account for a substantially greater proportion of total costs in
most industries than fixed costs. (For a detailed review of the factors
affecting the productivity of each input factor, see [2, Chapter 7].)
But the strength of such tendencies obviously differs among industries
and so do the counter-pressures generated by negatively sloped production
functions and by greater capital intensity in some industries.

Because it is determined by the difference between average product
prices and average total costs per unit of output, profit per unit of output
generally depends on the difference between the simultaneous upward and

downward movements in its two determinants. In other words, unit profits would generally be expected to increase not when prices rise and unit costs decline, but rather when prices rise faster than unit costs, or when costs are reduced more rapidly than prices.

The relationship between physical output and productive capacity, the third managerial control ratio, may be regarded as the point of inter-action between the volatility of market demand and the relative stability of capital facilities and production processes, or between factors subject to substantial changes in short periods and those tending to change materi-ally only over longer periods. In the short term, adjustments in the degree of utilisation of capacity are generally due primarily to variations in the level of output. In turn, changes in the output of a given plant or firm may be traced to the interaction between changes in the total market for such products and changes in the proportion of the total output accounted for by the given plant or firm. And the same approach may be applied to each product category. Thus, the resultant expectation of considerable short-term variability in the ratio of profit to total investment is enhanced by the fact that its remaining determinant, the rate of capacity utilisation, necessarily varies directly with output. In brief, management's efforts to maximise its rate of returns requires a continuous effort to realise the changing optimum balance among these interacting pressures. This might lead it to expand or contract output, to raise or lower product prices, and even to accept increases in unit costs and decreases in productive effi-ciency (despite an unwavering preference for decreases in unit costs and increases in productive efficiency). The course chosen for any one of these factors would thus depend on anticipated changes in the other factors and especially on management's estimate of their combined effect on the rate of returns.

8.4.2 Sources and Expected Patterns of Adjustment in the Long Term

Long-term changes in the rate of profit on total investment are determined not only by changes in capacity utilisation, in the productivity of fixed investment and in the internal allocation of capital, but also by any long run trends in average product prices and in average total unit costs.

There are no widely accepted economic theories supporting generalised expectations of either upward or downward long-term trends in average product prices or in average total unit costs. But various studies have found long-term upward and downward price movements in the United States and abroad as well as in numerous industrial sectors. Hence, until more persuasive theoretical guides can be developed, expectations concern-ing prospective long-term adjustments in these first two terms of the man-agerial control ratios may have to rest on available empirical findings for the particular industry, such as are presented in this chapter as well as those immediately preceding and following it.

Adjustments in capacity utilisation may be generated, of course, by changes in output or in productive capacity. Disparities between them may accordingly be attributed to: the carryover of facilities which can no longer be fully utilised because of permanent declines affecting older processes and markets; overexpansion in new areas of operation in anticipation of developing markets; and fluctuations in established areas of demand. But the long-term trend in capacity utilisation is most likely to be horizontal because capacity tends to be adjusted over time to the trend in physical output.

Changes in the ratio of productive capacity to fixed investment may be traced initially to the effects of two sectors of managerial decision making. The first concerns the relationship between: (a) the rate of decline in the effective productive capacity of the capital goods on hand as a result of progressive wear and aging; and (b) the rate at which depreciation and obsolescence charges are reducing the remaining investment in such goods. The second concerns the relationship between the increments contributed by new capital goods to productive capacity and to net fixed investment.

Over longer periods, expected changes in the productivity of fixed investment depend on the resultant of three developments. One is the widespread tendency to recover investment through depreciation charges more rapidly than any concomitant reduction in productive contribution —which causes a progressive increase in the productivity of fixed capital as a given stock of capital goods ages. A second is the tendency for new capital goods to yield greater contributions to productive capacity relative to their cost than was true of older equipment at the time they were purchased—although such gains may be partially offset if new capacity additions are concentrated in periods of inflated capital goods prices. And the third is the tendency for the ratio of capacity to fixed investment to decline when major modernisation programmes are undertaken. Because these latter involve the replacement of capacity based on heavily depreciated facilities and equipment by costly new capital goods yielding equivalent capacity, the sharp rise in the denominator cannot help decreasing the ratio. (For an extended discussion of these factors, see [2, pp. 135–145].) Empirical studies of resulting trends have yielded differing conclusions. Although these may be attributed partly to differences in the economic sectors studied, in the time periods covered and in the measures used, the conclusion can hardly be avoided that no single generalisation is likely to prove universally applicable. (Relevant findings are cited in Chapter 3, in [2, p. 100], in [1, p. xxxiii] and in [4, p. 211].)

Changes in the ratio of fixed investment to total investment reflect managerial estimates of the relative need for productive capacity (and other facilities determining the activity potentials of the firm) as compared with the need for working capital. The latter may be affected not only by adjustments in output and price levels but also by permanent changes in inventory levels and customer financing practices. But there is no theoretical basis and few empirical bases for developing persuasive expectations at this time concerning long-term adjustments in this ratio. (See [4, pp. 287–303] for a review of the relevant literature.)

Turning to interactions among the determinants of longer-term adjustments in the rate of profits to total investment, it is apparent that an increase in the productivity of fixed capital may be utilised so as to increase, maintain or reduce productive capacity, depending upon market prospects. If productive capacity is merely to be maintained, it makes possible a reduction in the level of fixed investment, thus tending to bring about a reduction in the ratio of fixed investment to total investment. And the latter development, in turn, would involve either an increase in working capital or a reduction in total investment—the latter affecting the structure of financing. Alternatively, an increase in capacity which is proportional to the gain in the productivity of capital might exert its primary impact on other managerial control ratios through the resulting pressure for expanding output, so as to prevent a burdensome increase in the under-utilisation of capacity. In this case, management might have to lower product prices, increase sales and advertising expenses, finance increased inventories, or extend further credit to dealers or consumers—the particular course chosen determining which control ratios will be altered.

Similar interactions might be considered in evaluating the effects of changes in the allocation of total investment among alternative uses. An increase in fixed investment is often likely to involve an increase in productive capacity. If capital goods prices are relatively high at the time, as is commonly the case during periods of general plant expansion, this may involve a reduction in the ratio of productive capacity to fixed investment. Moreover, increases in capacity through the introduction of additional facilities may involve at least a temporary reduction in the ratio of output to capacity, until such facilities are brought into efficient production and until markets are expanded accordingly. Such gains in capacity may also increase working capital requirements, thus tending to affect the level of total investment. On the other hand, the initial pressure for changing the allocation of investment may be engendered by increased needs for working capital. In that event, management may seek either to reduce the investment tied up in fixed assets—generally a slow process, unless certain operating units are sold—or to undertake additional financing.

It is also apparent from earlier stages of the discussion that changes in the structure of financing may interact with several of the other basic foci of managerial decision making, including costs, capacity levels, the productivity of fixed assets and the allocation of available investment resources.

For practical purposes, managerial decision making must also take account of the interactions between adjustments in the control ratios which tend to be variable in the short run and adjustments in the control ratios likely to undergo significant changes only over longer periods. Whenever substantial changes do take place in capacity, investment levels or the structure of financing, such adjustments constitute additional pressures for change in the more volatile control ratios—as has been indicated in several of the preceding examples. Short-term fluctuations in prices, unit costs and output levels are not likely to force significant adjustments in the productivity of capital, the allocation of investment resources, or the structure of financing. But these latter are likely to be responsive to persistent trends in price, cost and output levels.

Attention has already been called to the fact that persistent trends in output tend to engender similar adjustments in capacity, thus minimising the prospect of progressive upward or downward trends in the ratio of output to capacity. And managerial efforts to minimise the effects of unfavourable trends in prices and costs are likely to centre around reducing the relative importance of the input categories characterised by the most unfavourable trends in cost per unit of output. For example, in industries faced by trends in unit labour cost which are less favourable than trends in capital costs per unit of output, managements may intensify mechanisation and automation—with concomitant adjustments in the allocation of investment between fixed and working capital, as well as in other control ratios.

8.5 SOME FURTHER EMPIRICAL PERSPECTIVES ON MANAGERIAL CONTROL RATIOS

Even a cursory examination of Figure 8.5, based on the study cited previously [4], reveals wide differences among industries in the adjustment patterns recorded by their primary managerial control ratios between 1938 and 1958. The relative effects on the ratio of profits to total investment of changes in each of the five sectors of decision making and performance encompassed by these ratios seemed to cover a broad range over different industries, and also varied considerably within some industries over these twenty years. This suggests that effective managerial strategies might have to be differentiated accordingly among such industries, reflecting diverse long-term trends in certain of these ratios and differing degrees of short-term instability as well as disproportionate effects on profit rates.

The expectation of much greater short-term variability in Profit/Total Investment and in Profit/Output than in Capacity/Fixed Investment and in Fixed Investment/Total Investment was supported in all nine industries except electric power—with the implication that short-term variations in Profit/Total Investment tended to be dominated by variations in unit profits. This line of analysis might then be extended by determining the conditions associated with fluctuations in unit profits—including, for example, the extent to which relative increases in prices and in unit costs were responsive to changes in output as compared with changes in the general price level.

Over the longer run, there were significant disparities between the adjustment patterns of Profit/Total Investment and Profit/Output in the brewing, cotton textile, leather and tobacco industries, reflecting the influence of the three ratios which determine changes in Output/Total Investment. Capacity utilisation followed: an essentially horizontal trend in the cotton textile, leather and tobacco products industry; a generally upward trend in the electric power, newsprint and sugar refining industries; and extended periods of increase and of decrease in the remaining three. The productivity of fixed investment had a downward trend in six industries and a horizontal trend in the others. And the ratio of fixed to total investment was horizontal in six industries, upward in one, and had both upward and downward links in the remaining two industries.

Each of these findings clearly invites further analysis as a basis for evaluating the relative roles of wartime controls, postwar inflation and differential market expansion in accounting for the patterns revealed. Particular interest attaches to the dominance of downward trends in the productivity of fixed capital in contrast to the expectation of upward trends. This outcome seemed attributable in considerable measure to the heavy role of modernisation in most of the industries experiencing a downward trend in this ratio—replacements having been long inhibited by the depression of the 1930s and wartime controls through 1945—requiring large increments in fixed investment merely to replace worn and obsolete capacity. But further probing may help to indicate the role of technological advances, of tax policies and of trade union pressures in shaping such trends.

Figure 8.5 also illustrates some of the wide variations which may occur in the loci and timing of upward and downward adjustments in the three determinants of the ratio of output to total investment. In electric power, the sharp gain in this ratio during 1939–44 resulted from improvements in

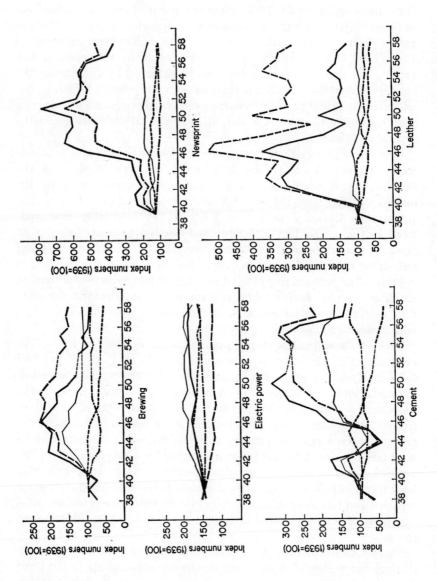

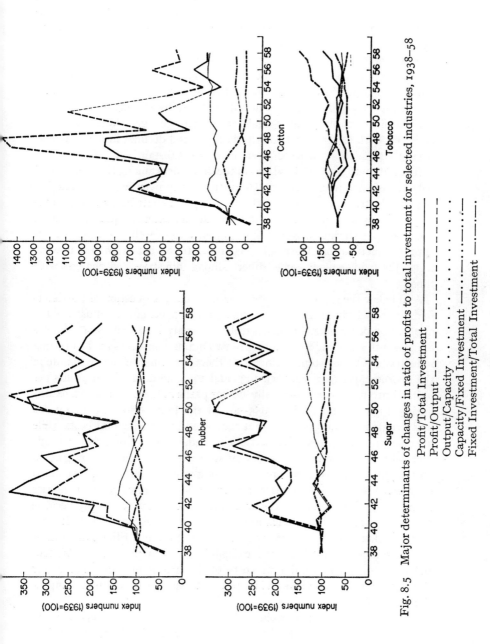

Fig. 8.5 Major determinants of changes in ratio of profits to total investment for selected industries, 1938–58

Profit/Total Investment ————
Profit/Output – – – – –
Output/Capacity · · · · · · ·
Capacity/Fixed Investment —··—··—
Fixed Investment/Total Investment —·—·—·—

the productivity of fixed investment and in the utilisation of capacity. Thereafter, comparative stability in all sectors kept Output/Total Investment within narrow limits. In the brewing industry, a major improvement followed by a decline in the utilisation of capacity during 1939–51 was accompanied by a reverse cycle in the internal allocation of investment. The productivity of fixed investment changed only between 1945 and 1948. In cement, 1939–54 was characterised by major, opposing cycles in the utilisation of capacity and in the productivity of fixed investment. Yet the internal allocation of investment underwent little change. During 1954–58, however, both of the first two criteria registered declines in performance, while the allocation for fixed assets increased substantially.

In addition to such explorations of the differences among the adjustment patterns of each managerial control ratio within given industries and between industries—as well as of their consequent contributions to profitability—these data may be used to seek out characteristic patterns within each industry during upswings and downswings as well as during periods of prolonged inflation. The results may indicate to what extent and in what ways 'the management game' differs among industries and changes with time.

And below the level of the industry, one faces the question of the determinants of relative performance among its competitors. To illustrate the application of the managerial control ratio analysis to such issues, Figure 8.6 presents some findings relating to two major companies in the brewing industry [4]. As one step in comparing their performance, one may note in the middle panel that, between 1939 and 1958, adjustments in profits per unit of output followed essentially similar paths in these companies, except during 1939–43 and during 1953–56. In the first period, Company A's unit profits rose sharply because it succeeded in reducing unit costs while average product prices remained unchanged, whereas Company B's unit costs and prices were both relatively stable thus preventing any gain in unit profits. Between 1953 and 1956, Company A's unit profits remained unchanged because the increase in average product price covered the rise in unit costs; but Company B's unit profits declined very sharply because its average product price remained virtually unchanged while its unit costs rose even faster than in Company A. Further probing of these differences in performance might then involve exploring the contributions to differential adjustments in total unit costs of disparities in individual factor prices, in factor proportions and in the effectiveness with which such inputs were utilised.

As an illustration of possible guides for control purposes, one may observe in Figure 8.6 not only the disparity between the adjustments in unit costs and in average product price in Company B between 1953 and 1956—

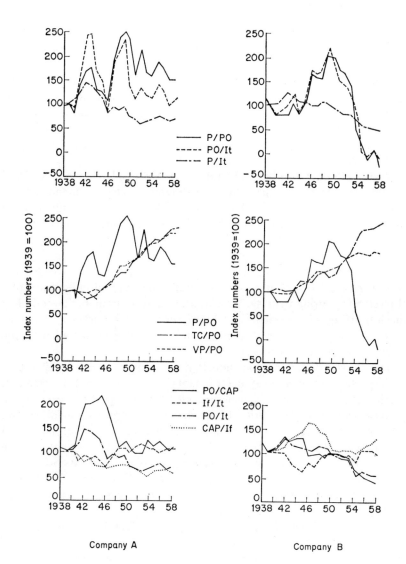

Company A   Company B

Fig. 8.6 Managerial central ratio adjustment patterns for two brewing
companies, 1938–58

which was referred to above—but also the offsetting of improvements in the productivity of fixed investment during 1954–58 by sharp, progressive reductions in the utilisation of capacity. With respect to Company A, Figure 8.6 calls attention not only to the reduction of unit costs while average product price remained unchanged during 1939–43, but to the increased lagging of average product price behind rising unit costs during 1949–58. And one may also note that the decline in Output/Total Investment was due primarily to steady reductions in the productivity of fixed investment.

Figure 8.6 may also be used to illustrate the availability of additional criteria for diagnosing the sources of differences in performance among companies in the same industry. In respect to the rate of profits on total investment, the top panel shows that Company A gained more than Company B during 1939–45; that A declined more rapidly than B during 1949–1953; and that B experienced the far greater reduction during 1953–58. What accounts for these differences? During 1939–45, A exceeded the performance of B both in profits per unit of output and in Output/Total Investment; during 1949–53, B's advantage derived from its slower decline in Output/Total Investment; and during 1953–58, A's enormous advantage arose solely from its slight decrease in unit profits compared with the sharp reduction experienced by B.

Digging still deeper, one may note that as among the two determinants of unit profits and the three determinants of Output/Total Investment, during 1939–45 A's performance surpassed B's in respect to each of these criteria except average price received, where there was no difference. During 1949–53, B's superiority in the productivity of capital more than offset A's higher utilisation of capacity, while all other ratios were essentially similar. And during 1953–58, A's higher capacity utilisation offset B's greater productivity of capital to yield comparable levels of Output/Total Investment, but A also achieved advantages in respect to average product price and unit costs.

Thus, each of the five criteria affecting Profit/Total Investment was a focus of major differences between these two companies in at least one of these three periods. Interestingly enough, compared with performance levels in 1939, A ranked higher than B: in respect to the utilisation of capacity in all three periods; in respect to unit costs in two periods; and in respect to average product price in one period. Company A also had a higher ratio of fixed to total investment in one period. On the other hand, B ranked higher than A in respect to the productivity of fixed investment in all three periods, and in respect to nothing else in even one of these periods.

In short, the primary, secondary and even lower level managerial control

TABLE 8.1 Changes in managerial control ratios, selected industries, 1939–58

A. Index numbers (1939 = 100)

	$\dfrac{\text{Profit}}{\text{Total Investment}}$	$\dfrac{\text{Profit}}{\text{Output}}$	$\dfrac{\text{Output}}{\text{Total Investment}}$	Average Price	Unit Costs	$\dfrac{\text{Output}}{\text{Capacity}}$	$\dfrac{\text{Capacity}}{\text{Fixed Investment}}$	$\dfrac{\text{Fixed Investment}}{\text{Total Investment}}$	$\dfrac{\text{Total Investment}}{\text{Equity Investment}}$	$\dfrac{\text{Profit}}{\text{Equity Investment}}$
Brewing industry	95	155	62	236	247	116	59	92	96	92
Cement	133	227	59	228	228	161	32	115	95	126
Cotton textiles	202	365	55	244	238	138	52	76	85	172
Electric power	140	79	177	85	90	136	116	100	110	154
Leather and products	130	284	46	275	275	101	58	78	104	134
Newsprint	345	431	80	263	240	130	72	86	67	231
Rubber products (1957)	184	245	75	207	205	89	75	112	77	141
Sugar refining	206	242	90	207	204	139	69	96	100	206
Tobacco products	142	214	66	182	179	87	71	107	123	174

B. Absolute rates, 1958

	Brewing	Cement	Electric Power	Newsprint
Profit/Total Investment	10%	10·1%	10·3%	11·1%
Fixed/Total Investment	56%	69·0%	97·5%	63·0%

ratios can become part of performance budgeting programmes, with planned targets for adjustments in aggregate results linked to a particular pattern of adjustments in lower level control ratios designed to effect the over-all objectives. The auditing would involve comparing performance in each sector with planned adjustments derived from integrated planning for the entire firm rather than from past standards unique to each sector.

Finally, Table 8.1 reveals some of the new perspectives on the specialised characteristics of different industries offered by managerial control ratios. Considerable effort proved necessary to develop reasonably comparable financial, physical output and productive capacity data for a reasonable array of industries. The nine used in this study were the only ones among an initial list of more than fifty for which this proved feasible. (For details of sources of data and estimation methods used, see [4].) The particular findings relate, of course, only to the extraordinary period 1939–58, with its sharp inflationary and growth pressures. Yet the wide range of adjustment patterns in Panel A indicates such disparate emphases among industries as to make judgements based on 'general industrial averages' or 'common norms' quite hazardous. Such diversity does not relate only to changes in the rate of profits on total (or on equity) investment—ranging from a 5 per cent reduction to a 245 per cent increase in respect to the first of these. It also relates to the directions and the relative magnitudes of the contributions provided by concomitant changes in unit profits and in Output/Total Investment.

Furthermore, the variety of component performance adjustments underlying comparable levels of aggregate performance may well stimulate explorations in the direction of modifying past patterns in given industries. For example, closely similar increases in unit profits (127–145 per cent) for cement, sugar refining and rubber products were associated with gains in Profit/Total Investment ranging from 33–106 per cent—emphasising the burden of differential disadvantages in Output/Total Investment. And comparable reductions of 38–41 per cent in the latter ratio for brewing and cement prove to have been the resultant of quite distinctive adjustments in the three determinants of Output/Total Investment: capacity utilisation; productivity of fixed investment; and fixed total investment. Panel B displays similar contrasts between the absolute levels of an aggregate performance ratio and one of its component ratios, indicating the magnitude of the differentials to be found among the other ratios in order to yield comparable aggregates.

9 Economic Effects of Technological Innovations

Although technological progress has been one of the most powerful forces reshaping our world during the past 200 years, remarkably little is known about the processes whereby such advances are created and brought into use or about their subsequent effects. The history of economic thought contains occasional evidences of such interest (for a comprehensive review of early contributions, see Gourvitch [21]), especially in some of the writings of Babbage [8], Bohm-Bawerk [10], Veblen [53] and Schumpeter [46], but these were clearly outside the mainstream of analytical efforts until twenty-five years ago. Indeed, formal definitions of the field long centred on the allocation of scarce resources among alternative uses at a given level of technology. Nor was this restriction of the analytical domain of economics considered particularly burdensome even as recently as the decades prior to 1940, when primary attention was focused on understanding and controlling business cycles. Resulting concentration on fluctuations in aggregate demand and in its major components yielded such important advances in what has come to be called macro-economics as to encourage continued general disregard of the role of technology in economic change.*

With the increasing emphasis on economic growth after the Second World War, it was inevitable that greater attention would have to be given to the supply side of economic forces, including technological innovations as one of the most powerful influences on output potentials and input factor requirements. Surveys of resulting contributions indicate, however, that the direction and effects of such innovations are still far from clear. (Early work in the field was summarised by Abramovitz [1]. The most recent and

* Notable exceptions include the productivity studies of the U.S. Bureau of Labor Statistics initiated in the late 1920s, Jerome's pioneering study of mechanisation [29] and its extensions through the National Research Project [56], Kuznets's early research on the rate of technological development [30] and, at least methodologically, Douglas's initial studies of the production function [15].

comprehensive survey is by Hahn and Matthews [26, note especially pp. 47–74 and 111–12].) Many recent studies (see [2, 35, 44, 47, 49] and for a bibliography, see [54]) have derived empirical production functions for the U.S.A. and major sectors of the economy showing that sharp increases in total output relative to total labour and capital inputs involved virtually no change in labour-capital ratios and hence should be attributed to 'technical change'. There can be no doubt about the importance of fuller investigation of the nature of such technical changes instead of continuing to regard them as beyond the interests of economists [16, 20, 25, 37, 41, 51]. But the dominance of findings that the torrent of technological innovations has been neutral in its effects on factor input proportions may reflect the inadequacy of our penetration into the processes whereby technological impacts are gradually absorbed into the structure of economic relationships.

In seeking to strengthen the analytical basis for estimating innovational effects, this paper will first review the approaches in common use for decision-making purposes; then compare resulting cost expectations with actual findings in six manufacturing industries and in 'all manufacturing' over 30 to 40 years; and, finally, explore means of bridging the gaps between them. The unexpected nature of these gaps accounts for subsequent efforts to explore four components of the readjustment processes triggered by technological innovations: the transformation of physical modifications of production into changes in unit costs, cost proportions, product prices and output; the transmission of changes from individual firms to the rest of the industry and to broader segments of the economy; the integration of short-term changes into longer term trends; and the progressive alienation of familiar concepts and measures by the reshaping of the essential nature of production activities by technological advances.

9.1 PREVAILING APPROACHES AND EXPECTATIONS

Technological progress in manufacturing has been shaped largely at the level of individual firms through managerial decisions to allocate resources for the development and adoption of particular innovations among the vast array of possibilities [12, pp. 19–20]. How are such choices made? Even where modern capital budgeting methods are used,* the results are frequently undermined by crude input data reflecting appraisals by engineers more competent to evaluate the technological than the economic effects of innovations [40] and based on the assumption that nothing else will change despite the ramified thrusts of major innovations. It is even

* For evidence that reliance on such rigorous methods may be uncommon, see [12, pp. 59–65] and [6, pp. 356–8].

more disconcerting to find that the specific techniques used to estimate the effects of individual technological innovations seem to be considered so self-evident that published descriptions are difficult to find. For example, descriptions of the procedure to be used in machine replacement problems begin with entries for the estimated savings on materials, wages and other outlays—or for total savings alone—without indicating how such estimates should be made. (See [3, p. 547]; [55, p. 56] and [9, Chapter 6]). Even in Terborgh's [52], Chapter 9, which is entitled 'Estimating the Annual Operating Advantage: Specific Instruction,' offers no guides beyond emphasising the need to consider indirect as well as direct effects both on operating costs and on revenue (pp. 95–7).

A generalised model for evaluating prospective innovations, based on textbook prescriptions and descriptions in business journals, concentrates not on expected profit increments but on the net cost savings determined by comparing each category of actual average unit costs in some recent period with expected costs when the new facilities are used at some defined level of output.* In particular,† estimates are made of expected changes: in man-hours per unit of output for each labour category; in the quantity of each material input per unit of output; in fixed investment; and in output as compared with recent actual levels. It is then assumed that unit labour and unit material costs will change in proportion to their input quantities; that fixed capital charges per unit will change in proportion to the investment level and inversely with output; and unit salary costs, if considered at all, are expected to vary directly with salaried employment and inversely with output. This model is flexible enough to cover a wide range of technological innovations, for it allows changes in each category of inputs, and it evaluates all alternatives in terms of expected net effects on average total costs per unit of output. It should be emphasised, however, that there is a remarkable paucity of publications comparing such estimates with actual results after some substantial period of time. (One of the few sources of relevant data, although based on a small sample, is [12, pp. 89–91].) And regrettably, Terborgh's explanation of the obstacles to such post-evaluations also applies to pre-decision estimates: 'The overwhelming majority of business investment projects are of this segmental or component type—replacements, improvements, expansions or some combination thereof. They become a part—usually a small part—of an existing operation. Since it is impossible in most cases to compute their separate

* Reliance on such more limited criteria would have obvious appeal for engineers seeking to exclude possible market effects. This cost emphasis also finds some support in Marshall [34, pp. 350, 359].

† Although this procedure is seldom presented in textual discussions, it is commonly encountered in the accompanying illustrative problems. (For example, see [52, pp. 154, 158, and 179] and also [22, pp. 366 and 368].)

revenue generation and operating cost incurments after they are in service, it is even more impossible to predict these magnitudes before the projects are acquired' [52, p. 52]. Of course this admitted inability to make such determinations obviously places difficulties in the way of assuming the applicability to a wide range of industrial operations of Griliches's interesting finding that the pattern of adoption of a new technological change in agriculture was closely associated with its relative profitability in different regions [23].

Because decisions about individual innovations require broader strategic guides, one may also assume widespread managerial efforts (though they are seldom recognised explicitly) to estimate the effects of whole networks of innovations as the basis for planning longer term technical improvement programmes which concentrate on mechanising labour tasks, or saving materials, etc. The impracticability of preparing detailed estimates for each of the many component innovations comprising each of the alternative programmes suggests that decisions must reflect judgements about the expected effects of broad classes of innovations. And in view of the continued scarcity of relevant research findings, such judgements may likewise be rooted in the original model, suggesting that unit costs tend to parallel adjustments in unit input requirements for groups as well as for single innovations. Nor has any other systematic approach turned up in literature and field surveys of engineering and managerial expectations.

The foregoing would seem to support the following hypotheses with respect to the cost effects of the major technological innovations of the past few decades: (a) improved materials, reduced waste and the development of by-products have tended to lower material inputs per unit of output, thereby reducing unit material costs and their proportion of total unit costs (for an illustration of a logical projection from changes in physical input requirements to assumed changes in cost ratios (i.e. the relationship of material costs to value of product), see [17, p. 279]); (b) task specialisation, methods improvement and mechanisation have tended to reduce unit labour requirements and, hence, both unit wage costs and the ratio of wages to total cost. (For an illustration of such a logical but empirically unwarranted assumption concerning the effects of increasing mechanisation on the ratio of wages to value added, see [29, pp. 227–8]); (c) increasing mechanisation tends to decrease average unit wage costs sufficiently to more than offset any increase in unit machine costs during periods of low utilisation; and (d) technological progress over the long run tends to increase the capacity of equipment relative to its price. Thus, each type of technical innovation is expected to generate a distinctive pattern of cost effects. And managerial efforts to cope with labour cost pressures would presumably counsel different strategic decisions about innovational programmes than growing pressures from material costs.

9.2 ACTUAL COSTS IN SELECTED INDUSTRIES

The following analysis of actual cost adjustments over periods of thirty to forty years is based on cost data from the U.S. Census of Manufactures, physical output estimates by Fabricant [18] and the Wholesale Price Index of the U.S. Bureau of Labor Statistics. The industries covered are: Blast Furnaces; Steel Mills; Coke Ovens; Cement; Petroleum Refining; and Canned Fruits and Vegetables. To facilitate comparisons, data are also included for All Manufacturing Combined.

Each of these industries was subjected to all of the major categories of technological innovations discussed above, including a continuing stream of minor improvements as well as occasional spectacular advances.* According to the preceding expectations, these innovations should have engendered downward trends in total unit costs, in unit wage costs and, except for Canning, in unit materials cost. Some capital goods innovations might have increased average fixed investment charges per unit, albeit presumably by less than accompanying decreases in unit variable costs, while others reduced such charges—thus limiting expectations to a reduction in the ratio of variable to total costs. As for unit salaried costs, the innovations analysed were not among those considered earlier as bases for standardised cost expectations. Finally, variations in the nature, timing, and magnitude of innovations in each industry would have tended to yield comparably varied adjustments in component unit cost categories as well

* Among the more important developments during the period in the Blast Furnace Industry were: the increasing use of Mesabi ores; increases in the average size of furnace; increasing mechanisation and automation in materials handling; improvements in control of the reduction process and in heat economy; and increasing control of the quality and uniformity of mineral inputs. In Steel Works and Rolling Mills, major advances included: the introduction of scrap steel; enlargement of furnace capacity; improvements in control of the reduction process and in heat economy; improvements in materials handling; and enormous advances in the mechanisation of rolling and other processes. In the Coke Industry, major innovations included: the shift from beehive to by-product coke ovens; expansion of the variety of by-products; increases in the scale of operations; and improvements in control of the reduction process and in heat economy. Advances in the Cement Industry included: the increasing mechanisation of extraction operations; increases in the size of kilns; improvements in heat economy and process control; and the increasing mechanisation of materials handling, bagging, etc. Advances in the Petroleum Refining Industry included: the development of straight-run distillation and of thermal and catalytic cracking; the increasing size of refinery units; the increasing automation of controls; improvements in heat economy; and the expansion of product variety. And in the Fruit and Vegetable Canning Industry, major advances included: the increasing mechanisation of materials handling and of fruit and vegetable preparations; increased control of processes; improvements in canning and crating; and increases in product variety.

7+

as in cost proportions—along with comparably pervasive dissimilarities among industries.

The findings relating to each industry are presented in Figures 9.1 to 9.7 in three panels, Panel (a) depicts actual changes in physical output and in average unit material, unit wage and unit salary costs as well as in an unwieldy residual comprising the sum of overhead, all other costs and profits per unit of output.* Thus, it is the panel which is most directly relevant to the common form in which the expected results of technological estimates are expressed. In Panel (b), costs have been adjusted for fluctuations in the general price level. Finally, Panel (c) presents the proportions of total product value accounted for by materials, by wages, by salaries and by the residual—whether deflated or undeflated.

Panel (a) in each of the seven charts shows that actual average unit costs seldom displayed the significant downward trend which was expected. Unit material costs were higher in 1937 than in 1909 in every case except Petroleum Refining (5 per cent decline). Unit wage costs were likewise higher in 1937 than in 1909 in every case except Coke. Unit salary costs over this period declined heavily in Blast Furnaces and Canning, were reduced by 14 per cent in Petroleum Refining and rose in all of the others. The residual category of overhead and all other costs plus profit per unit of output rose in each series between 1909 and 1937. These findings also indicate that average total costs per unit of output rose significantly in All Manufacturing Combined and in each of the industries except Petroleum Refining (where it seems to have been unchanged). This conclusion may be drawn, despite the absence of profits data, by comparing the increase in material, wage and salary costs combined per unit of output with the accompanying increase in total product value per unit over the entire period and then using the cost proportions in Panel (c) to estimate how much of the 'residual ratio' would have to be attributable to profit and also how much profits would have had to rise in order to have prevented any increase in total unit costs.

Panel (b) shows that unit costs fail to support expectations of substantial downward trends even when deflated for changes in the general price level. Between 1909 and 1937, deflated unit material costs declined by more than 12 per cent only in Petroleum Refining, and deflated unit wage costs declined by more than 9 per cent only in Blast Furnaces and Coke. Deflated unit salary costs declined by more than 10 per cent in Blast Furnaces, Petroleum Refining and Canning over this period, while all other costs plus profits per unit of output after deflation rose in every series except Canning (which declined by 6 per cent). Hence, deflated total unit

* That such a residual may nevertheless serve as a useful focus for theoretical analysis is suggested by Manne [32, p. 9].

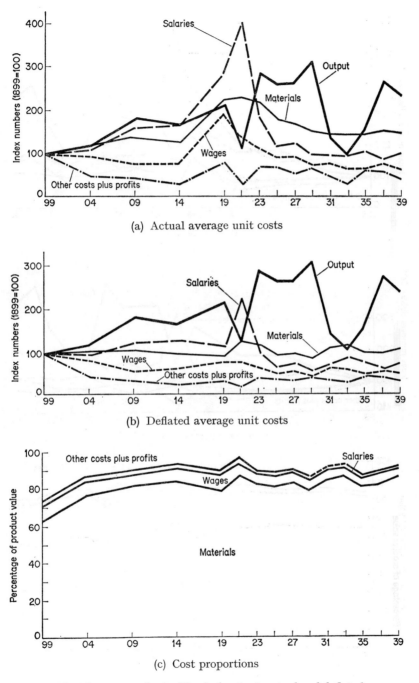

(a) Actual average unit costs

(b) Deflated average unit costs

(c) Cost proportions

Fig. 9.1   Blast furnace products. Physical output, actual and deflated average unit costs and cost proportions, 1899–1939

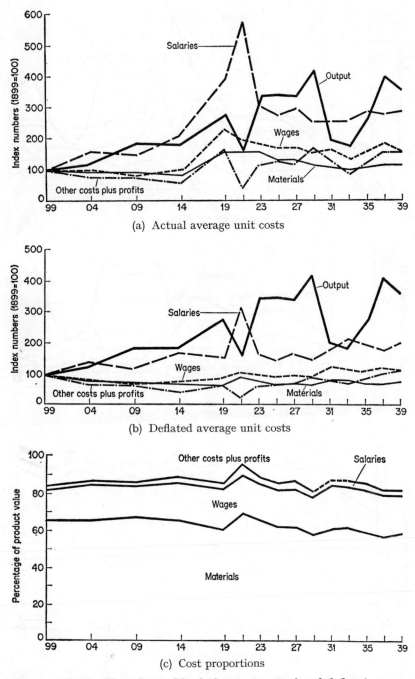

(a) Actual average unit costs

(b) Deflated average unit costs

(c) Cost proportions

Fig. 9.2 Steel mill products. Physical output, actual and deflated average
unit costs and cost proportions, 1899–1939

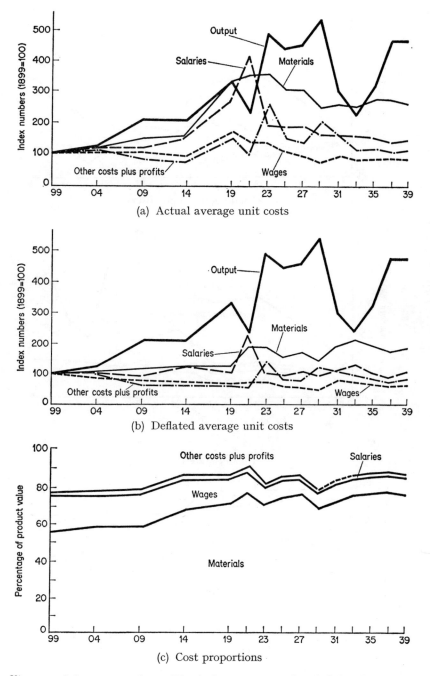

(a) Actual average unit costs

(b) Deflated average unit costs

(c) Cost proportions

Fig. 9.3   Coke oven products. Physical output, actual and deflated average
unit costs and cost proportions, 1899–1939

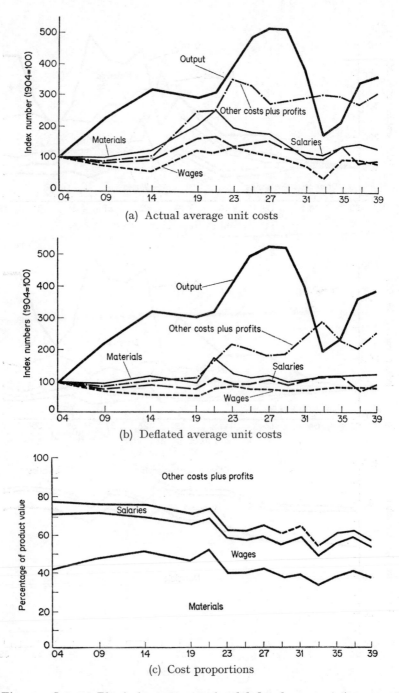

Fig. 9.4   Cement. Physical output, actual and deflated average unit costs and cost proportions, 1904–39

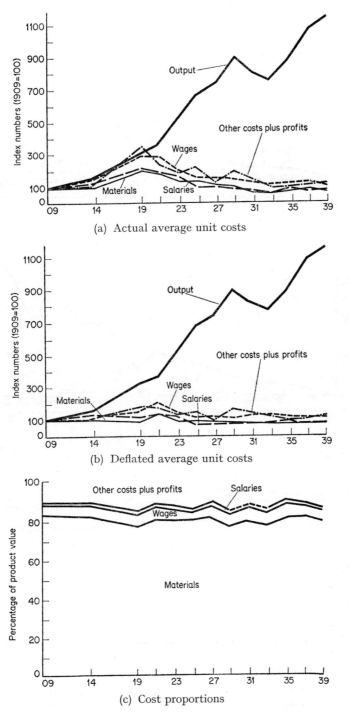

(a) Actual average unit costs

(b) Deflated average unit costs

(c) Cost proportions

Fig. 9.5   Petroleum refining. Physical output, actual deflated average unit
costs, and cost proportions, 1909–1939

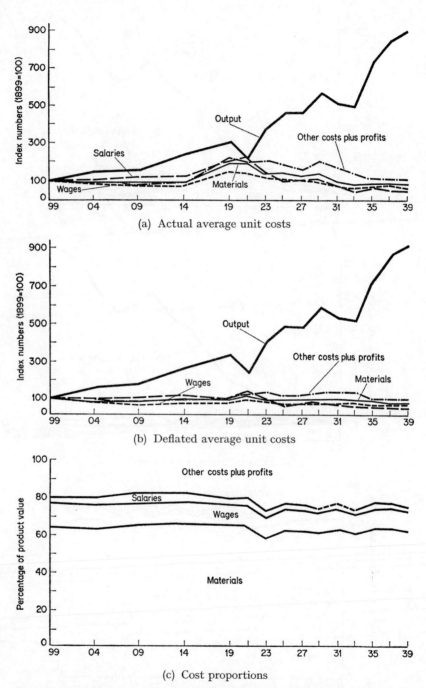

Fig. 9.6   Fruits and vegetables, canned. Physical output, actual and deflated average unit costs, and cost proportions, 1899–1939

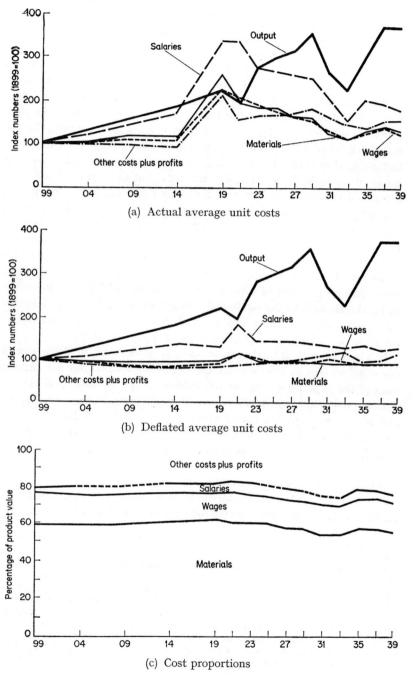

(a) Actual average unit costs

(b) Deflated average unit costs

(c) Cost proportions

Fig. 9.7 All manufacturing combined. Physical output, actual and deflated average unit costs, and cost proportions 1899–1939

7*

costs probably declined by roughly 20 per cent in Petroleum Refining and 10 per cent in Blast Furnaces, while rising in each of the other industries and exhibiting no change in All Manufacturing Combined.

Panel C reveals that cost proportions had horizontal trends in most of these industries over considerable periods of time. Lasting changes of significant magnitude were few and they occurred in the early years. Such major adjustments affected the material and wage cost ratios in Blast Furnaces only between 1899 and 1909. In Steel Mills, the wage ratio changed between 1909 and 1914, while the materials ratio changed between 1923 and 1929. Progressive changes in the material and wage cost ratios were apparent in Coke between 1909 and 1921, but these trends, too, were horizontal thereafter. In Cement, the wage ratio changed between 1909 and 1914 as did the materials ratio, and the latter also underwent a reverse pattern of change between 1914 and 1923. On the other hand, Petroleum Refining and Fruit and Vegetable Canning were free of major adjustments in the trend of cost proportions and this was also true of All Manufacturing Combined. It is also of interest that materials plus wages accounted for more than 70 per cent of total product value in each of these industries and in All Manufacturing Combined throughout the period studied, except for Cement, and the latter also experienced the only sharp reduction in the ratio of variable to fixed costs between 1909 and 1937.

In short, actual adjustments in average unit costs, in deflated unit costs and in cost proportions for the industries studied did not support most of the expectations associated with the major technological innovations experienced by each.* Moreover, although many of these innovations pervaded wide sectors of manufacturing, the data for All Manufacturing Combined likewise failed to confirm such cost expectations, suggesting that the selected industries need not be seriously atypical.

These findings cannot be interpreted as contradicting the earlier cost expectations because the latter concerned the effects of single innovations within a given plant, assuming all else to be unchanged, while the empirical results reflect the net effects on the industry of many technological innova-

---

* The extent of these deviations from expectations may be further illustrated by the fact that the major change in Blast Furnace cost proportions between 1899 and 1909 coincided with a doubling in the proportion of total United States iron ore supplied by the Mesabi Range, from 26·4 per cent in 1899 to 54·3 per cent in 1909, after which the ratio remained stable (57 per cent in 1939). And the major change in Coke Oven cost proportions between 1909 and 1921 coincided with the rapid adoption of the more economical by-product oven in place of the beehive oven, with the former's proportion of total coke production rising from 15 per cent in 1909 to 78 per cent in 1921. Oddly enough, however, both of these shifts were accompanied by sharp increases rather than decreases in the proportion of total costs accounted for by materials.

tions as well as market and other adjustments. In building a bridge between these frameworks, intermediate stages may be identified which represent quite practical foci for decision making and, hence, call for a corresponding array of analytical models.

9.3 ANALYTICAL FOUNDATIONS OF MAJOR UNIT COST FINDINGS

Exploration of the network of influences underlying the finding that major categories of deflated unit costs tend to follow horizontal trends will begin with the problem of appraising alternative replacements for given equipment, or alternative innovations for performing a given function. Despite its conformity with the focus of the model in section 9.1, even this application requires some elaboration of the original framework in addition to identifying its implicit conditions. Restrictive assumptions include: no change in the nature of inputs from preceding operations; no change in the nature of the outputs provided by the new facilities; and conformance of the capacity of new facilities with those of adjacent operations. Explicit allowances must also be made for changes in the interest rate, expected equipment life, time pattern of depreciation charges and maintenance costs.

The model seems adequate to cover the cost effects of innovations which merely reduce unit input requirements for materials or capital within one plant, leaving factor prices unchanged. But allowance would have to be made for the possibility that labour-saving innovations may engender increases in average hourly earnings, either directly through piece rates and incentives or indirectly through stimulating the renegotiation of wage rates. Related salaries may also be raised to maintain customary differentials. In addition, innovations may alter the flexibility as well as the level of input requirements, thereby requiring adjustment of the model to consider estimates of unit input levels over a range of output levels rather than for only one level.* In turn, such modifications invite two new hypotheses: that labour-saving innovations within a single plant are more likely to generate offsetting factor price increases than other input reductions; and that the cost effects of changes in the flexibility of inputs will tend to increase with the amplitude of fluctuations in the plant's output.

In the case of widely adopted innovations, two further elaborations of the model seem necessary. One would consider the effects of widespread changes in each category of unit input requirements on corresponding factor prices. The other would reach beyond unit cost criteria to include the

---

* This contrasts with Terborgh's proposal, as well as most others, involving a single output level [52, pp. 94–5].

effects of widespread innovations on product prices, especially when inno-vational economies are sizeable and competition is brisk. Such expanded analytical horizons invite the formulation of more detailed hypotheses con-cerning the economic readjustments triggered by spreading innovations.

In exploring direct factor price responses, one might begin by assuming that a given percentage reduction in one industry's unit inputs of various resources would tend to exert: little effect on the total demand for capital funds, because such markets serve broad sectors of the economy; pro-gressively larger effects on individual materials as the given industry accounts for an increasing share of total demand for that resource; and still greater effects on labour markets which are narrowly delimited by trade unions. It might also be assumed that innovation-induced reductions in unit input requirements tend to reduce factor prices, except in materials markets where competition is restricted enough to minimise such effects and in labour markets where trade unions can exploit such economies to raise wage rates on grounds of higher productivity. Such assumptions would lead to the hypothesis that the cost benefits of resource-saving innovations tend to be: offset in the case of labour by rising wage rates; accentuated in the case of many materials by lower prices; and unaffected in the case of capital because of the unresponsiveness of interest rates—although the magnitude of such reactions would vary with the conditions specified above. And a related hypothesis might suggest that labour-saving innovations tend to spread more rapidly than others because resulting increases in the industry's wage rates accentuate the pressures on laggard firms, whereas resulting decreases in material prices may ease pressures for adopting material-saving innovations. One might also hypo-thesise that, farther along in the readjustment process, widespread reduc-tions in unit costs may lead to lower product prices, thereby reducing the net income benefits anticipated on the basis of cost reductions alone.*

Suggested modifications of the original model are traceable, therefore, not to changes in the informational requirements involving engineering expertise, but to the need to strengthen managerial evaluations by in-cluding a larger sector of the interactions generated by innovations. Such elaborations also open the possibility, however, that similar innovations may lead to dissimilar outcomes in different industries, and even within the same industry if associated conditions change.

---

* Such a broader model was presented in earlier chapters. This may explain why Mansfield [33] has not found closer relationships between the adoption of innovations and profit levels. Although Minasian reported more favourable results in relating research and development activity to profits among a sample of chemical firms [36], Hitch commented that 'others have made similar at-tempts in other industries with negative results [28, p. 193].

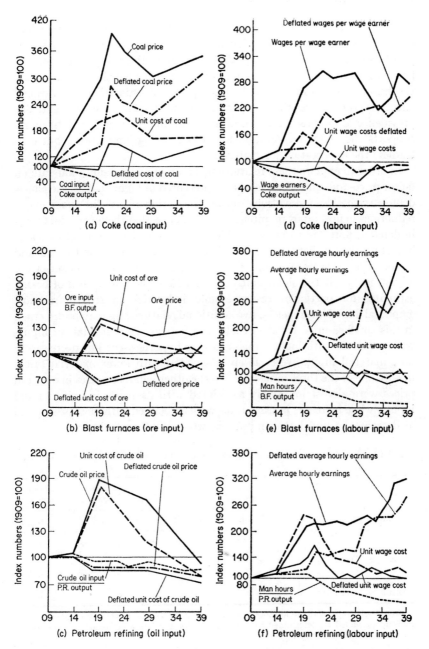

Fig. 9.8 Unit material and labour input requirements; factor prices and unit costs, actual and after adjustment for changes in the general price level for selected industries, 1909–1939

The industry findings presented earlier have no bearing on unique adoptions, but those which seem relevant to widely adopted innovations support some of the preceding hypotheses and not others. For example, cost fluctuations in Panel (a) graphs reinforce the earlier conclusion concerning the hazards of assuming fixed factor prices in estimating innovational effects, especially over the long periods affected by durable equipment. The prevalence of long-term horizontal trends for unit costs in Panel (b) charts supports the above expectation for labour-saving innovations, but contradicts the expectation for materials.

In order to explore these relationships more directly, additional data on factor prices and unit input levels are presented in Figure 9.8. These panels demonstrate that innovations during the period really did effect major reductions in unit input requirements and, hence, that the horizontal trends in deflated unit costs were traceable to comparably substantial increases in factor prices rather than to the relative stability of both unit inputs and factor prices. It is also apparent that the detailed patterns of such offsetting adjustments differed significantly, emphasising the importance of basing estimates for particular resources and industries on strictly relevant empirical data. Nevertheless, two additional relationships may be discerned in this small sample. First, virtually every decrease in unit labour inputs was associated with higher wage rates, as hypothesised; but decreases in unit material inputs were closely associated with lower material prices in only one of the three industries. On the other hand, increases in material prices were almost invariably associated with decreases in unit material inputs, while increases in wage rates were associated with increases as well as decreases in unit labour inputs in two of the three industries.

TABLE 9.1   Changes in unit input levels and in actual and deflated factor prices (from Figure 9.8)

Input per unit	Factor price	Material panels			Labour panels			Input per unit	Deflated factor price	Material panels			Labour panels		
		A	B	C	D	E	F			A	B	C	D	E	F
−	+	24	11	5	24	17	20	−	+	24	20	0	24	21	20
−	−	6	15	16	0	4	0	−	−	6	10	21	0	0	0
+	+	0	0	5	0	5	10	+	+	0	0	5	0	9	10
+	−	0	0	0	6	4	0	+	−	0	0	0	6	0	0
−	=	0	4	0	0	0	0								
Blank		0	0	4	0	0	0	Blank		0	0	4	0	0	0

Frequencies represent the number of years during 1909–1939 in which the indicated relationship prevailed as determined by comparisons for the following periods: 09–14, 14–19, 19–23, 23–29, 29–33, 33–39.

The foregoing suggests that the apparent contradiction noted earlier may be resolved by closing the original causal loop: supplementing the view of innovations as the stimulus and factor price adjustments as the response with the reverse sequence. Thus, material-saving innovations might well tend to induce lower material prices, as hypothesised; but declining material inputs might be associated with rising material prices whenever the latter stimulate material-saving innovations which, in their early stages of adoption, may only moderate rather than reverse such price pressures. Similarly, the close association between lower unit labour inputs and higher wage rates may be due not only to innovation-induced increases in wage rates, but also to the stimulus of rising wage rates in the adoption of labour-saving innovations. One might offer a hypothesis of asymmetry in this connection: that the response of factor prices to innovation-induced reductions in unit input levels is likely to be faster than the response of new resource-saving innovations to factor price increases. Incidentally, while such initiating increases in factor prices are usually attributable to expanding production in the industries using these resources, at least some of the expansion in the given industry may be due to price reductions resulting from earlier cost-cutting innovations.

In short, the revised analytical model which has been developed up to this point, and whose structure is shown in Figure 9.9* (along with a few additional refinements to be discussed later), helps to account for the general finding of horizontal trends in major categories of deflated unit costs by outlining readjustment processes involving offsetting interactions *within* each unit cost category between factor prices and unit input requirements.

Finally, analysis of the additional data provided for Figure 9.8 also indicates some empirical support for the earlier deductive expectation that innovations may alter the shape as well as the level of the relationship between average input requirements per unit of output and changes in production levels. Because such relationships are assumed to be stable only during periods when technology and facilities are fixed, the relationships redrawn for this purpose in Figure 9.10 may be considered relevant only during comparatively short periods in each panel. From these one may infer that successive innovations seem to have changed the shape of such relationships at least at the level of industry averages. And it is apparent that major changes in slope, such as are illustrated in several panels, may have a significant effect on the cost benefits of the innovations responsible for them—especially where production fluctuations are

---

* Briefly summarised, it shows that the effects of innovations can be traced by reaching beyond adjustments in the unit input requirements of single input factors to cover adjustments in its factor price and in other costs of the given plant—and continuing on to include adjustments in competing plants and in product as well as factor markets.

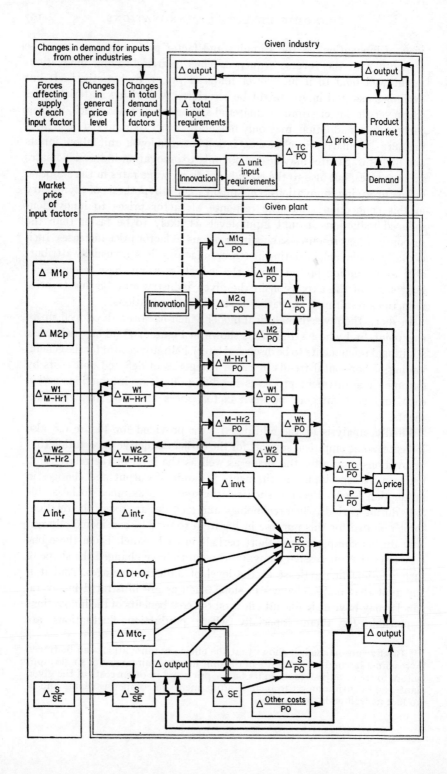

	Inputs			Other
	Quantity	Price	Unit costs	
Materials	M_{1_q}, M_{2_q}	M_{1_p}, M_{2_p}	$M_1/PO,$ M_2/PO	PO: Physical Output
Labour	M-Hr$_1$, M-Hr$_2$	$\dfrac{W_1}{\text{M-Hr}_1}, \dfrac{W_2}{\text{M-Hr}_2}$	$W_1/PO,$ W_2/PO	TC: Total Costs
Salaried	SE	S/SE	S/PO	P: Profit
Capital	Invt	Int$_r$; Depr + Obs$_r$; Maint$_r$	FC/PO	Substripts: t = total; r = rate; 1, 2-different kinds of inputs

Fig. 9.9 Revised model for estimating effects of technological innovations

substantial. Indeed, some innovations may actually be designed with a primary view to changing the *shape* of such relationships.

9.4 ANALYTICAL FOUNDATIONS OF STABLE COST PROPORTIONS

Efforts to trace the influences responsible for the emergence of relatively stable cost proportions over long periods for each of the industries studied* can be more meaningfully related to managerial efforts to develop long-term technological improvement programmes involving a succession of innovations than to the single innovation decisions considered in the preceding section. The planning and adoption of such programmes is a commonplace in business, one group concentrating on reducing average total unit costs and another on developing new products with attractive profit potentials. Although the first of these has the longer history, the literature still does not present any formalised models to guide such decisions. It is conceivable, therefore, that reliance has been placed, at least conceptually, on the original model presented in section 9.1 by treating each major sector (such as a programme to reduce labour inputs or material inputs) as one coherent innovation. Thus, successive reductions in unit input requirements in any given resource sector would be expected to reduce unit costs in that sector along with its share of total costs. And because choices would be made among alternatives solely on the basis of

* For a negative reaction to the significance of stability in a related sector of economic relationships, see Solow [48]. It should be noted, however, that his analysis was restricted to the wage share of value added for entire groups of industries and even larger economic sectors, thus reflecting the interaction of inter-industry differences both in wage proportions and in cyclical adjustment patterns.

prospective reductions in total unit costs, cost proportions might be expected to vary randomly through time [11; 25, p. 2; 19; 24].

In order to adapt the original model to its present purpose, one might begin by introducing the revisions suggested in the preceding section. These would tend to moderate the expected reductions in unit costs because the longer time perspectives involved in the planning of extended programmes would permit even fuller development of offsetting interactions between resource-saving innovations and corresponding factor prices. These longer time perspectives would also counsel replacing the current values for inputs, factor prices and costs as used in the original model and in the preceding section by projections of established trends and cycles for each variable. (Such needs were recognised by Joel Dean, who warned that, 'Future changes in wages costs, prices and operating volume may wipe out estimated revenues in future years' [14, p. 30], but he did not suggest how the consideration of such possibilities might be encompassed within the analytical framework.) Identification of the factor prices likely to exert the strongest adverse pressures, and of the average resource economies likely to be achieved by competitors over the planning period, would tend to ensure the proportioning of performance targets to the magnitude of the prospective competitive disadvantages threatened by neglecting them. And a third modification might involve introducing cost proportions into the revised model (as shown in Figure 9.9) whenever expected unit cost adjustments have to be expressed in relatives rather than absolutes—as tends to be the case in estimating the prospective effects of a complex of innovations over a period of years—because one cannot determine the comparative impacts on total unit costs of a 10 per cent reduction in unit material costs as against a 20 per cent reduction in unit labour costs until each is weighted by its share of total costs.

Direct consideration of cost proportions in the estimation model may also influence decisions in important respects. For example, this would permit allowances for management's reputed concern with the flexibility as well as the level of total unit costs, such flexibility being assumed to vary inversely with the ratio of fixed to total costs. Differences in cost proportions among competitors may also engender disparate evaluations of given innovations, the effect of any prospective percentage reduction in input levels on total unit costs varying directly with that factor's proportion of total costs. Moreover, clarification of the disparate patterns of cost proportions among industries may help to explain differences in the foci of their technological improvement programmes as well as the sequential transmission of innovations from their points of origin to other industries. In view of this potential, it may be worth noting that, among the six industries covered in this study, the materials ratio ranged between

40 and 80 per cent, the wage ratio between 8 and 20 per cent, the salary ratio between 2 and 5, and material plus labour costs combined accounted for 60–90 per cent of total costs. These findings reveal not only the wide range within each cost category, and the wide disparity in cost proportions between materials and labour, but also the overwhelming dominance of these two combined as compared with fixed costs. (Significant differences in cost proportions may also exist within individual industries as a result of differences in make-or-buy decisions, levels of mechanisation, degrees of product specialisation, etc. See [34, p. 355].)

Attention may now return to exploring why the elaborated analytical framework tends to encourage decisions which maintain relatively stable cost proportions. Three approaches will be considered: that such stability is a by-product of management's basic commitment to reduce total unit costs; that it results from a variety of external pressures on the firm; and that stable cost proportions have become a direct objective of managerial control efforts.

The first approach is exemplified by management's efforts to prevent externally generated factor price increases from raising corresponding unit costs by intensifying engineering programmes designed to reduce unit input requirements of such resources. In addition to such readjustment processes *within* each cost category, already discussed in the preceding section, the finding of stable cost proportions suggests the operation of a second network of readjustment interactions among cost categories. Thus, residual disparities among concomitant changes in different unit costs—due to the inadequacy of innovational offsets within some categories or to differential adjustments in factor prices—may also be reduced by shifting input proportions in favour of less costly resources. Recourse to such expedients may be less readily recognisable from empirical data than is commonly realised, however, for they involve decreasing the unit input requirements of the more costly factor and increasing those of the less costly factor—thereby tending to disguise the fact that the latter's lower cost may have been caused by differentially greater resource-saving innovations in the first place. And the tendency toward maintaining stable cost proportions would also be reinforced by the fact that progressive reductions in any sector's share of total costs decrease its relative impact on total unit costs, thereby reducing the incentive to further reductions in this sector while increasing the prospective benefits of reductions in other costs.

In support of the externally dominant view, it might be suggested that stable cost proportions result because the common factors affecting all unit costs in any industry (e.g. changes in output and in the general price level) are more influential than the specific factors affecting each. And another route to this same conclusion would argue that differential changes in the unit input requirements of various resources tend to reach equilibrium in their effects on corresponding unit costs through long-term price responses in factor markets—and vice versa. (Reder [42, p. 196] says 'If labour's share is constant over time, and if factor markets are cleared by the forces of demand and supply, we must either accept the Cobb-Douglas function as the proper relation among aggregates of output, labour and capital or argue that constant shares result from secularly constant ratios of factor quantities and factor prices. This second possibility is not to be dismissed lightly'.) Instead of having to choose between these internally-oriented and externally-oriented viewpoints, Figure 9.9 shows that both may be regarded as sequential linkages in the cycle of interactions between the individual plant and its operating environment.

To illustrate the third approach, one might ask whether increasing specialisation in large corporations has made the maintenance of established cost proportions among functionally differentiated parts of the firm a more practical focus for managerial control efforts than the presumably more fundamental (but actually more tenuous estimates) of their respective contributions to aggregate performance or net profits [20, pp. 50–4]. This behavioural view suggests the hypothesis that increases in the share of the sales dollar absorbed by given cost categories, even when traceable to reductions in other categories, are likely to intensify managerial efforts to reduce such unchanged absolute outlays to 'normal (ratio) levels' or to control costs which have 'got out of line'. Alternatively, it is possible that the maintenance of past relative shares may represent the most common outcome of efforts to resolve bargaining conflicts among interest groups within the firm in the absence of objective or authoritative determinants [13, p. 33, Chapter 5, p. 120].

In addition to clarifying some of the origins of stable cost proportions, the preceding exploration suggests several broader conclusions. It is apparent, for instance, that the two major empirical findings which have been discussed so far—horizontal trends in deflated unit costs and stable cost proportions—are mutually reinforcing instead of necessarily reflecting unidirectional causality. More important, the variety of influences tending to maintain stable cost proportions, and their conformity both with managerial cost reduction objectives and with organisational pressures, suggests that the tendency towards stable cost proportions is less likely to prove a coincidence in the few industries studied than one of the most pervasive sectors of economic stability yet uncovered in industrial operations. And this likelihood is enhanced by the fact that the current findings cover periods marked not only by tremendous technological innovations, but also by substantial economic growth, a great war, major changes in the general price level and the deepest depression yet experienced. Such results also suggest that statistical studies may characterise many innovations as technologically neutral not because they really left physical input proportions unchanged, but because their substantial immediate impacts on such proportions were (a) masked by coupling the finding of parallel gains in returns to both factors (or stable cost proportions) with the assumption that factors are paid at rates corresponding to their marginal products; and (b) neutralised over longer periods through the readjustment processes which have been discussed. This assumption has tended to divert attention from the possibility that one of the early impacts of new innovations may be to disrupt prevailing relationships between the productive contributions and distributive shares of the factors and thus initiate readjustment processes which tend to restore such relationships only over extended periods. (See [16, pp. 319–321] and [7, p. 357]. Such disruptive effects might also intensify the cyclic impacts of innovations suggested by Hicks [27, pp. 299–302].) Finally, it may also be of interest to note that the maintenance of stable cost proportions implies that the continued development of resource-saving innovations is likely to be accompanied by comparably rising factor prices over the long run—and vice versa; and it also implies the feasibility of developing generalisations about trends and cycles in innovations to parallel those relating to the factor prices with which such innovations interact.

9.5 ANALYTICAL FOUNDATIONS OF HORIZONTAL TRENDS IN TOTAL UNIT COSTS

It should be emphasised that the findings of horizontal trends in deflated total unit costs over periods of thirty to forty years relate to industries each of which experienced numerous major technological improvements. Then what accounts for the apparent meagreness of resulting cost benefits?

Were the impressive gains in production technology offset by the introduction of more complex products with higher unit costs? This question may be answered empirically by referring to the heavy reductions in unit input requirements illustrated in Figures 9.8 and 9.10, for output covered new as well as old products. But it is even more important for analytical purposes to explain the differing concepts of output reflected by such a question. To have relevance for managerial evaluations of business operations, measures of total output must reach beyond purely physical dimensions, such as the number, weight or volume of various products, so as to aggregate the output of different product units in terms of their relative

economic values; and resulting changes in the value of output can be converted into changes in physical output by excluding the effects of inflationary or deflationary changes in product prices. In the general procedure
used, as noted earlier, the output quantity of each product in two periods

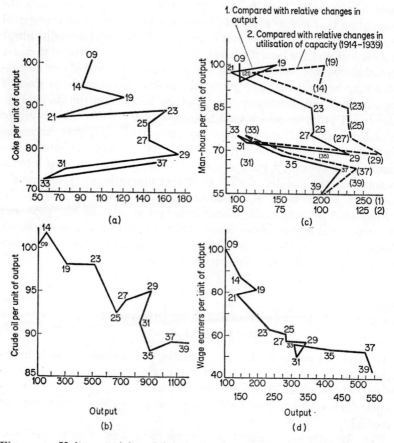

Fig. 9.10   Unit material and labour inputs relative to output of selected
industries, 1909–1939

(a) Blast furnace: coke input; (b) Petroleum refining: crude oil input; (c) Steel
mills: labour input; (d) Canned fruit and vegetables: labour input

is multiplied by its average price in both periods and the percentage change
between the totals for the two periods measures the change in total
product value not due to price changes, i.e. the change in physical
output.

The formula for the change is:

$$(\Delta PO)_{1-2} = \frac{\sum\left[Q_{A_2}\left(\frac{P_{A_1} + P_{A_2}}{2}\right) + Q_{B_2}\left(\frac{P_{B_1} + P_{B_2}}{2}\right) + \cdots\right]}{\sum\left[Q_{A_1}\left(\frac{P_{A_1} + P_{A_2}}{2}\right) + Q_{B_1}\left(\frac{P_{B_1} + P_{B_2}}{2}\right) + \cdots\right]}$$

where Q = quantity; P = price; A and B = products; 1 and 2 = base and comparison periods.

Thus, the relative contributions to output of different products is measured by their relative economic values, or by the cost of all resources absorbed into each along with its overlay of profit. (For further explanations of this approach, see [17, pp. 23–24, 358–67] and [20, pp. 92–7]. For related approaches, see [50, pp. 19–20] and [5, p. 144].)

This emphasis on the economically oriented aspects of production flows has major implications which are often unrecognised. First, resulting measures of output change may differ substantially from those obtained by using the technological criteria of engineers, or the weight and volume criteria of freight handlers, or the service criteria of consumers. For example, when the average mileage per tyre was doubled by the addition of some chemicals to the rubber, consumers could count each tyre as two in terms of mileage expectancy, but production managers could not count each tyre as two in terms either of resources absorbed or revenue generated. Second, use of this concept means that the introduction of more complex new products need not raise total costs per unit of total output because their higher cost per unit of product tends to be paralleled by the greater (price) weight given to each such unit in computing total output. Third and even more disconcerting, technological improvements which lead to lower unit costs and prices for given products also engender reductions in the (price) weights given to such product units in computing total output. Attendant changes in total output tend to be moderated, however, because the given product's price may be reduced less than its total unit costs and also because, in computing total output, the quantity of the given product is weighted not by the new price but by an average of the old and new prices. Fourth, this measure is often criticised for ignoring product improvements because averaging a product's price for two years in order to eliminate inflationary effects implies that the product remains unchanged. Such attacks are often justifiable on grounds of understating consumer satisfactions, but they are clearly mistaken on the grounds of managerial evaluations. If an improvement affects only technological and service features, leaving resource inputs as well as factor and product prices unchanged, each unit may yield greater consumer satisfaction without increasing the market-determined value which is management's criterion for appraising contributions to total output. If the improvement increases resource requirements, the resulting price increase should exceed that for unchanged products, thus enhancing the (price) weight of such product units in computing total output.

In short, this economic approach facilitates managerial evaluation of operations by aggregating flows of physically differentiated products into a measure of changes in total output. But the procedure used also tends to diminish the magnitude of variations in total unit costs, relative to expectations based on comparing total costs with the sheer number of units produced. This would result whenever the prices of affected products move in the same direction as cost changes, because the economic weights attached to such product units in computing total output are thereby altered in the same direction as their contributions to total costs. Contrary to possible first impressions, this does not constitute a defect in measurement concepts and techniques, but rather offers a valid representation of still another channel of readjustment interactions—this time among resource economies, unit costs and prices—which are of central concern in analysing the economic effects of technological innovations. Reviewed sequentially, a decrease in a product's factor prices or unit input requirements tends to reduce total costs per unit of total output whenever the product's price, and hence the weight attached to each of its units in computing total output, is unchanged. As such cost reductions spread among competitors, however, the product's price is likely to decline, reducing the weight attached to such units in computing total output. As a result, the original beneficiaries will find their total output declining relative to their total costs, thus pushing average total costs per unit of total output upward again. Of course, the speed with which such reversals develop depends on how rapidly the original sources of cost reductions become available to all competitors and on how rapidly these are converted into price reductions. Accordingly, factor price changes which affect all competitors immediately are likely to yield shorter lived benefits to producers in highly competitive industries than resource-saving innovations which spread only gradually among competitors.

Deflation for changes in the general price level also contributes to the generation of horizontal trends in the total unit costs of individual industries. Resource-saving innovations and factor price adjustments tend to affect one another, to spread from their points of origin to other firms and industries using such inputs, and to engender changes in the unit input levels and factor prices of substitute resources. Changes in the general price level represent an average of the resulting price changes experienced by a large array of commodities. Hence, deflating the total unit costs of any plant or industry by changes in the general price level can be interpreted most effectively as indicating the extent to which the given unit costs have changed as compared with accompanying changes in the average cost of resources absorbed (plus profit) per unit of output in the rest of the economy. A horizontal trend in deflated unit costs does not mean an absence of technological progress or an absence of benefits from such progress, but simply that these unit costs have moved in unison with the average price of all products.* Such a relationship could signify that economies in the industry have paralleled those in the economy; or that the industry has withheld the benefits of its differentially greater economies from consumers to be shared by its input factors through higher wage rates, salary levels and net profits,† or that the industry has been absorbing the burdens of its differentially smaller economies through lower payments to its input factors. It follows, therefore, that the deflated total unit costs of any industry could deviate from a horizontal trend over extensive periods only if there were a progressively expanding margin (either upward or downward) between its factor prices and profits and those in other industries—a condition which tends to be undermined over time by the mobility of resources and by competition from substitute products.

This suggests two further hypotheses: that innovations resulting from internal research and development programmes are likely to yield longer-lasting competitive advantages than the acquisition of innovations available to all competitors; and that long-term technological improvement programmes are not likely to yield progressively lower total unit costs when measured according to economically meaningful rather than purely physical concepts of output. Conversely, such expectations imply that lagging behind the technological progress achieved by competitors tends to impose higher unit costs; and that such lagging is unavoidable unless the adoption of developments available to all competitors is supplemented by internally generated research and development advances which are at least roughly equivalent in competitive advantage to those pioneered by others in the industry. At any rate, such interactions among industries represent still another sector of the readjustment processes involved in absorbing the impacts of technological innovations into the structure of economic relationships.

---

* See Figure 9.7, which shows what was happening in manufacturing as a whole, as an indication of the broader base relative to which the differential adjustments in each industry were being compared. And it is instructive to note in turn that long-term changes in the unit costs of All Manufacturing paralleled changes in the general price level.

† Such a view of increases in coal wages is suggested by Adelman [3, pp. 21–2].

9.6 SOME BROADER IMPLICATIONS

This study emphasises the need for extensive re-orientation of the basic concepts entering into appraisals of the economic effects of technological innovations. The traditional view in economics that such innovations are exogenous developments [23, pp. 32–8] should be replaced by recognition of the close interactions between the economic pressures and the allocation of resources for developing and selecting particular kinds of advances*. The prevailing managerial notion that innovations affect economic relationships in manufacturing through their influence on the quantity of unit input requirements of the particular resources directly involved needs to be broadened to encompass concomitant changes in the kinds and quality levels of these and other resources, on the flexibility of such input requirements, on the design, quality and market potentials of individual products and on the resulting composition of total output in multi-product operations. The common technician's view that such appraisals can be made within the context of a single stimulus-response cycle limited to the plant must be transformed into a dynamic process encompassing an expanding network of ramifications triggered by such innovations—reaching beyond the firm into factor and product markets as well as into the reallocations of resources by competing firms—and yielding results subject to significant changes over progressively longer periods. In short, the massive technological changes which are transforming our economy cannot be evaluated effectively within a conceptual framework which assumes that innovations arrive from extra-economic space, that their effects are limited to their immediate impacts on input–output ratios and attendant unit costs at their points of application, and that these can be appraised by ignoring attendant changes in the nature of inputs and outputs as well as in factor and product prices.

Major analytical implications of this study include the identification of important subsectors for which differentiated models may be developed. The design of such matrices might involve consideration of such distinctions as the following: (a) between single innovations and whole innovational or technical improvement programmes; (b) among adoptions unique to the given firm (usually internally generated), early adoptions of innovations likely to spread gradually to competitors, and late adoptions serving to catch up with major sectors of the industry; (c) between estimating the differential effects of alternative innovations, thus yielding only preference rankings, and estimating the absolute effects of a given innovation—the

* Increasing awareness of this relationship has characterised recent work, as shown by Machlup [31, pp. 163–5], Schmookler [45, pp. 211–12, 226–8], Nelson [39, pp. 580–3] and Carter and Williams [12, pp. 136–48].

latter encompassing not only the expected direct effects of the adoption but also their interactions with established economic trends and cycles; and (d) between short-term and progressively longer term effects. Two additional analytical implications relate to the observed wide range of differences among industries and among factor and product markets, thus stressing the need for directly relevant empirical guides in appraising specific situations, and to the various kinds of expertise required to supply the data entering into effective managerial evaluations of this kind, including the contributions of accountants, procurement specialists, production supervisors, market analysts and industrial relations personnel as well as plant engineers.*

The most fundamental implication of the empirical findings which have been presented is that the economic effects of technological innovations seem to be widely at variance with the expectations of economists and engineers as well as of industrial management. Successive substantial reductions in material inputs per unit of output have not consistently reduced unit material costs, nor have they effected sustained reductions in deflated unit material costs in the individual industries studied or in All Manufacturing Combined. The same findings hold for unit labour costs despite even greater reductions in the quantity of such inputs per unit of physical output. And the cumulative effects of thirty years of the most rapid technological progress in American history effected little or no change either in cost proportions or in deflated total costs per unit of physical output. Such findings might well generate doubts about the frequency and importance of innovations during the period, were both not thoroughly documented. Accordingly, there is obvious need for the detailed explorations which have been initiated in this study into the processes whereby economic interrelationships are readjusted to absorb the impacts of a multitude of variously oriented technological advances.

Each of the major findings seems to imply that such readjustment processes range more broadly than is commonly recognised. Horizontal trends in deflated total unit costs, for example, do not signify that technologies were stagnant within each of the industries studied, but rather that technological progress was so pervasive that even the impressive advances in the industries studied hardly surpassed the average gains of all other industries. Despite its enormous absolute benefits to consumers, therefore, such progress yielded little sustained competitive advantages over other

---

* In place of Terborgh's argument for a single specialist to cover this entire area [52, pp. 21–2], this would suggest a formalised procedure for securing competent estimates from appropriate specialists and processing these to yield final estimates, with all efforts co-ordinated by someone in central management. This need for co-operation among different functions was also recognised, albeit in a far more limited form, in [43].

surviving industries, as represented by the average price of their products, because temporary gains by one industry forced competitors to intensify efforts to catch up. Similarly, horizontal trends in the major categories of deflated unit costs may be due less to localised interactions between resource-saving innovations and corresponding factor prices tending to minimise variations within each sector of unit costs than to two more roundabout processes involving interactions with other factor costs. One of these, suggested by the sharp contrast between the highly fluctuating actual unit costs and the stable horizontal trends in deflated unit cost categories shown in Panels (a) and (b) of the industry charts, indicates that only those unit cost increases which exceeded concomitant increases in the general level of costs and prices tended to engender offsetting efforts to reduce corresponding unit input requirements. And the second reflects the fact that reductions in the unit input requirements of a given resource can be effected not only by adopting more resource-saving innovations, but also by using less costly factors in its place. In addition, the resulting shifts in factor demands would tend to redress disparate increments in factor prices and thus add another, longer term sequence to the processes affecting trends in deflated unit costs. And the third major finding—stable cost proportions—suggests that basic economic readjustment processes may be significantly reinforced by the behavioural responses of management officials in the absence of effective objective guides to the allocation and utilisation of resources among the many specialised operations and organi-sational units within large corporations. Thus, although management's in-ability to determine the putative profit contribution of each input unit defines a gap within the structure of economic guides to resource allocations, the processes for resolving conflicts among individual motivations, group interests and organisational pressures must become stable enough to assure continuity in operations, and the results must also conform over reasonable periods to the surrounding framework of economic valuations as discussed in preceding chapters.

10 The Framework of Decision for Major Technological Innovations

Our surprisingly limited understanding of the processes whereby technological progress is effected may be traced in part to the long prevailing belief that each major technological advance was essentially unique, being ascribable either to inexplicable genius or to an extraordinarily lucky accident. Oddly enough, however, growing realisation of the organised structure of science and increasing success in extending its boundaries have likewise failed to enrich our grasp of how technical advances take place— no longer because these are still regarded as incomprehensible, but because they are now assumed to be quite transparent. Thus, technological gains are widely regarded as the virtually inevitable product of organised research and development, with reasonably regularised yields roughly proportioned to the resources applied and effects centred around the guiding objectives of improved products and lowered costs.*

Such superficial conceptions would be of little moment were it not for the increasing need to learn how this cornucopia functions. The rapid acceleration in the rate of technological progress, the enormous resources which must be invested in its pursuit, the seeming randomness in the volume and direction of its benefits,† and above all, its threats to the competitive position not only of individual firms, but of entire industries and even nations—all emphasise our need to clarify the processes involved. One root of the following analysis is the proposition that technological advances not only modify the values and behaviour of society, but are themselves shaped by the carryover values and implementing beliefs of those who determine

---

* Proponents of this general view include: Schumpeter [105, p. 132], Maclaurin [69, p. 104], Galbraith [28, p. 9] and Machlup [66, p. 153]. Opposing views have been offered by: Jewkes, *et al.*, [47, pp. 28–32, 225–30 and 237], Kuznets [61, pp. 47–8], Heald [120, pp. 1, 111] and Wiesner [123, p. 214]. For an excellent general review, Nelson [88].

† For example, see Jewkes [47, *ibid*], Kuznets [61, *ibid*], Nelson [89, pp. 299–301], Markham [77, p. 601], Sanders [101, p. 68], Bush [124, p. 1102] and Wirtz [121, p. 43].

how much resources, if any, should be allocated for developing various kinds of innovations. To illustrate, Klein, tracing the original notion to Schumpeter, suggests that 'the forces making for efficiency in the narrower sense are deeply ingrained in our society and stand in the way of more rapid progress' [57, p. 497]. Others emphasising the role in resisting innovations of behaviour patterns conditioned by long prevailing values concerning what is considered proper, safe, and sound include Maclaurin [70, pp. 178–89], Williams [127, p. 125], Rubenstein [97, pp. 385–93] and Arthur D. Little, Inc. [125, p. 634]. Accordingly, attention will be focused first on some prevailing conceptions of the bases for such managerial decisions and then on the nature and implications of alternative guides for directing the major innovational programmes of industry.

Analytical structures for exploring new problem areas tend to become useful only as successive probings transform initially naïve speculations into progressively more sharply delineated variables, relationships, processes and criteria. One reason for slowness in developing an effective framework is that reliance on the traditional ritual of the scientific method —moving smoothly from hypothesis formulation to data collection to analysis to conclusions. (For indications of the need for more pluralistic conceptions of scientific method, see [50, pp. 27–31] and [92, p. 19].) This seems to be less helpful than choosing among alternative explanations. Indeed, it is surprising that endless strictures to adhere to this idealised procedure are so infrequently coupled with warnings about the probable wastefulness and aridty of hypotheses crystallised without even reasonable immersion in the complex activities and environments whose characteristics are to be diagnosed and explained.*

This discussion begins with the assumption that major technological innovations come to fruition within individual firms (or organisations) and are the result of managerial decisions shaped by interactions between changes in external pressures† and adjustments in the firm's internal goals,

---

* On the general aspects of this problem, see Bridgman [7, pp. 18, 26]; for common shortcomings of analytical models developed in this way, see Kaplan [50, pp. 275–88], Littauer [65, p. B 27] and Bross [8, p. 1, 330]. For an illustration of concern about such models in economics, see Carter and Williams [16, pp. 5, 29, 59–62 and 151–2]. For such illustrative constructs, see Kennedy [54, pp. 541–7] and the critiques of Hicks and Keynes by Carter and Williams [16, pp. 160–3] and by Leontief [64, pp. 66–71].

† One significant environmental pressure consists of changes in available technical knowledge (cf. Nelson [86, p. 13], Peck [90, p. 298], Rubel [122, p. 34] and Freeman [27, pp. 21–39]). A second major environmental pressure takes the form of shifts in product and factor markets (cf. Hicks [41, Chapter 6], Brozen [11, pp. 288–302], Salter [100, pp. 43–4], Fellner [25, pp. 171–194] and Kennedy [ibid]). Cross-sectionally, new technical knowledge may be conceived as flowing from one firm to others in the industry, to other domestic industries and abroad, as well as in the reverse directions. For example, see

resources and performance prospects—thus suggesting the possibility of developing initially separate (if eventually overlapping) analytical frameworks for each. And resulting decisions, in turn, will initiate new internal and external pressures. Within the chain of relevant managerial decision-forming and decision-implementing processes, analysis will be concentrated on three early links:

(1) the role of major technological innovations in promoting the organisation's objectives;

(2) the processes involved in establishing the technological foundations for major innovations; and

(3) the analytical perspectives used in guiding and appraising innovations.

The discussion has been concentrated on major technological innovations both in order to minimise concern with the ambiguous outer boundaries of most attempts to define technical innovations and also in order to centre attention on adjustments large enough to compel overt managerial consideration.

10.1 ELEMENTS OF A SYNOPTIC MODEL

Although the rapidly expanding literature relating to technological innovations is dominated by narrowly focused studies of particular parts of this extensive domain, many seem to reflect essentially similar, though unstated, conceptions of the basic system of relationships involved. It may be useful to outline a structure of such implicit hypotheses so as to crystallise views which appear to be widely accepted and to highlight the contrasting hypotheses to be offered later.

One of the four major building blocks of such a synoptic model is the belief that technological innovations are inherently attractive, especially in terms of the economic rewards which are considered to be overriding in business organisations.* In one direction, innovations are expected to

Mansfield [71, pp. 741–66] and [73, pp. 290–309], Rosenberg [96, pp. 424 et seq.], Strassman [115, pp. 16–22] and Woodruff [128, pp. 479–97].

* For reflections of such business attitudes, see Holland [45, Chapter 2], Larrabie et al. quoted in Silk [109, p. 170] and Keezer, et al. [52, pp. 355–69]. Economists expressing similar views include: Schmookler [112, pp. 183–90], Carter and Williams [15, p. 38], Nelson [88, p. 101], Brozen [12, pp. 204–17], Sutherland [116, pp. 118–35] and Minasian [82, pp. 93–141]. Those placing primary emphasis on expanding markets include: Sayers [102, pp. 275–91], Coales [18, pp. 239–42], Brown [9, pp. 406–25], Ulin [119, p. 27] and Peck [90, p. 295]. In this connection, special attention should also be given to Penrose's view that 'a kind of "competition in creativity" has become a dominant motif in the pattern of competitive behavior in many industries' [91, p. 106].

reduce production costs through decreasing waste, increasing the productivity of inputs, or permitting shifts to cheaper factors of production. Other innovations yielding new or improved products are expected to enhance sales revenue through expanding old markets, opening new markets, or permitting higher product prices. Such impressive potentials are held to explain the special predilection for promoting technological advances which is deemed to characterise management, at least in American industry.

A second major building block centres around the view that technological innovations in individual firms are generally the product of processes which are planned and accordingly tend to be concentrated in the areas chosen by management.* As for the controllability of innovation generating processes, this is usually taken to bear less on the proportion or speed of successes achieved than on the capacity to choose: between pioneering and following others; between high risk-high reward and low risk-low reward alternatives; and between continuing with a succession of interrelated innovations and stopping such a sequence at any given stage.

Another major building block is the view that major technological advances are generated through a chain of essentially rational decisions organised with self-improving feedbacks.† Specifically, the objectives of such innovational efforts are assumed to derive from the organisation's defined goals. In turn, it is assumed that alternative means of promoting such technological objectives are appraised by scientists and engineers in order to estimate prospective benefits, risk and costs on the basis of procedures which are reasonably reliable and likely to become increasingly accurate as the result of cumulative experience. This is supplemented by subsequent managerial decisions on the availability of needed resources, the attractiveness of estimated returns as compared with attendant burdens, and the most propitious time to initiate projects. It is also supposed that actual results are compared with earlier expectations, so that

---

* For assertions that such control is exercised, see quotes from Kreps and Galbraith in Nelson [88, p. 111], as well as Maclaurin [69, p. 104] and Harrel [38, Chapter 8]. For implied acceptance of this view via assertions that businessmen only do what seems profitable to them, see Machlup [66, p. 153], Fellner [25, pp. 171–94] and Griliches [36, p. 349]. A rationale for approaching such decisions is suggested by Nelson [89, p. 300]. Choices about the degree of pioneering and risk to be undertaken are suggested by Mansfield [73, pp. 290–311] and by Anthony and Day [3, p. 128]. Such assumptions are also implicit in the wide range of studies which seek to deduce decision processes and rules by working backward from actual results, as though these represented an essentially planned or reasonably probable outcome.

† For the relationship between management goals and research criteria, see Rubenstein [98, pp. 95–105]. For references to the elements of such evaluative processes, see Hertz [40, p. 212], Siegal [108, pp. 161–77], Mottley and Newton [83, pp. 740–51], Spengler [114, p. 434] and Jones [48, p. 1094].

significant deviations may be used as bases for improving future evaluations.

One additional building block is the increasingly pervasive belief that research and development programmes constitute the most important means of effecting significant technological progress within individual firms and, hence, of enhancing growth and profitability.* This view seems to rest on such assumptions as the following: that many, and perhaps most, major product and processes are surrounded by technological frontiers which offer reasonably numerous opportunities for achieving major advances; that the most promising of these can be identified by experts in the relevant technical fields; and that the chances of succeeding in such attempts can be substantially improved by increasing the resources applied to them. An alternative source of encouragement to this heavy emphasis on research and development programmes seems to be the increasingly common tendency to trace the outstanding successes of selected firms back to earlier achievements in research and development, often without serious attention to other possible influences.

Taken together, these building blocks yield a model which combines the appeals of simplicity, rationality and seeming relevance both to widespread interpretations of recent business experience and to common conceptions of the decision-making processes of management.

10.2 WEAKNESSES IN THE SYNOPTIC MODEL

Studies of technological change in recent years have yielded a confusing patchwork of new concepts and empirical results, which may well be characteristic of the exploratory period in new fields before the centripetal pressures of rigorous analysis begin to produce a coherent nucleus shading off into at least vaguely discernible frontiers. Both the difficulties of effectively grasping such a large and chaotic domain and the common assumption of the nonspecialist that whatever is familiar is probably understood have encouraged reliance on relatively simple notions by those who are concerned only with particular bits of the field, or who wish only to use part of it as a foundation for models centred around their own

---

* For comments at the level of industries or higher levels of aggregation, see Freeman [27, pp. 21–39], Terleckyj [118, p. 143] and Rubel [122, p. 44]. For expectations and empirical findings that research inputs may be expected to rise on the average with increases in research outputs, see Silk [109, p. 170], Ulin [119, p. 27], Mansfield [74, pp. 319–49] and [75, pp. 310–22] and Comanor [20, pp. 182–90] as well as Machlup [66, pp. 152–3], and Griliches [36, pp. 349–350]. For a penetrating study of the limited extent to which even firms famous for their research capabilities have relied for growth on internal discoveries, see Mueller [85, pp. 80–6] and [84, pp. 323–46].

8+

specialties. Serious examination of the relevant literature, however, reveals ample basis for doubt about virtually every major element in the preceding synoptic model.

In presenting the synoptic model, attention was given first to the motivation for undertaking major innovational programmes. The claim that this is to increase profitability through increasing markets and reducing costs would seem to be reasonable enough, but too superficial to be helpful. Such guides do not explain how choices are made between allocating resources for new innovational programmes rather than for production, marketing and other functions presumably serving the same purpose. Nor do they explain how choices are made among alternative innovations or even how profit criteria are applied in balancing a low probability of gaining substantial rewards after an extended period of uncertain duration against the certainty of significant and perhaps mounting outlays over an indefinite period. Until a more effective bridge is developed between eventual general objectives and the quite specific choices which managers must make, there is likely to be continuing resort to the meaningless rationalisation that *if* managers made a given decision, they must have expected it to be profitable. Moreover, it would seem to be worth exploring the possibility that increasing concern with research and development programmes may be engendering new perspectives in managerial definitions of the composition, dimensions and patterns of profit and related desiderata—thus opening the way to new strategies and decision criteria.

Field studies also suggest the need to consider a variety of other direct motivations, some of which may, of course, be traced back to the general goal of profitability [39, p. 263; 116, pp. 118–35; 16, p. 56; 88, p. 124; 55, pp. 161–2; 2, pp. 355–6.] For example, some managers feel that because the future will undoubtedly be different, survival requires participation in the stream of change even if they are not sure of where it is leading and cannot contrive persuasive estimates of attractive returns from individual projects; and a rather similar view holds that innovations which are technically sound will eventually pay, although attendant investments usually do not seem justifiable at the time. What may be regarded as a bootstrap argument is that innovations are necessary to maintain the quality and morale of development staffs; and some have extended this argument to affect the image of progressiveness of the firm and its capacity to attract good personnel. From a seemingly far distant viewpoint, Keynes argues that many major business decisions are taken 'as a result of animal spirits—of a spontaneous urge to action rather than inaction'. And still others see such decisions as traceable to 'policy', regarded as an undefined complex of strategies which overshadows whatever quantitative assessments of outlays and returns can be made for individual proposals.

Although almost every empirical contribution is valuable in view of the paucity of information, most studies have been confined to such fragmentary coverage of the surrounding domain as to advise against the generalisation of their results. Not only have they tended to include only a few outstanding industries and companies instead of anything approaching 'representative' coverage, but most have concentrated on successful projects rather than examining a cross-section of all undertakings, and most have also been restricted to recent, as well as relatively short, periods. In addition, the analytical integration of these various undertakings is hampered by the continuing absence of effective bases for classifying different kinds of innovational undertakings [61, p. 30].

At levels beyond the firm, numerous challenges have been offered to the thesis that R & D outlays lead to major innovations which, in turn, engender economic growth. Some note that beneath the average association between aggregates for R & D and for economic output may be found wide variations in successive time periods, different regions, and different industries. Others go on to stress that such statistical relationships may be quite misleading until they can be based on more careful explorations of the nature of research and technological changes and the means whereby these are likely to alter the loci, composition, quality and magnitude of goods and services [122, pp. 30–1; 123, p. 214; 125, p. 642; 34, p. 274; 15, p. 19]. At the level of the firm, despite an array of perceptive studies by Mansfield and a few others, there is widespread agreement that available evidence of correlation between innovation and profits or growth are still far from convincing.* The preceding chapter has also presented some empirical evidence suggesting that a succession of major innovations failed to lower average total unit costs significantly, even after deflation, in each of a number of large industries.

One of the most critical elements of the synoptic model is whether management can choose or control: the specific areas in which innovations will originate; the balance between high, medium and low 'payoff-and-risk' projects; and the proportions of undertakings which are far from, or near, fruition. Although almost all students agree that research and major developmental undertakings are subject to great uncertainties, such general warnings are frequently brushed aside in the course of constructing rational models to guide managerial decisions in this area. Unfortunately, the overwhelming evidence from empirical studies so far is that, except

* For supporting evidence, see Mansfield [74, pp. 319–40] and [75, pp. 310–322] as well as Minasian [82, pp. 100 *et seq.*] and Comanor [20, pp. 182–90]; for expressions of continuing doubt, see Griliches [36, pp. 349–50], Hitch [44, p. 193], Sanders [101, p. 64], Mueller [84, p. 344], Hershey [39, p. 263] and Quinn and Cavanaugh [93, p. 118].

for relatively routine improvement projects, unpredictability is pervasive. It seems to be difficult to predict: the kinds of inventions or discoveries likely to occur; the kinds of applications likely to be made of new discoveries; how close to success given undertakings are; and even how alternative designs or carefully developed theoretical models will turn out [47, pp. 150, 225, 230, 237; 88, pp. 112, 118; 89, pp. 299, 301; 61, pp. 47–48; 84, pp. 323, 358; 80, p. 463; 56, pp. 478–9; 57, p. 508; 15, p. 19; 18, pp. 239–42; 122, pp. 35, 43; 124, p. 1080.]

However compelling the logic of rationally structured and quantitatively scaled models for evaluating innovational proposals as a basis for management decisions, most of the evidence from field studies indicates that these are either not used at all, or play only a minor role. Indeed, the need to account for such seemingly widespread perversity reaches beyond innovations to investment decisions at large. Probing somewhat deeper, empirical studies suggest that, when evaluative models are used, the target or cut-off criteria prove to be either vague or quite flexible in most instances and are further cushioned by a variety of often partially concealed allowances [16, pp. 59–65, 73, 105; 88, p. 124; 127, pp. 116–18; 2, pp. 355–6; 116, pp. 118–35.] For a recent critique of the state of investment theory, see [62, Chapter 5]. Moreover, post-mortems reveal that actual costs and returns are frequently at considerable variance with expectations, [16, pp. 89–92; 80, pp. 471–5; 122, p. 35] that relationships between innovational inputs and outputs fluctuate over a wide range and that, for all the hope of improvement through feedbacks, there is no evidence of increase in the 'productivity' of persons engaged in innovative activities. [24, p. 310; 36, p. 349; 44, p. 193; 84, pp. 342–4; 101, pp. 64, 68; 77, p. 601; 129, p. 234; 93, p. 118; 120, pp. 1,111; 124, pp. 1,102.]

10.3 CHANGING GUIDES IN MANAGERIAL DECISION MAKING

In exploring management decisions in respect to major innovations, it seems useful to begin by considering the general guides which management adopts in sifting information and weighing alternatives in taking action on individual proposals. Such deep-rooted value orientations are particularly influential when issues are not obviously determined by the available evidence alone, i.e. when important elements of the evaluation process are missing or largely indeterminate and hence have to be filled in by judgements for whose consequences executives must accept responsibility. Indeed, such value orientations are even likely to condition conceptions of how much and what kinds of information should be gathered before decisions can be made [16, p. 103]. It is to these foundations that it may be necessary to turn, therefore, both in seeking to account for consistent patterns of decision among an array of individually varied proposals and in seeking to design strategies for altering such patterns [127, p. 125].

Several decades have passed since a foreign visitor characterised American managers as tending to rely on action in place of thought and optimism in place of analysis. However true it may have been then, students of management realise that it has been subject to far-reaching transformations under continuing pressures from changes in technological imperatives and potentials as well as from changes in social objectives and political constraints.

The general nature of such re-orientations in decision frameworks may be illustrated by the familiar sequence of metamorphoses which led from producing goods for one customer at a time to producing simultaneously for many customers by increasing the number of production units using essentially small scale methods and on to mass production techniques incapable of producing small quantities economically. Distribution progressed similarly, of course, from servicing one customer at a time to servicing many customers simultaneously by multiplying the utilisation of small scale methods (more salesmen, more small stores hooked into chains, etc.) and on to mass marketing techniques (e.g. national advertising) not economical for small scale operations. Both in production and in marketing, each of these transformations necessitated extensive changes in the tasks to be performed, skills required, risks involved, organisational adaptations developed and even in the time perspectives for planning and evaluating performance. The resulting need to reshape the values and supporting behaviour patterns underlying managerial decisions has always been clearly perceived in retrospect. But it can hardly cause any surprise that managers, like other people, tend to face new problems and situations by relying on the knowledge and judgements tested by past experience and hence seem unresponsive to innovations. Thus, production and marketing innovations either had to be cut down into small, trial doses or face long delays. The latter has been illustrated by the even more shocking changes, as viewed in the upper echelons of production-dominated companies, forced by the fact that mass production methods have enhanced reliance on mass marketing for survival—with attendant shifts in budget, organisational power and the influence of ideas which seemed distasteful as well as alien to specialists in manufacturing.

Although analogies are notoriously unreliable, it may be of interest to consider the implications of adjustments in research and development functions similar to those undergone by production and marketing. A shift from a few scientists and engineers working individually to laboratories with large staffs continuing to employ small scale methods has already occurred with some frequency in the U.S.A. and Western Europe. Even larger scale and more specialised operations may emerge increasingly, perhaps along lines already reflected by some governmental installations. And the very power of mass marketing to saturate existing markets more rapidly may tend to encourage the intensification of R & D programmes in some industries to create the new products for which their marketing organisations are waiting to stimulate demand—a possibility which has been illustrated during the past twenty years by the pharmaceutical drug industry's sharp increase in research budgets [19, pp. 377–82].

Readjustments in the managerial ethos have also been forced by (a) industry's expanding array of highly specialised functions, necessitating efforts to integrate their quite distinctive contributions and to determine changes in the relative need for each; and (b) increasingly comprehensive and sophisticated criteria for evaluating corporate performance, urging the justification of an increasing proportion of decisions on objective grounds. Together, these and other major industrial developments, it may be hypothesised, have induced gradual shifts in such general guides within the decision-making framework of management as the following:

(1) favouring short-term profitability over prospective long-term gains; but the increasing need for heavy capital facilities and the mounting concern of investors and prospective employees with growth potentials have tended to alter the balance between these goals;

(2) favouring direct revenue-producing operations over activities offering only indirect benefits; but the increasing problems of coordinating complex organisations has led to a rapid expansion of staff functions, e.g. accounting, finance, budgeting and corporate planning;

(3) favouring continued specialisation on established products and processes over trying to invade the established specialties of others; but increasing diversification has been encouraged by demonstrations that the disadvantages of less experience with given products and processes may be more than offset by advantages in selling or distribution of servicing facilities, etc.;

(4) favouring the benefits of maintaining the prevailing allocation of budget and influence among major components of large organisations over the possible gains offered by adjustments likely to disrupt such harmony; but the development of new technologies combined with needs which cannot be dealt with adequately within existing organisational units has forced acceptance of quality control, data processing, market research and executive development;

(5) favouring efforts to maximise the efficiency of established operations over diverting resources to explore new kinds of undertakings;

but new technological potentials and market pressures have led manufacturers to consider backward and forward integration, new distribution arrangements and financing terms for customers as well as the expansion of product lines;

(6) favouring proposals amenable to fairly rigorous estimates of prospective outlays and returns over those resting primarily on qualitative judgements of prospective results;

although this tendency has been intensified by the popularity of capital budgeting and cost-benefit analysis, the continuing importance of other appeals seems to be evidenced by many recent entries into international operations, integrated data processing systems and research; and

(7) favouring the extension of tight managerial controls over pressures in the opposite direction;

this has led to progressively tighter controls over sales and office operations, but its limitations seem to be gaining recognition in respect to advertising, executive development and corporate planning.

Some of these illustrative 'guidelines' overlap, of course, while others might have been added, but the point being emphasised here is that the bases for managerial decisions have already responded, albeit slowly, to the pressures generated by technological and other changes—though they continue to lag sufficiently to slow the adoption of innovations and to moderate, if not minimise, efforts to develop new advances. In order to understand more clearly how such generalised pressures are brought to bear, it is necessary to examine the successive stages of such decision-making processes and this will be the primary task of the remainder of this chapter.

First, however, it seems useful to suggest a broadening of the concept of managerial decisions. Instead of regarding them as climactic acts which can be effectively isolated for analytical purposes, it may prove more useful to regard them as elements in a stream of successive temporary commitments, each of which is heavily conditioned by the network of previous decisions and is subject to repeated later alterations on the basis of additional information, adjusted goals and newly emerging pressures and alternatives. This shift in concept would serve both to decrease the significance of demonstrated deviations between *final* results and the expectations leading to the *initial* decisions and also to increase the importance of informational feedbacks and of organisational adaptability in determining the effectiveness of managerial responses to the changing determinants of successful performance.

10.4 ON THE ROLE OF MAJOR INNOVATIONS IN PROMOTING ORGANISATIONAL OBJECTIVES

Efforts to develop a more useful analytical framework may be initiated by comparing technological innovations with other means for promoting the objectives of the firm and then examining the role of research and development in advancing defined innovational goals.

Basic hypotheses which may be hazarded in this area include:

(1) that in most firms top management tends to have a reasonably stable preference for the means of promoting its primary objectives (such as improving or maintaining: profitability; growth; market position; security of assets; relative stability of operating levels; and a favourable public image);

(2) that the first preference is generally for the continuation, or only moderate intensification, of familiar operations involving little risk to established organisational structures or patterns of resource allocations (e.g. modest improvements in products and distributive arrangements; relatively limited additions to productive capacity not involving major innovations in processes; and reductions in production costs via gradual improvements in techniques and facilities as well as progressive reductions in waste);

(3) that the generation or pioneering adoption of major technological innovations is likely to rank low because it tends to involve heavy investments, substantial risks and readjustments in existing organisational arrangements, and budgetary allocations affecting many functions and operating divisions;* and

(4) that such lower ranking preferences are seldom resorted to except: (a) when more favoured means prove inadequate; (b) when extra-market factors (e.g. governmental pressures or subsidies) alter the relative potentials or costs; (c) when technological advances by compentitors threaten mounting disadvantages; or (d) when continuing internal technological development programmes yield unexpectedly substantial potentials; and

---

* Evidences of such tendencies are presented by Keezer *et al.* [51, p. 59], Williams [127, p. 125], a study by Arthur D. Little, Inc., [125, p. 634], and Wiesner [118, p. 214]. Jewkes *et al.* even point to industrial research laboratories as sources of resistance to change [47, pp. 184–5]. For indications of pressure to retain or restore established allocation shares among parts of the organisation, see Chapter 9 and Cyert and March [21, pp. 30, 120].

(5) that the belief is nevertheless widespread that technological progress is inevitable and important in the long run and hence cannot be entirely neglected without serious hazard.

One implication of these hypotheses is that in most organisations technological progress is not a primary or self-justifying objective at all, but merely one among an array of means of promoting more fundamental desiderata. This means that evaluation of given innovations might yield different results depending on the relative importance of various criteria (e.g. preventing increases in unit labour costs; improving product quality; matching a competitor's product modification). Recognition that technological innovations are usually part of a complex of policies and actions designed to be mutually reinforcing raises additional doubts about simplistic efforts to assess the outcome of technological innovations as though these could easily be isolated from the interacting system. In short, it seems analytically untenable to assume that the effects of technological innovations can be soundly assessed in terms of concomitant—or, for that matter, lagged—adjustments in profits. Instead, it would seem desirable to construct more intricate models indicating the complex of parallel and serial linkages through which technological innovations undertaken for any purpose interact with other adjustments in input and output flows and in product and factor prices to shape cost, revenue and investment patterns.*

Another implication of the preceding hypotheses is that the extent of reliance on programmes involving the promotion of technological progress would tend to differ among industries and firms at any given time, [53, pp. 248–75; 47, pp. 156–8, 184; 122, pp. 34, 39; 16, p. 18] and would also tend to differ within individual firms and industries, according to the adequacy of preferred alternatives for achieving organisational objectives both over the course of business cycles and over the course of longer term growth patterns.† This view opens the way to a variety of interesting speculations. For example, are there major 'cultural differences' among industries in the continuity and seriousness of their reliance on technological progress? If so, are these traceable to the conditioning generated by the rate of past major technological advances (e.g. as reflected by the

* The need for more complex models is also indicated by Carter and Williams [16, pp. 5, 29, 151–2 and 160–4] and by Williams [127, pp. 117 et seq.]. A crude model illustrating some of these complexities was presented in Chapter IX. For general philosophic support of such a position, see Kaplan [50, pp. 316–19].

† For cyclic and other intermediate-term variations in pressures for technical changes, see Hicks [42, pp. 299–302], Sayers [102, pp. 275–91], Brozen [10, pp. 239–57], Holland [45, p. 15] and Cyert and March [21, pp. 278–9]. Longer term factors affecting interest in technological advances are discussed by Burns [14, pp. 120–58], Kuznets [60, Chapter 9] and Schmookler [104, pp. 1–19] as well as in Chapter 9.

differences between chemicals and electronics on the one hand as compared with railroads and food canning)? Does concern with technological progress tend to be stimulated more by rising or by declining profits? by rising or by declining growth rates? Are technological potentials expected to contract as an industry grows older? It may be well to probe the range of experiences with technological leads and lags at considerably greater length than has been done so far before assuming the universality of the stimuli and effects as well as of the processes involved. Surely, it is too early in the development of this field of inquiry to reject the possibility that greater understanding may be achieved by permitting the emergence of various kinds of models to cover different sectors of industry and different sets of concomitant economic conditions. (See Chapter 7.)

Still another implication of these hypotheses is that seeking to generate major technological innovations may rank low in management's hierarchy of resource allocation preferences because the uncertainties involved in estimating the timing and magnitude of prospective benefits (including the effects of attendant disruptions in other aspects of company operations) prevents their effective assessment within the analytical frameworks used to make decisions among more familiar allocation alternatives. For example, field studies have emphasised the need to consider—along with the extreme difficulties of estimating—the chances of achieving technical success on individual projects, of extending this to the development of commercially viable products and of then finally reaping rewards through efficient manufacturing, marketing and distribution. And, in addition, it is also necessary to estimate how long these stages are likely to take, how much investment they will require, probable changes in price and demand over the five to fifteen year periods commonly involved and concomitant advances achieved by competitors [47, pp. 150, *et seq.*, 220–1, 237 and 266–7; 16, pp. 89–92; 127, pp. 121–2; 24, p. 305; 84, pp. 342–4; 80, pp. 461, 465, 471–5; 56, pp. 478, 480; 57, p. 508; 15, p. 19; 119, p. 27; 93, p. 115; 39, p. 236]. Faithful adherence to formal capital budgeting procedures when so wide an array of required input data is unpersuasive provides little assurance to managements asked to stake huge sums on the undertaking, however much the introduction of assumed or subjective probabilities may facilitate the solution of classroom exercises.

Indeed, it is even conceivable that this area of inapplicability is less exceptional than appears to be the case—i.e. that the analytical techniques most widely used in the economic theory of the firm to provide rational solutions to decision-making problems may be directly applicable only to relatively routine issues of limited consequence, offering little more than vague conceptual guides and generalised computational procedures for coping with the really strategic decisions confronting top management. Thus, it may be necessary to experiment with new kinds of analytical frameworks to deal not only with allocations for developing major technological innovations, but also with other far-reaching decisions affecting additions to productive capacity, drastic shifts in the breadth of product lines, the invasion of new markets, the reorganisation of distributive channels, acquisitions or mergers with other firms, etc. [55, pp. 149–50; 16, pp. 5, 29, 151–2, 160–4; 2, pp. 355–6; 58, p. 362; 127, pp. 121–2; 62, pp. 122–46; 32, pp. 48–54]. And the usefulness of such frameworks will probably rest less on the logic of computational procedures for aggregating, discounting and comparing assumed outlays and incomes than on the degree of penetration of their conceptions of the underlying processes.

Finally, the combination of the preceding hypotheses implies a need for managements in many industries to develop a strategy for coping with two broadly opposing pressures. One, generated by extensive past experience indicating that the incidence of major technological advances is small and randomly distributed through time, suggests a low probability of such development within any given operating period. The other, which may be rooted in the same experience, in addition to being reinforced by prevailing attitudes in industry at large, warns that when such major advances do emerge their effects on relative competitive positions may be drastic. Formulation of a policy would seem to require the clarification of objectives in this sector followed by elucidation of the conceptual bases for implementing specified intentions—both of which will be discussed in the following sections.

10.5 MANAGERIAL APPROACHES TO ADVANCING TECHNOLOGICAL LEVELS

The following hypotheses suggest some of the bases which may enter into the shaping of managerial objectives affecting the level and composition of allocations for advancing the technological base of its activities:

(1) that, instead of seeking to achieve a significant technological lead over all competitors, most managements have sought only to keep pace on the average with their competitive peers, and some have even been willing to condone lags behind such peers, provided that such lags were either no greater than could be offset by the given firm's superiority in other respects (e.g. marketing) or no greater than could be overcome within, say, one year through feasible increases in allocations for this purpose [52, pp. 355–69; 93, p. 119; 107, p. 370; 16, pp. 65–6];

(2) that, within the complex domain of technology, most managements have tended to exhibit well-developed preferences among the possible foci of efforts to achieve advances:

    (a) favouring improvements in products over adjustments in production operations, favouring modification in the design and properties of established products over attempts to create entirely new kinds of products, favouring changes in operating methods over the redesign of facilities and equipment; and being still less favourable towards efforts to alter the foundations of basic processes [6, pp. 603–17; 123, p. 214; 19, pp. 374, 377–8; 77, p. 595; 16, p. 56];

    (b) preferring *tinkering* with minor improvements based on *ad hoc* suggestions over developing successive evolutionary gains along established lines of scientific and engineering progress, and preferring the *adoption* of major innovations developed and proved to be commercially practicable by others (via purchasing licences or equipment or designs) over undertaking *basic research* in the hope of generating major advances [67, pp. 385–96; 51, p. 62; 126, pp. 483–97]; and

(3) that progressive experience with R & D tends to increase the resources devoted to such programmes, to enhance their role in determining the rate and direction of technological progress in most firms and to reduce the ratio of 'low risk–low payoff' projects. (For opposing viewpoints, see [51, p. 62; 12, pp. 273–6; 122, p. 40].)

One implication of these hypotheses derives from the fact that similar tendencies toward limited commitments characterised early managerial approaches to other new corporate functions, including marketing, international operations, corporate planning and computerised information and control systems. But each developed gradually as increasingly knowledgeable specialists became available, as management became more familiar with the range and importance of its potential contributions, and as new criteria for evaluating such activities emerged. Accordingly, it may not be unrealistic to anticipate a similar exfoliation of R & D, or of a more broadly conceived innovational function reaching beyond products and processes alone. Effective appraisal of such possibilities, however, would seem to require supplementing the numerous studies of current resource allocations, organisational arrangements and work foci of R & D programmes by analyses of historical changes in such patterns and of the factors associated with them. In particular, it seems important to learn to what extent the vague, global concept of R & D has been giving way in managerial thinking to an awareness of its more sharply defined components, e.g. separating quality control and the minor modification of products for special customer needs from more far-reaching explorations of new kinds of products and processes. And an associated need relates to the evolution of more clearly formulated conceptual bases for determining allocations for R & D projects and for the programme as a whole.*

A second implication concerns the likelihood of wide differences among competitors in their reliance on, and in their expectations of, the innovational programme. In part, this might merely reflect perceptions of relative strength in other major determinants of the firm's competitive position. But such differences may also derive from divergent views of the relative benefits of pioneering against 'following the leader'. In a culture which regards it as an heroic virtue, executives are almost compelled to pay at least lip service to pioneering not only in publicity releases, where even fake lions can roar, but in the form of R & D budgets to be noted by security analysts and by stockholders. Is there evidence, however, to support the mythology? Have the largest or the most profitable firms been the most prolific in generating major technological advances? Has the enormous growth and influence of the autombile industry and of its dominant firms, for example, been associated with a continuing torrent of major research advances? Relevant evidence would require long-term studies of whether the rewards of consistent technological pioneering are frequent and large enough to offset the cumulative drains; of whether 'catching up' with the actual discoveries made by others is a feasible strategy and also economically advantageous; and of whether the delays and difficulties involved in effective commercialisation of proved technological advances seriously limits resulting benefits to the originating firm as compared with competitors tending to place a heavier emphasis on marketing strength than on technological pioneering. Moreover, the possibility must be considered that such questions may evoke disparate answers in different industries and that even objective analyses may yield results which differ with the length of the evaluative period used [78, pp. 175 *et seq.*; 91, pp. 112–15; 116, pp. 118–35; 29, pp. 93–112; 72, pp. 1023–51].

Such considerations also suggest the possibility of fundamental contradictions between the actual roles assigned to R & D in many company programmes and the criteria used by managers and external analysts to

* For comments on the circularity, inconsistency and variability of the rationales offered by some respondents, see Jewkes *et al.* [47, pp. 142–3] and Nelson [88, p. 122]. But the impression of groping confusion yielded by such cross-sectional studies may be quite different from the progressive (if still not complete) clarification of purposes emerging within companies over the years of experience in this area. One of the quite uncommon sources of support for the above view that R & D may be expected to move in the direction of more far-reaching projects is Kornhauser [59, Chapter 3].

appraise resulting contributions. It is a commonplace, of course, that R & D covers a wide range of activities, but greater emphasis is needed on the fact that evaluative criteria may cover an equally broad spectrum and, hence, that relevance depends on carefully matching planned with actual performance. Even where R & D is dominated by essentially routine efforts to effect successive small increments in the manufactured quality and in the service features of established products, efforts to appraise its success in terms of adjustments within one year or two in product sales, market shares and profitability may be considered appropriate only when one can persuasively neutralise the effects of concurrent changes in market conditions and all other company programmes and policies—and when R & D was not devoted primarily to safeguarding established positions by keeping pace with competitive advances. But it might be quite misleading to apply these same criteria to R & D programmes involving heavy commitments to more far-reaching advances which are likely to require longer periods, to absorb greater resources and to produce a higher ratio of failures. On the contrary, yields in such cases might have a greater bearing on long-term growth and even survival than on shorter term sales and profits; and might lead to diversification into new fields instead of increasing shares in present markets.

It is frequently difficult even to define the specific outcomes of such projects, since major innovations often produce ragged edges in the surrounding technological frontier, thereby establishing pressures and even partial commitments in given directions which may not only limit management's freedom in choosing next steps, but also represent a continuing fall-out of effects from earlier innovations. Thus, the use of the short-term criteria by management might well serve to transform an R & D programme with ostensible commitments to major advances into one with progressively dwarfed objectives. And the use of short-term criteria by external analysts could accordingly vary widely in relevance according to the patterns of dominance of the programmes being studied.

10.6 ON THE PROCESSES OF EFFECTING MAJOR TECHNOLOGICAL ADVANCES

In order to develop and compare alternative strategies for effecting major technological advances, it would appear necessary to begin with some conceptions, however vague, of the structure of variables and inter-relationships which constitute the *terra incognita* to be explored, of the means by which the existing boundaries of knowledge may be extended, and of bases for choosing the more promising targets among the innumerable possibilities which seem available.

Relevant hypotheses which may be suggested in this connection include:

(1) that, contrary to widespread managerial beliefs (or hopes), most scientists and engineers do not have access to widely accepted models of the terrain beyond current research frontiers (including the identification of promising targets and of the means as well as the risks of reaching them) and that such models as may have emerged tend to have but very limited claims to validity;*

(2) that, as a result, research specialists faced by the necessity to make specific choices among the seemingly endless array of possibilities tend to recommend proposals which are likely to gain managerial acceptance and which are also likely to enhance their own records of performance as appraised and rewarded by management—thus being closely responsive to, rather than independent of, the structure of managerial preferences [47, p. 133; 16, p. 65; 108, pp. 161–77; 94, p. 417]; and

(3) that the virtual absence of any effective analytical framework prevents the formulation of wholly rational or rigorously consistent decisions in most R & D programmes, prevents cumulative improvement through the feedback of results, and tends to produce low levels of success in identifying high potential targets, in estimating the likelihood of effecting major advances, and in assessing resulting costs, time requirements and benefits [47, pp. 150, 225, 230, 237; 88, pp. 112, 118 and other references near top of p. 218].

One implication of these hypotheses is that many managers have tended to over-estimate the capacity of scientists and engineers to see beyond the frontiers of their respective fields, partly because of an understandable desire to shift some of the uncertainties of decision making to others and partly because of a superficial conception of the nature of technological progress. (On the reasons for using 'expert' opinion as a safeguard against the possible penalties of decisions which yield disappointing results, see the quotation from von Braun in [17, p. 404], as well as [56, p. 504]. For more general warnings about exaggerated views of R & D potentials, see

---

* Among the numerous sources tending to support this modest view of scientific capacities, the following are especially notable: Jewkes *et al.* [47, pp. 150–1, 225–7, 237], Klein [57, pp. 480, 508], von Braun [124, p. 1080], Carter and Williams [15, p. 19] and Marshall and Meckling [80, p. 463]. Although the temptation seems to be strong for laymen (and perhaps some managers) to outline seemingly infallible logical bases for attacking the unknown, and to assume that 'good' scientists have correct 'hunches', the grounds for such views seem meagre indeed: see Nelson [89, p. 300], [87, p. 571] and [88, pp. 114–15], and as a moving glimpse of the fallibility of distinguished scientists, see Feynman's recent Nobel Prize address [26].

[120, p. 111; 124, pp. 1, 102].) The remarkably tight-knit structure of science seems to support the view that advances represent the progressive extension of well-defined development paths, somewhat like adding courses of brick to build walls higher. Unfortunately, this perspective tends to overlook the frequency with which major advances have resulted from striking off in new directions, necessitating the tearing down of earlier accretions of brickwork and replacing them to provide underpinning for the new findings which seem to be sounder and more promising. In view of top management's inescapable responsibility for all major corporate functions, it would seem urgent that more knowledgeable bases be developed at that level for choosing among alternative programme recommendations.

Another implication is that management cannot retain the authority to hire, evaluate and reward research personnel without thereby curtailing their independence from managerial conceptions of performance desiderata. If the latter seem to favour short-term undertakings, a high ratio of successful project completions and immediately discernible contributions to increased sales or reduced costs, these are obviously likely to become the dominant foci among research proposals, whatever scientists and engineers may consider to be the potentials of other kinds of undertakings. And such tendencies may be further reinforced by more subtle efforts to make R & D administrators, and even technical staff members, more 'profit conscious'. Viewed more broadly, such pressures would tend to encourage continuing concentrations on taking small steps, and on remaining within the fields, and even along the specific paths, of investigation which have been fruitful in the past.

It would seem to follow, therefore, that the more effective development of R & D potentials may require both the redefinition of managerial objectives in this area and more vigorous leadership in formulating policies and organisational arrangements to reinforce such altered perspectives. A promising, and perhaps necessary, point of departure for such efforts is to dig beneath the superficialties imposed by viewing R & D as merely a special case either of the general problem of profit maximisation under uncertainty or of the only slightly narrower problem of investment decisions. Innovational decisions can be fitted into these groupings, of course, but the distinctive problems confronting management in this area begin precisely at the points where they differ from the purchasing, production, marketing and other problems which the prevailing decision-making framework evolved to handle.

In respect to R & D objectives, for example, it may be necessary to reach beyond the hope of generalised contributions to profitability and growth by spelling out intermediate objectives relating to gains in information,* the strengthening of personnel quality,† the prevention of erosion in market shares through the lagging of 'ordinary' improvements in products and processes behind the stream produced by competitors, the provision of safeguards against the severe consequences of 'breakthroughs' by competitors through retaining a strong ability to catch up with advances by others, the continuous exploration of diversification possibilities, etc. In defining such an array of targets, managements may also see the need to redress imbalances involving neglect of the deeper scientific roots of potential major advances in products and processes. And in addition, it may be important to emphasise the integral relationship of an effective R & D programme to all other company operations and to specify objectives for developing such mutual reinforcement [16, pp. 85–86; 2, p. 355].

Managerial efforts to strengthen innovational programmes may also consider several aspects of organisational arrangements. One concerns the possible need to separate the estimation of technical potentials and risks from the estimation of economic potentials and risks in the interests of increasing the independence of scientists and engineers and of enabling them to concentrate on their areas of specialised competence. A second relates to the possible need for more effective separations between longer term 'high risk–high payoff' projects and shorter term 'low risk–low payoff' projects to permit the differentiations in performance criteria and incentives without which an increasing proportion of the total effort is likely to gravitate towards the more cautious programme. Another concerns the possibility of reprofiling the structure of management controls bearing on R & D activities so as to tighten controls at points where universities, too, have found discipline valuable (e.g. increasing the scientific rigour with which proposals are examined—including evidence of a careful survey of the literature, the outlining of proposed search procedures, the definition of initial targets, etc.—and also providing for comparably rigorous periodic reviews of achievements, difficulties and planned next

---

* The emphasis on aggregate measures of the performance of the firm as a whole often encourages the neglect of more directly relevant measures of component sectors. Neither profitability nor growth provides an effective measure of the contributions of accounting or engineering, or even of production or marketing for that matter. Surely such measures are at least equally inapplicable to the evaluation of R & D. Instead, there is obvious need for a structure of differentiated performance criteria. For some partial approaches to this, see Chapters 3, 5 and 8.

† For emphasis on the extraordinary importance of the quality of personnel in determining research output, see Jewkes et al. [47, pp. 145, 149], Williams [127, pp. 126–7], Rubel [122, p. 44] and Cherington et al. [17, p. 405]. Unfortunately for the prospects of developing R & D production functions and related analytical models for decision making, the capacity of individuals to make important research advances is not yet detectable to any large degree; nor have many achieved a sizeable number of major advances.

steps) and loosening them at points representing unjustifiable carry-overs of supervisory practices from other kinds of corporation activities. There may also be valuable returns from organising regular means of inter-relating research programmes and personnel with other operations and those staffing them, partly to facilitate the communication of questions, suggestions and puzzling experiences and partly to develop greater recep-tivity towards innovations by those responsible for facilitating their commercialisation. (For references to delays in the utilisation of R & D findings because of inadequate understanding and organisation biases, see [124, p. 214; 97, pp. 388–9].)

10.7 SOME STRATEGIC CONCEPTIONS UNDERLYING R & D PROGRAMMES

The processes intervening between R & D inputs and eventual outputs seem commonly to be regarded as enclosed in a black box of technicalities which can be ignored in the formulation and evaluation of relevant managerial strategies. It seems apparent, however, that the programme proposed by research personnel must rest on implicit if not overt concep-tions of 'the game against nature' to be played, that the form of such conceptions may influence the selection of projects entering into the pro-gramme and that subsequent results ought to help test the relevance of such guiding conceptions. Accordingly, however incomprehensible the highly sophisticated models underlying individual projects may be to non-specialists, it may be increasingly necessary for management to become familiar with the more generalised models responsible for broader pro-grammes, including the assumptions on which they rest as well as the wider implications of their expected outcomes. The following hypotheses are offered to illustrate the range of alternatives which may underlie current programmes as well as to indicate their prospective bearing on resulting allocational decisions:

(1) programmes designed to generate a succession of *small* improvements may rest upon hypotheses which view the opportunities for achieving individually modest technological gains:

(a) as uniformly distributed around current outposts and hence likely to yield steady though modest rates of return to develop-mental efforts in any direction—like mining a surrounding bed of low grade minerals; or

(b) as distributed continuously only along certain developmental paths and hence likely to yield reasonably steady but modest rates of return, though subject to occasional failures when new undertakings are found to diverge from optimal paths—like following a coal seam; or

(c) as dotted around randomly—like a diamond field—and, hence, while not all digging is fruitful, a broad sweep may be expected to yield a fluctuating but reasonably rewarding average level of returns;

(2) programmes expected to yield a sufficient rate of *major* advances despite primary commitments to generating a succession of *small* improvements may rest upon such hypotheses as the following:

(a) that major advances are merely the cumulative outcome of progressive small improvements; or

(b) that major advances represent the establishment of effective new equilibria after improvements in various components of a technical system make possible their re-integration; or

(c) that major improvements, or 'high-payoff' nodes, are randomly distributed, cannot be effectively hunted directly and, consequently, are just as likely to be discovered as the by-product of a continuing emphasis on small increments; and

(3) programmes specifically focused on generating *major* advances may rest upon such hypotheses as the following:

(a) that major advances represent giant steps along established lines of development and, hence, high potential targets may be identified by experts capable of extrapolating discernible 'trends' in the relevant sectors of technology—perhaps like aiming at 200 miles per hour trains or super-large or Mach 3 aircraft; or

(b) that major advances require shifts to new directions of development and targets may, hence, be identified by bringing in specialists in other techniques or fields—e.g. computer experts or laser specialists; or

(c) that promising new fields are most likely to be uncovered in the course of basic efforts to advance the frontiers of knowledge rather than through aiming directly at specific targets—like studying macromolecules instead of seeking a new synthetic fibre from the outset.

Thus, the number of possible combinations is large enough to make it hazardous for the outside analyst to guess the strategic conceptions underlying particular R & D programmes. Similarly, it would be apparent in the course of managerial review that there might be reasonable alternatives to any particular conception which should be discussed and periodically reconsidered on the basis of subsequent experience. Even more important, it is apparent that these several strategies would be expected to differ substantially in the ratio of inputs to outputs, in the variability of such relationships, in the levels of attendant risks and in their prospective contributions to competitive advantage. (Differences in programme strategies may well account for some of the wide differences in empirical findings cited in references above.)

For example, in the case of evolutionary advances along recognisable paths—as covered above—technological progress may indeed be roughly proportional to increases in inputs, because more searches within a limited domain enhances the likelihood of finding the most promising improvements. But resulting innovations are also likely to yield short lived, as well as modest, competitive advantages because chance factors would tend to distribute individual successes among the competing groups and also because the intensive exploration of common ground tends both to sensitise each group to the potentials of new developments and also to strengthen its capacity to duplicate advances by others in a reasonably short time.

In the case of major technological innovations, however, the relationship between the magnitudes of inputs and of outputs may be much more tenuous because: the range of possible approaches by competitors is so much greater that searches are unlikely to reach high densities, thereby leaving more to chance; and the prospects of success may be determined in far greater measure by the qualitative characteristics of the personnel engaged (including their capacity to see holes in seemingly solid walls and including the representation of new kinds of expertise) than by their sheer numbers; and the correct path to the next high-payoff node may be so long and costly as to discourage many even among those who happen to find it—as has happened with the cessation of drilling in dry holes only to delay the discovery of rich oil fields at greater depths. Major advances would seem to offer larger and longer lasting competitive benefits because striking off into new territory is likely to leave competitors farther behind in developing relevant kinds of specialised personnel, new knowledge, facilities and operating skills. Of course, catching up with a major advance may be less costly than effecting it originally, because pioneers often have to explore many blind alleys before finding a path which proves rewarding, while followers can concentrate more directly on the revealed target. But the time taken to catch up also enables the pioneers to achieve further advances especially on the basis of their greater momentum in exploring the new possibilities opened by the advance.

All of the foregoing assumes that outcomes accord with intentions, but conceptions such as that in (2) immediately above, which bridge between the other two extremes, would seem to urge caution in assuming that the boldness, or even the direction, of R & D plans can be correctly inferred from their eventual results—as is often implied by *ex post* analyses. On the

contrary, past experience suggests that many major technological innovations may appropriately be characterised as representing 'unintended
revolutions', being the outcome of undertakings with far more limited
objectives than came to be achieved.

While each of the preceding conceptions as well as others ought to be
drawn into the development of generalised models for designing R & D
programmes, attention should also be given to the need for additional
guides to cover the array of critical managerial decisions involved. For
example, another common problem concerns when to terminate particular
lines of exploration. If it is assumed that most major advances involve substantial periods of groping before promising new perspectives appear, and if
it is also recognised that many treasures ahead can keep receding just out
of reach for maddening periods, it is apparent that deciding when to continue and when to stop may often be more difficult and more influential
in determining R & D payoffs than choosing which projects to initiate.
A related vexing problem concerns how to determine the prospective 'relevance' of new findings to the guiding objectives of the firm. Since effective R & D programmes frequently reveal promising new paths of inquiry
in various directions, the progressive dispersion of efforts can only be
avoided by deliberately ignoring some (most?) of these—despite the
tantalising possibility that any one could prove highly rewarding. The still
vague conceptions underlying such decisions would seem to exert major
influence on the extent to which R & D is used to promote diversification
as against strengthening concentration in established products and
markets—thereby tending either to increase competition via cross-
entry or to limit competition by enhancing the dominance of past leaders.

In short, a number of the decision foci confronting managers dealing
with R & D pose the need not only for analytical models capable of being
refined to yield increasing relevance in given sectors of industry, but also
for empirical guides for judging the returns from various courses of action
—e.g. does taking twice as long to go half as far as expected at double the
outlay represent an exceptionally unfavourable experience or is it rather
more favourable than the average in seeking to effect major advances?
There is even urgent need to clarify the form in which R & D output may
emerge—e.g. new information, new hypotheses, rising staff capabilities,
new empirical findings, patent applications, product or process improvements, higher sales or lower costs—and the extent to which the latter
may be attributable to factors largely separate from R & D activities.

And before leaving the question of how invasions of unknown territory
come about, it may not be entirely amiss to express a bit of scepticism
about the comprehensive rationales which are often offered by research
executives to inquiries about why given programmes were undertaken.

Seldom is it admitted, lest it be considered unseemly or even evidence of incompetence, that able scientists and engineers were simply allowed to grope in the hope that 'corners' might be turned which would reveal possibilities not discernible from the frontiers of the time. Yet technologies which have persisted for long periods would seem to attest to the existence of daunting obstacles on all sides. Under such conditions, waiting for a new theoretical vision may be less fruitful than sending out competent scouts to hunt, putter and dig for possible openings. At any rate, there was obviously widespread resort to such quasi-scientific tactics in the past— and penetrating field inquiries might well reveal that similar expedients are still far from uncommon.

10.8 ON REVISING ANALYTICAL PERSPECTIVES IN DEVELOPING MAJOR TECHNOLOGICAL INNOVATIONS

Just as closer scrutiny tends to dispel the seeming uniformity seen from afar in any landscape or field of study, the intensive analysis of actual technological innovations soon compels the replacement of highly general-ised (and often superficial) concepts by more distinctive means of dealing with their various, clearly differentiated aspects, with the complex of pressures influencing their development and their different impacts on surrounding economic and other relationships.

Some of the hypotheses which may be hazarded concerning the nature of technical change and technological innovations include:

(1) that the concepts which predominated in early economic studies of technical change can now be recognised as too narrow to encompass the multiple dimensions of technological development and to provide a realistic grasp of the intricate interweaving of technological inno-vations with economic and other adjustments [1, pp. 5–23; 111, pp. 312–20; 112, pp. 89–104; 113, pp. 76–86; 23, pp. 709–29; 81, pp. 547–57; 110, pp. 281–301; 49, pp. 1–17; 32, pp. 109–65];

(2) that, partly as a result of such conceptual shortcomings and partly as a result of statistical limitations which are often pointed out and then ignored during the course of subsequent analysis and interpretation, most of the measures which have been used to assess the extent and consequence of technological innovations are open to serious question; and

(3) that effective exploration of the implications of increasing techno-logical progress both for managerial decision making and for broader economic problems has been impeded by the heavy concentration of efforts to determine the universal long-term effects of highly abstract technological innovations on traditional economic variables—to the comparative neglect of a wide range of questions which may prove

more interesting from the standpoint of elucidating relevant economic processes and also more productive of useful guides to policy issues at the levels of the firm, the industry and the national economy. (The long history of such disparate analytical foci is indicated by the strong contrast between Ricardo's brief chapter 'On Machinery' [95, pp. 263–71] and Babbage's comprehensive discussion [5]. For a recent comment on the chasm between theory and reality, see [37, pp. 111–12].)

One of the implications of these hypotheses is the need for an analytical framework which reaches beyond the long prevailing central focus on changes in input–output ratios and unit costs at the point of application as the primary basis for measuring the dimensions and appraising the effects of technological innovations. The wide array of industrial operating characteristics which may be affected by technological innovations may be indicated by the following illustrations merely at the physical level:

(1) *changes in physical inputs* involving not only the quantity of each per unit of output, but also: the kinds, quality grades and uniformity of the various purchased materials used; the specific skills and the composition of skills in labour inputs as well as attendant restrictions on work loads; and such aspects of capital facilities and equipment as productive capacity, degree of specialisation, normal working life, flexibility of use levels, alternative levels of scale and prospective obsolescence rates;

(2) *changes in physical outputs* involving not only the aggregate quantity but also: the variety of products; the extent of design changes in each line; the range of quality grades and sizes in each; and alterations in their respective service features for buyers (including capacity, precision, service life, liability to breakdown, convenience, safety, etc.); and

(3) *changes in physical aspects of production flows* including the degree of integration of successive operations; the controllability of output rates and the speed with which they can be altered; the variability of different inputs with changes in output levels and in product-mix; the average duration of the production cycle; incidence of downtime and attendant work-in-process inventory requirements; requirement of special working conditions; and accident and health hazards.

One reason for probing the complex machinery underlying the simple abstract concept of technological advances is that only at this level can managerial choices be made among real alternatives. And it is apparent that management cannot either assess the effects of various past innovations, or select which alternatives to promote in the future, except by penetrating beneath measures of aggregate effects to identify the distinctive outcomes (including disadvantages as well as benefits) likely to be associated with each. In addition, focusing on the working parts also provides the basis for studying the rich and still developing texture of technological progress, for innovations interact with adjacent arrangements often engendering a chain of adjustments before a workable equilibrium is reached—as in cases where improved product design necessitates alterations in processing methods, which lead to the introduction of new kinds of materials, whose effective utilisation forces additional modifications in processing facilities. Thus, the analytical purview, already broadened to include arrays of component input–output ratios, might be extended further towards developing sequential flow measures designed to detect common interaction patterns as shown in Chapter 3.

Even more important, however, is the possibility of using this structure of technical adjustment alternatives to explore the network of economic adjustments triggered by each of the preceding kinds of changes in the physical aspects of production. For example, shifts in the kinds (and sometimes merely in the grade) of materials required may alter supply availabilities, factor price responses to variations in demand, transportation and inventory requirements, and even locational advantages. Changes in the composition of labour requirements may similarly affect the available supply, training requirements, the average wage level as well as the structure of wage differentials, the variability of employment levels with output fluctuations and the nature of issues to be negotiated with trade unions. In short, it is apparent that changes in physical inputs, production processes and physical outputs tend to engender direct economic adjustments through repercussions in factor and product markets as well as through alternations in the responsiveness of operations to managerial controls. These and other adjustments in physical quantities and prices of inputs and outputs may then be encompassed by an analytical framework elaborated to permit tracing the successive interactions involved in shaping production functions, factor and cost proportions, fixed and variable unit cost functions, and gross and net average revenue per unit of output— as has been suggested in earlier chapters.

Finally, it is apparent that efforts to appraise the effects of technological innovations effectively must reach beyond individual firms—to cover diffusion rates and competitive responses, etc.—and must also search for the pattern of changing effects between the point of initial application of an innovation by one firm and its acceptance into general use by the industry, without concentrating solely at either end or at any single point. Indeed, there is good reason to believe that studies attempting to determine the lasting effects of technological innovations are bound to be insensitive to the network of reallocations by means of which the economy absorbs and gradually adapts to the succession of innovational impacts—as well as to the complex of intervening pressures which encourage, and influence selections among, new technological advances. Incidentally, past field studies also suggest the need to differentiate among innovational effects according to such special conditions as: (a) whether output levels are expanding or contracting; (b) whether the output potentials of the basic facilities involved are facilities-dominated (as in power plants) or resources-dominated (as in smelting plants) or labour-dominated (as in certain service activities); and (c) differences in the levels of industrialisation of the economies (or economic sectors) studied, including the possible need to allow for the effects of progressive industrialisation in long-term studies [32].

Another basic implication is that many of the measurements now used to appraise the effects of technological innovations are of very limited value, and may even be misleading, for reasons other than the coverage and precision of the data employed. Illustrations of such vulnerable measures would include our widely used indexes of physical output, price changes, unit costs and productivity adjustments as well as most measures of capacity and of 'physical capital'. One reason for such shortcomings is that most of these measures are designed to be blind to technological innovations by assuming, in the interests of statistical comparability, no change in the nature of the inputs or outputs which they cover—despite the overwhelming evidence that they are in fact being altered progressively and substantially, and that much of this is attributable to technological innovations. A second source of limitations, attributable to the same concern with statistical comparability, is the frequent assumption of no change in the composition of aggregates being measured—as when changes in the skill composition of labour inputs are ignored in measuring increases in average wage rates, although this is a common point of impact by technological innovations. Inasmuch as the validity of such measures to assess the effects of technical change depends on fully separating out concomitant changes in costs and prices, it is apparent that errors on one side are mirrored on the other—as when technological improvements in products are discounted by attributing all of attendant price increases to pricing power.

The fundamental difficulties of separating changes in price from changes in the nature of the commodity may be illustrated by the case of capital facilities and equipment. The very concept of capital aggregates consisting of homogeneous units is as unrealistic as the concept of capital units remaining essentially unchanged through time (or as the concept of a meaningful index of capital goods prices over extended periods), because technological development has demonstrated both the economic superiority of designing production facilities so as to integrate the specialised contributions of individually differentiated kinds of equipment and also the tendency in increasingly industrialised economies to apply technological advances to production in substantial measure through altering capital equipment and facilities.*

Finally, it may be worth noting that efforts to apply economic analysis to the management of R & D have already gone through two disappointing stages. The first, in response to the prevailing enthusiasm for input–output studies in all directions, produced a shower of aggressively quantitative determinations of research productivity and of research production functions at company, industry and national levels. To this there has developed an increasingly powerful counter-pressure proclaiming that there are no effective measures either of research inputs or of research outputs. While the critical input is recognised to be the utilisation of scientists and engineers, there is also general agreement that the numbers employed have far less bearing on the outcome than their levels of creativity, imagination and other admired but inadequately defined and still unmeasurable qualities [61, p. 42; 66, p. 147; 101, pp. 53–63]. Even the cost of inputs, which is considered to be a less significant determinant of results, is often difficult to determine because of the deliberate or unavoidable intermixing of costs for an array of activities ranging from conventional testing and customer servicing through fundamental research, development programmes, pilot plant operations and even later stages of commercialisation [47, pp. 147–9; 101, pp. 58–60; 93, p. 111]. On the output side, serious deficiencies are reported in the usefulness of patents and in attempts to measure the amount of new information or the number of inventions and discoveries. This has led to suggestions that the best measure of R & D outputs may be the magnitude of its inputs (although this assumption of a fixed relationship between them is based neither on logic nor on evidence), thus completing a fruitless circle for, as was just noted, the inputs cannot be measured either [101, pp. 63–75; 129, p. 234]. Nor can the practical manager by-pass these difficulties by concentrating on the control of unit costs, because these cannot be measured until units of output are defined.

Perhaps the most astonishing feature of this situation has been the general failure to recognise that these difficulties are inevitable, widespread and

* Efforts to deal with such problems include Shaw [106, pp. 287 et seq.], Denison [22, pp. 215–84], Ruggles [99, pp. 387 et seq.], Gordon [33, pp. 937–57], Kendrick [53, pp. 34–6, 51–4], Gold [32, pp. 18–30] and Marquard [79]. Quite another area of statistical problems underlying the testing of economic hypotheses is suggested by Godfrey [30, pp. 315 et seq.].

inconsequential. There are no authoritative measures of the 'productivity' or 'efficiency' of any corporation as a whole, nor of any subsector of corporate activities providing nonrepetitive services (which covers virtually all staff functions as well as supervisory, technical and policy-making personnel). Nor can such measurements be made of professional services anywhere else, whether in universities or government, and even their usefulness in major sectors of national production are open to serious question. Yet all of these have managed to function because input–output measurements are essentially a means of summarising the results of complex activity systems rather than the basis for understanding or managing the intricate and usually highly specialised processes involved. Indeed, such measurements are likely to become useful only as a result of progressive understanding of the functioning of whatever system is of concern— for only in that way can we learn which variables and which relationships are important for particular control or evaluative purposes. In short, as was emphasised in Chapter 3, when we do not understand the system—as is patently true of R & D—we cannot devise strategically significant measures of its 'productivity' or 'efficiency' or determine its production function.

10.9 GOVERNMENTAL AND PRIVATE ROLES IN PROMOTING TECHNOLOGICAL ADVANCES

The following hypotheses bear upon some of the issues in this area which have attracted increasing attention during recent years:

(1) that the national interest in advancing and diffusing technological progress is stronger, and also broader in scope, than that of individual firms or governmental agencies, to say nothing of universities;

(2) that governmental agencies are no more committed to R & D, or to its basic research components than private corporations, each tending to regard such activities as merely one means of promoting its more fundamental objectives;

(3) that, although the R & D interests of governmental and private organisations overlap to some extent—mostly in respect to joint or cooperative undertakings—their largely disparate roles in the functioning of the U.S.A. economy tend to ensure substantial differentiation of their operational interests, with consequent limitations on the spillover from advances in one sector to the other; and

(4) that the continued expansion and diversification of private needs and public responsibilities combined with the continued unfolding of R & D potentials suggests that a variety of new policies and organisational forms will have to be explored by private, public and nonprofit

agencies to provide the larger array of differentiated innovative services likely to be required.

These hypotheses contest the common assumption in relevant economic analyses that 'the government' is inherently more deeply committed to technological progress and basic research than private industry, because the social benefits of such efforts may be expected to exceed what is privately appropriable [10; 126, pp. 483–97; 89, pp. 297–304; 4, pp. 616–619]. The relevance of such a proposition for the shaping of policies over the next fifty years or more depends, however, on: (a) how close we are to the point where privately appropriable benefits from technological innovations are recognisedly less than attendant private costs over major portions of the private sector of the economy; and (b) the extent to which the behaviour of actual governmental agencies is likely to coincide with theoretical conceptions of the bases for promoting the general welfare over the long run.

With respect to the first of these, frequent insinuations that we are close to, or already at such a point, are unsupported by any evidence whatever. Indeed, in view of the infant stage of our grasp of R & D processes and potentials—perhaps akin to the development of manufacturing seventy-five years ago—such gloomy forebodings about their imminent limitations would seem to border on the ludicrous. As for the second question, it takes little exploration of the literature of political theory and the history of governmental performance to indicate the enormous gulf between idealistic visions of unflagging devotion to the general welfare and the actual achievements of individual government agencies, and of entire 'administrations' for that matter, under the inescapable pressures of conflicting interest groups, limited funds, short-term performance criteria, the career interests of government officials and the frequent absence of policy guides which are scientifically authoritative and also politically appealing. (For a detailed illustration of the enormous power of such pressures even under mobilisation conditions, see [31, pp. 487–543].) Hard evidence shows that the government lagged far behind industry in pioneering and supporting technological progress and basic research over many decades preceding 1940; that its commitments since then have been far more narrowly concentrated than those of private industry; that resulting programmes have been overwhelmingly dominated by strongly mission-oriented objectives centring primarily around defence; that attendant allocations for basic research have been restricted to quite minor proportions of the total; and that much even of these meagre contributions seems to be more convincingly attributable to the government's concern with producing more scientists and engineers, and to its statutory responsibilities for supporting higher education, than to any generalised dedication to advancing all frontiers of knowledge in the hope of eventual social benefits of some kind.*

The foregoing obviously does not imply that government agencies are incapable of making major contributions to basic research and technological progress. On the contrary, growing awareness of these needs in our culture has helped to stimulate (and to enable) such agencies to follow the earlier lead of industry in seeking to harness R & D potentials on an increasing scale; and there is every reason to expect comparably rewarding results. But sound policies to promote the general welfare through enhancing technological progress and basic research must encompass both the vast unmet needs still to be found within the public sector and the seemingly limitless possibilities in the private sector—indicating the necessity of making the most of all sources of contributions.

Another implication of these hypotheses is that effective utilisation of the limited resources available to further basic research and technological progress will require tougher appraisals of the strengths and limitations of each of the major contributors. For example, while private firms are likely to have their innovational horizons limited by the pattern of expected or hoped-for profit, government agencies may have their horizons limited by the relative popularity of, or political support of, alternatives; and even universities seem to have horizons which are responsive to the grant-generating or fame-promising potentials of different lines of exploration.

Although the uncertainty of innovational outcomes tends to be discouraging to all who undertake them, its effects on the optimality of allocations may be distorted by the divergent impacts of expenditures on projects which turn out unsuccessfully: in private industry, they represent outright losses which may be justifiable but only within specified limits; in universities, they involve little or no financial burden because such projects are usually supported by outside funds or by the unpaid extra efforts of faculty members; and in government agencies with operational responsibilities, it is not uncommon to find both the prospective beneficiaries of solutions and the representatives of the regions in which the funds were spent reacting by supporting renewed or even expanded allocations for such unsuccessful projects. Indeed, the point has been made that in many

* Recent Congressional hearings concerning the role of research and technology in the economy have elicited a wide array of data and judgments. For example, see Rubel [122, pp. 30–45], Bush [124, p. 1091] and Seaborg [122, p. 1100], Kistiakowsky [94, p. 1102], and Wiesner [124, p. 1106] and also the summary report of the House of Representatives Select Committee on Government Research [121, pp. 11, 26 and 34]. It is also interesting to note the report in *Business Week* (May 21, 1966, p. 109) that the pressure for fast practical results is so great in some government programmes as to concern even directors of industrial research programmes.

government projects (especially in defence and space) results are all that count and, therefore, that projects are adjudged successful on the basis of performance criteria, even when increases in cost would have characterised them as catastrophes within the private framework. Turning in still another direction, it would appear that private industry may be better staffed and organised than government agencies to convert new laboratory findings through to practical application, whereas universities usually have little or no capacity to do so. In short, these and other possible illustrations —including the relative degrees of stimulus from competition—would seem to suggest that comprehensive analyses along these lines might serve both to sidetrack further disputes about which single channel for innovational developments is best and to provide additional constructive bases for guiding such division of labour in the future [122, p. 35; 93, p. 113; 4, p. 624; 44, p. 626].

One remaining implication of the hypotheses is that R & D activities seem to be far more highly differentiated than had been expected—or even realised until recently—either by analysts seeking to generalise about the economic, organisational or psychological aspects of such activities, or by administrators seeking to integrate such groups into existing corporate structures. As a result, the spillover of technological advances has been surprisingly limited both among industries and between the defence programmes and civilian manufacturing. And questions have also been asked about the effectiveness with which findings in university laboratories have been digested and utilised by industry [118, p. 214; 122, pp. 30, 34–35, 43; 124, pp. 1, 227]. Another result has been the increasing need by all but the largest laboratories for help in coming effectively to grips with problems bearing upon, but technically outside, the firm's relatively narrow areas of specialisation. Such developments may be regarded as reflecting the need for new forms of organisations to serve as intermediate nodes (containing specialised knowledge and offering specialised services) in networks which interconnect private corporations, government agencies and universities [15, pp. 38–41; 47, pp. 242–3; 44, p. 626; 43; 124, pp. 1085, 1088; 125, pp. 642–51; 107, p. 372; 35, pp. 128–138]. Responses may include not only the proliferation of nonprofit organisations like the Mellon Institute and the Battelle Institute as well as research-oriented consulting firms like Arthur D. Little, Inc. and the Stanford Research Institute, but the pioneering of new kinds of co-operative (or jointly sponsored) organisations supported by industry and the government, by industry and universities, and by the universities and the government. In addition, industrywide research may be reinvigorated; interuniversity groups may grow in numbers; and new undertakings at the municipal and state government levels may also take root.

The point to be emphasised is that efforts to choose among the forms which have emerged during the past twenty years of groping, or to design 'optimal' arrangements on the basis of the relatively limited and highly differentiated experiences encompassed to date, may prove far less useful than seeking to determine current pressures for change, to identify needs not being met, and to assess the nature of difficulties emerging in R & D organisations which are growing in size and which are gradually expanding their spheres of service. Similarly, efforts to increase spillover may well benefit less from recent emphases on multiplying communication channels through publications and conferences than from bridging the gap between the mutually alien problems, skills, facilities and expertise of different industries through new organisations committed to becoming expert enough in the characteristics of several to actively assist in making such transfers. For example, such intermediaries may facilitate the transformation of steel and aluminium companies into a more broadly oriented materials engineering industry.

10.10 ON EXTRA-QUANTITATIVE GUIDES TO MANAGERIAL ALLOCATION DECISIONS

Widespread empirical evidence that rigorous quantitative models play only a minor role in managerial decisions relating to major innovations and other investments suggests that redoubled efforts to convert 'the heathen' may be less rewarding than trying to learn how executives supplement (or surmount) inadequate analytical guides and data in making decisions involving large sums and possibly severe penalties. Instead of urging the bumble bee to reshape itself and stop flouting prevailing notions of aerodynamics, more attention might be given to studying executive bumble bees in the process of coping with problems reaching beyond the restricted boundaries of available normative models. Pioneering along these lines has already been initiated by Simon and his associates, yielding valuable idiosyncratic models of the criteria and evaluative processes used by executives in making certain actual operating decisions [76, 21]. In order to comprehend broader policy decisions, however, such as are involved in adopting major innovational programmes, or in major extensions of the scope and scale of R & D, it may prove necessary to explore the determinants of changes in the structure of top management's values and supporting behaviour patterns, which underlies all major decisions.

Accordingly, one may inquire how changes are induced in top management's conceptions: of acceptable trade-offs between current profits rates, longer term growth prospects and other desiderata; of acceptable levels of risk; and of minimum acceptable responses to innovational pressures. And in respect to R & D in particular, another set of inquiries might probe into how changes are induced in top management's conceptions: of the kinds of contributions to be expected realistically of such programmes; of the length of time needed to evaluate resulting performance; and of the desired degree of boldness in research targets, perhaps as represented by changes in acceptable rates of project failures.

Such foci obviously illustrate the values by which top management makes major decisions. Hence, field studies which penetrate these decision-making foundations are likely to prove necessary to increase our understanding of responses not only to available and potential technological innovations, but also to a wide range of other major allocational issues.

10.11 CONCLUDING OBSERVATIONS

1. Although a number of valuable contributions have already been made, studies of the sources, effects and means of guiding technological innovations are still very rudimentary.

2. It is not surprising that the concepts and tools borrowed from other areas of study in order to fill the initial void have proved quite inadequate; nor that the harvest of our first fragmentary studies still resembles a bramble bush of conflicting observations and insights.

3. Although, to paraphrase Carl Sandburg, we academics have always tended to be nervously loquacious in the face of the unknown, there seems to be no reason to doubt that increasing research, especially with an enriched mixture of field studies, will soon yield more useful analytical models for dealing with at least some of the variety of already discernible problem foci.

4. It may also be worth emphasising, however, that R & D is itself in such an early stage of development that analysis must be focused on its changing patterns of growth as well as on the relative efficiency of different policies and organisational arrangements at any given time—thus urging increased study of the problems and adjustment experiences of laggard companies and industries as well as of the leaders.

11 Industry Growth Patterns: Theory and Empirical Results

Efforts to develop an effective theory of economic growth seem to be yielding progressively more meagre results in recent years. That this may reflect the limitations of continued concentration at the level of entire economies is suggested by mounting evidence that input–output and other economic relationships may differ significantly among major sectors of production and distribution. Resulting national statistical aggregates would then represent only the passive resultant of disparate changes among such components. Growth studies may accordingly be enriched by seeking to develop models which encompass the adjustment patterns of products, firms, industries and regions as well as their interactions in shaping changes at higher levels of aggregation. By way of supporting such efforts, this chapter will concentrate primarily on the growth patterns exhibited by industries, with only peripheral attention to exploring the growth patterns of firms and products.

11.1 EARLY FINDINGS

The search for uniformities in the growth patterns of individual industries rose to a peak nearly forty years ago in the explorations of Simon S. Kuznets [18] and in the subsequent comprehensive work of Arthur F. Burns [4]. Partly because of the widespread acceptance of these results and attendant explanations of their inevitability, and partly because of the compelling attractions of other economic problems, little additional work was done in this area for an extended period [9]. Recent portents of a revival of interest stem from three sources: the growing output of long-term forecasts for individual industries, which invites a search for generalisations; efforts to reinvigorate research and theory relating to economic growth by probing the behaviour of disaggregated sectors; and the combination of these approaches involved both in planning resource allocations in under-developed nations and in appraising the adequacy of resources for future growth in advanced economies [20].

9+   247

The following discussion will review Burns's expectations and compare them with actual results over the following 25 years as a basis for: suggesting revisions in the interpretation of his original findings; outlining needed modifications in the theory as well as the pattern of industrial growth paths; and exploring the possibility of developing expectations • covering the growth patterns of individual commodities and firms.

Burns's findings consisted of a few elegantly simple generalisations set within a larger framework of carefully developed qualifications and limitations. His basic generalisation in respect to the long-term growth pattern of individual industries was that 'an industry tends to grow at a declining rate, its rise being eventually followed by a decline' [4, pp. 171–3]. As a corollary, he attacked two alternative views: arguing that 'the conception of indefinite growth of industries can neither be supported by analysis nor by experience'; and also asserting that there is neither sound rational basis nor empirical evidence for 'the notion that industries grow until they approximate some maximum size and then maintain a stationary position for an indefinite period . . . once an industry has ceased to advance, . . . (it) soon embarks on a career of decadence' [4, p. 170].

This conclusion was based on a study of 104 continuous series beginning between 1870 and 1885, of which 92 showed retardation, and of 43 supplementary discontinuous series, of which 38 showed retardation. The basic technique involved fitting a 'logarithmic' parabola $\Big(\text{Log } y = c + (\log A)x$

$+ \dfrac{(\log B)}{2} x^2, [3, \text{ p. } 97]\Big)$ to decade rates of growth centred on every fifth year, although additional modifications were introduced to minimise the effect of cycles and of certain extraordinary adjustments. No specific equations are given for individual industries, but his monograph presents the following for each series: average annual rate of growth for 1885–1929 or longer; variability of 'decade growth rates'—using the average growth rate for each decade; average rate of retardation (per cent per decade); and the stage of retardation (as measured by the date of the maximum point of the fitted parabola relative to 1930 as a common reference point).

Such impressive evidence led to widespread acceptance of his resulting generalisations. But Burns's own extended exposure to the complexities of detailed production patterns led him to emphasise a variety of limitations which have, nevertheless, been widely neglected—perhaps because they tend to undermine both the clarity of the basic finding and the possibilities of applying it. Specifically, he warned that the progressive retardation of growth rates need not be manifested during an industry's 'precommercial stage' nor in the stage of 'late decadence'; that it need not hold for the secular trends of even established industries, 'though it does hold for their primary trends, which are movements of longer duration than secular trends'; and that it will hold before and after 'a structural change', but not for the period as a whole during which such a change took place [4, p. 172]. The first of these presents minor problems compared with the second, in view of Burns's statement that, 'While secular trend, as we have defined it, can be measured with a fair degree of precision the primary trend cannot. There is considerable latitude for judgment in choosing a curve to represent the primary trend . . .' [4, p. 45]. Analytically, however, the most troublesome limitation is the attempt to exclude the effects of structural changes by stipulating, 'when as a result of a structural change, a progressive industry is invigorated or a senescent industry rejuvenated, the rule of retardation . . . may not hold for a period overlapping the (before and after states)' [4, p. 172].

In order to determine whether retardation should apply or not, obviously one needs carefully defined independent criteria of structural changes. In the absence of these, there is clearly opportunity for selective reinforcement of the basic thesis by including all cases which exhibit retardation, without bothering to explore whether any structural changes had been experienced, and by excluding all cases which do not exhibit retardation through attributing non-conformance to presumed structural changes.

And there are hints of additional complications as well. Although the study is focused on the development of individual industries as reflected by secular changes in the volume of productive activity [4, p. 9], one brief comment recognises that 'industry . . . does not have a uniform signification, since series differ appreciably in the degree of generality of their industrial reference' [4, pp. 15–16]; and another acknowledges some weaknesses in measuring output, 'our data are expressed in units which are inconstant over time . . . although changes in the qualitative characteristics of the units are generally very gradual' [4, p. 9]. The limited scope of uniformity in growth patterns is highlighted by Burns's observation that, 'irrespective of the number of stages of industrial development that may be distinguished, or how they may be defined, given stages will be found to differ in duration and intensity from industry to industry, as will the relative durations of the several stages' [4, p. 172]. Moreover, he even warns of the restricted applicability of the trend pattern used in his own study, 'If we had complete records of the life histories of many industries, we would almost certainly find that a logarithmic parabola could describe accurately the entire development of very few industries, and that any other single mathematical curve would serve the task just as badly' [4, p. 171]. Resting such scepticism on the grounds that virtually all research has been limited to data covering 'mere segments of the histories of industries, and almost exclusively (the) progressive segments at that' [4,

p. 171], opens the way to two further difficulties: the possibility of dismissing nonconforming growth patterns as representing merely transitional deviance (i.e. pending the availability of fuller information); and the possibility that his own findings might not remain applicable, for they too are based on only a limited segment of the past.

Thus, Burns's starkly simple though widely based findings were rooted in an impressive matrix of searching questions which will continue to offer valuable guides to new research even if his empirical results should be subject to modification. His monograph has commanded widespread acceptance since its publication and its continued influence may be illustrated by the following:

'We are not surprised to find evidence of retardation in the output of virtually all established industries making a relatively narrow range of products. In *Production Trends in the U.S. Since 1870*, Arthur F. Burns amply demonstrated this retardation to be a characteristic of a progressive economy' [25].

'To me, the book (Burns's *Production Trends . . .*) holds a magnificent portrayal of the dynamic growth of industrial America, implying an intricate theoretical structure' [26].

'Arthur F. Burns has established a marked tendency towards retardation in the growth of individual industries' [1].

'The problem of retardation in economic progress was explored by Arthur F. Burns in . . . 1934. This study has become a classic, and not much can be added to its findings . . . A declining rate of growth after a certain point is the general law in individual industries, just as it is in organic growth' [27, 3a].

' . . . exhaustion of the possibilities of innovation contributes to the maturing and eventual decline of (an) industry. Kuznets and Burns used this line of reasoning in their explanations of retardation in the rates of growth of individual industries, and I think they were right to do so' [8].

II.2 LATER EMPIRICAL PERSPECTIVES

The results to be reported now are based on extensions of 35 of Burns's 104 series from his terminal date of 1929 to the mid-1950s [24]. Such coverage is more significant than it seems because, as shown in the Appendix, only 74 of Burns's series represent actual production rather than imports, consumption, financial values or other trade indicators; and also because even these 74 include some quite minor economic sectors (e.g. raisins, flaxseed, non-Portland cements, whaling, antimonial lead, nails and traffic on the Erie and Saulte Ste. Marie canals). All series are identical with those used by Burns except where revised (mostly in the case of agricultural series) by the authorities responsible for the original series.

Efforts to characterise the 'basic' or 'underlying' shape of intricately varying statistical series are subject to recognised technical difficulties as well as to aesthetic preferences. Edwin Frickey long ago outlined some of the uneasy compromises to be made: increasing the closeness of fit against retaining essentially simple curves; seeking to express the central tendency—or average or net interaction of all counter pressures—of the series against highlighting its dominant thrust; seeking to portray the effects of particular causes against separating the components representing different time periods. And he also went on to present his provocative display of the twenty-three different mathematically fitted secular trends which have been applied to pig iron production between 1875 and 1932 [10].

The primary purpose of this analysis is not to seek means of surmounting such problems, but rather to explore the perspectives on Burns's basic hypotheses provided by an additional twenty-five years of experience. For this purpose, it will suffice to rely on simple determinations of whether earlier evidences of retardation have been reinforced during succeeding decades and, if not, whether the earlier evidences might themselves have been subject to alternative interpretations. Accordingly, all series were charted on semi-log paper and long-term trends were then fitted by least-squares technique or 'method of linear linkages'. It should be emphasised that none of Burns's adjustments were made to the original data, either to remove cycles or for other purposes, thereby avoiding a source of controversy [6, 7, 28, 5], but also tending to increase the standard error of slope parameters (especially as trends approximate the horizontal) in proportion to the average amplitude of the cycles in each series. Resulting individual adjustment patterns are summarised in the following tables.

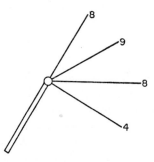

Fig. 11.1   Simplified summary of industry growth patterns

TABLE 11.1   Simplified representations of individual series growth
patterns (from Table 11.5)

Simplified Pattern	Frequency	Industries and year of curve's starting point or inflection points
	8	Petroleum ('85), Tobacco, raw ('85), Cigarettes ('85), Cattle ('90), Hogs ('90), Aluminium ('95), Natural Gas ('95), and Barley ('02)
	9	Wheat ('97), Potatoes ('04), Iron Ore ('05), Coke ('05), Pig Iron ('05), Steel ('05), Rolled Steel ('05), Beet Sugar ('05), and Railway ton-miles ('05)
	2	Corn ('05, '40), and Rice ('16, '35)
	5	Cotton ('11), Oats ('12), Copper ('16), Bitumin Coal ('18), and Total Coal ('18)
	1	Fish Total ('28, '37)
	4	Buckwheat ('05), Coal, anth. ('17), Rye ('22), and Sheep ('43)
	1	Lead ('28, '37)
	1	Railway, passenger-miles ('20, '44)
	1	Cane Sugar ('04, '26)
	1	Wool ('25, '31, '43)
	1	Vessels ('20, '43)
	1	Mercury ('76, '16, '43)

Actual data and fitted trend lines are shown in the attached semi-log charts
of individual industry output. Parameters may differ widely, of course,
among industries with similarly shaped growth patterns, as shown in Table
11.5.

Table 11.1 summarises the relatively simple trend patterns which were
fitted to the original data as presented in the four panels, Figure 11.4 on pp.
270–3. These seem to lie within the reasonable range of aesthetic discretion
as well as within the zones of reasonable fit, as shown in Table 11.5 on
pp. 267–8, although no insurmountable arguments can be adduced in favour
of this approach. Four patterns account for 28 of the 35 cases. Undiminished growth rates for at least 50–70 years account for eight series (barley,

raw tobacco, hogs, cattle, petroleum, natural gas, aluminium and cigarettes). Nine more series can be represented by two linear segments indicating rapid growth followed by slower growth, but with the latter continuing at an undiminished rate for at least fifty years (wheat, potatoes, beet sugar, railway ton-miles, iron ore, coke, pig iron, steel and rolled steel products). Another eight series reflect extended periods of stable production at peak levels: cotton, oats, copper, bituminous coal and total coal followed essentially horizontal trends after 1911–18; corn's trend was horizontal for thirty-five years before turning upward in 1940; rice had a horizontal trend from 1919 to 1935 before likewise turning upward; and total fish levelled off in 1936 after growing slowly up to 1928 and then rising sharply over the next eight years. Growth to a peak followed by a declining trend—which most nearly approximates the full pattern envisioned by Burns—was exhibited by only four series (buckwheat, anthracite coal, rye and sheep). Most of the six remaining cases display more complex combinations, including sharp reversals from decreases to increases in four (railway passenger-miles, cane sugar, mercury and vessels). The four leading patterns are summarised in Figure 11.1.

Infrequent agreement with Burns's expected development path is but one finding based on Table 11.1. Another is that post-1929 trends were continuations of those which current hindsight suggests had been in effect for significant lengths of time prior to 1929: for at least twenty-five years in eighteen cases and for more than ten years in another seven cases. This does not imply that Burns's interpretation of trends was erroneous at the time of his analysis. It does emphasise, however, the amorphous nature even of apparently well established trends in time series—a wide range of trend alternatives lying undiscerned beneath the seemingly prevailing pattern pending delineation by later data.

Further evidence of deviations from the expectations yielded by Burns's analysis is provided by Table 11.2, which compares the year in which the logarithmic parabola fitted by Burns reached its maximum and actual production peaks up to 1955. What makes these findings especially disconcerting is not merely that the actual peak was within plus or minus ten years of the estimated peak in only eight of the twenty-eight cases in which such comparisons could be made (the other seven had estimated peaks beyond 1950). Rather, it is the unexpected finding that the proportion of estimated peaks which fell within this twenty year range was not substantially higher for successively earlier decades. Thus, the estimated peak was within ten years of the actual peak in only one out of two or three cases for peaks expected to have occurred prior to 1900 as well as between 1900 and 1909 and between 1910 and 1919—with actual peaks deviating from these estimates by twenty-six to fifty years despite the

TABLE 11.2   Comparison of estimated and actual year of peak output for individual series (from Table 11.6)

Year of estimated peak	Number of cases	Gap between estimated and actual peak year so far			
		No. less than ten years	No. more than ten years	Number uncertain	Size of gap when greater than ten years
Pre-1900	2	1	1	0	(49)
1900-09	2	1	1	0	(50)
1910-19	3	1	2	0	(26) (33)
1920-29	11	1	10	0	(15) (17) (20) (22) (22) (24) (24) (26) (32) (32)
1930-39	5	2	3	0	(15) (15) (23)
1940-49	5	2	3	0	(12) (12) (12)
Post-50	7	0	0	7	

From Table 11.6. The estimated peak represents the year in which the logarithmic parabola fitted by Burns reached its maximum (A. F. Burns, *Production Trends in the U.S. Since 1870* (N.Y., National Bureau of Economic Research, 1934, Tables 22-5).

TABLE 11.3   Number of successive all-time peaks separated by significant intervening declines (from Table 11.6)

No. of peaks	No. of cases
1	3
2	7
3	4
4	11
5	9
6	1

tremendous experiential basis for making such appraisals after 1930. It is less surprising that only one of the eleven estimated peaks expected to fall between 1920 and 1929 came within ten years of the actual peaks in view of the more limited perspectives for evaluating comparatively recent developments. But this pattern of declining accuracy was reversed again, for peaks estimated to occur between 1930 and 1939 and between 1940 and 1949 proved to be within ten years of the actual peak about as often as during the periods prior to 1920: two cases out of five in each of these later decades.

Perhaps the most provocative findings, however, are those in Table 11.3. These reveal that, by 1955, twenty-five of the thirty-five series had experienced at least three successive all-time peaks separated by significant intervening declines—and twenty-one had experienced at least four. It is quite conceivable, therefore, that contemporary analysts might have found quite satisfactory evidence for predicting the continuation of apparent senescence on each of these occasions—each time casually extending the upward trend past the earlier peak and decline to the new heights reached thereafter, but unable to envision repeated extensions of the process in the future. Hazarding new forecasts in this area on the basis of such discouraging results is bound to be a trying experience. And this is especially true because errors can be made about current series by overestimating as well as underestimating the period and rate of continued growth, whereas errors about peaks presumed to have occurred in the past can be in only one direction.

The findings in Table 11.3 also raise questions about the practical usefulness of Burns's unquestionably sound warnings about structural changes. It seems probable that one could identify at least one and perhaps several changes affecting inputs, or production processes, or product characteristics, or market levels and competition in each period when such earlier continuous declines were so gloriously reversed. And yet, Burns's trends were fitted over repeated experiences of this kind in most of the series examined in this paper. Moreover, many of these structural changes may also have occurred during periods not characterised by spectacular deviations from past production trends. Hence, a workable strategy for dealing with 'structural changes' in estimating long-term trends in production is not easily formulated or justified.

In short, such findings deviate from Burns's most widely remembered conclusions in three ways: by showing that progressive retardation may be far less pervasive than had been suggested by his comprehensive coverage of an earlier period; by demonstrating that undiminished rates of growth for individual series may be more frequent and persist for longer periods than he—or any other economist who comes to mind—considered likely; and by revealing that even horizontal trends may continue for long periods in a significant number of industries. Further indications of the wide disparities between Burns's estimated growth patterns and those found in this paper are presented in Table 11.5 on pp. 267–8, which compares the slopes (with confidence limits) of our linear linkages with the rates of change derived from our attempted approximations of Burns's unpublished equations. On the other hand, these results also tend to reinforce some of his less well remembered, but even more fundamental, hypotheses about industrial growth processes: that any simple mathematical curve, including the logarithmic parabola, is likely to fit very few industries closely; and that detailed growth paths are likely to vary widely among industries. The results in Table 11.2 also underline the soundness of his warning that trend

9*

lines fitted to particular historical series represent generalisations about that period rather than predictions about future periods [4, p. 102].

An even more recent study, covering annual physical output through 1966 of seventeen major industries, similarly failed to support the universal applicability either of Kuznets's and Burns's expectations of progressive retardation after an early period of rapid growth or Gaston's expectation of universally applicable Gompertz curves [11].* Instead, the summary of growth patterns found tends rather to parallel those presented in Figure 11.1: with 'undiminished growth rates for sixty-five years in five industries and for forty years in a sixth; rapid growth followed by a slower growth rate which has, however, remained steady for at least twenty years in six more industries; and a rapid growth rate followed by a horizontal trend for thirty to fifty years in three more cases [13, p. 152]. It may be of interest to add that the findings of this study also tend to cast doubt on certain other frequently expressed expectations. For example, newer industries need not offer more rapid growth than many older ones; raw material industries need not be slower growing than those engaged in manufacturing; nor can such consistent differences be found between capital and consumer-oriented industries' [13, pp. 152–3].

11.3 SOME BROADER IMPLICATIONS

One of the direct implications of these results would seem to concern the validity of Burns's accompanying structure of explanatory hypotheses. Those selected for emphasis in Wesley C. Mitchell's summary may be stated in the form of the following propositions [4, pp. xvi–xvii]:

(1) that the introduction of new commodities restricts increases in the demand for old ones;
(2) the faster the early growth, the harder it is to sustain such rates for long;
(3) technological progress in one industry causes retardation in competing industries;
(4) reclamation of raw materials limits increases in demand for fresh production;
(5) new industries attract resources from older industries, thus limiting the latter's growth;

* Industries covered: cement, steel, glass, coal, natural gas, petroleum, manufactured gas, electricity, cigarettes, cigars, metal cans, autos, airlines, bus lines, truck lines and oil pipelines. The last four series covered thirty-six to forty years; all of the others covered sixty to seventy-five years. For details, see [13].

(6) progressive consumption of natural resources forces increasing resort to inferior resources;

(7) the rate of technical progress tends to abate as an industry grows older because of declining possibilities for major new advances; and

(8) protective efforts of industries experiencing retardation—e.g. increased salesmanship and research—tend to limit the expansion of their competitors.

It should be recognised, however, that Burns did not test these propositions empirically, although he did introduce interesting illustrations. Hence, neither his finding of pervasive retardation nor the essentially different findings just presented have any direct bearing on the validity of these propositions.

Serious attention to these hypotheses is merited, nevertheless, because they constitute a pioneering effort to establish some analytical foundations for the theory of growth of individual industries. Even if one suggests flaws in such propositions, or calls attention to unstated assumptions underlying them, or detects possible conflicts between them, or demonstrates the incompleteness of Burns's framework, resulting advances in the development of industry growth theory will rest on these very foundations. Thus one may argue with respect to (1) above that some new commodities may replace one another while old commodities continue to enjoy active demand; and also that, in an expanding economy, the new is not restricted to growth at the expense of the old. Although (2) is a mathematical truism, as Burns says, it clearly does not follow that the inability to maintain early growth rates necessitates continuously declining growth rates. With respect to (3), alternative views might suggest that many technological advances may expand factor and product market potentials, while others may induce comparable advances by competitors. Then, again, (4) would seem to offset some of the burdens associated with (6); and (5) and (8) would seem to rest on the same assumption of static conditions as (1), instead of being considered as possible generators of increased supplies of needed inputs. Finally, (7) has such an air of archaicism as to discourage serious consideration. Yet each of these comments merely emphasises the need to clarify the concepts involved and to develop objective bases for evaluating such influences.

A more general critique might emphasise that such propositions seem rooted in the acceptance of inevitable retardation for the economy as a whole—not only because this concept seems recognisable in several of the individual propositions, but because such an outcome seems to be the inescapable result of all the propositions combined. Yet, one of Burns's outstanding conclusions is contrary to this: asserting that the decline of individual industries goes hand in hand with the growth of the general economy—and he took this position during a period when few economists would have considered it true or even likely. Hence, the major implications for Burns's hypotheses of the widespread discrepancy between his empirical findings and those presented above are: that he has not adequately covered the factors tending to delay or prevent retardation in individual industries (including the reverse effects of some of the forces mentioned in the above propositions); and that he has also underestimated their influence on the outcome—both having presumably been encouraged by the overwhelming one-sidedness of his statistical results.

Closer examination of the nature of Burns's data also leads to some important implications. Because almost all of his series relate to quite narrow product categories, it would follow that his findings of pervasive tendencies towards retardation really referred to individual products rather than individual industries [12] and, hence, that all of his associated hypotheses about stages of growth and about the factors promoting retardation might likewise have greater relevance to individual products. But this would also imply that the growth paths of industries would merely be some weighted average of the growth paths of their individual products. And, since industries need not have any fixed number of products, it would seem to follow that individual industries might have widely differing growth paths depending on the extent to which the contributions of rapidly growing new products offset or fall short of the decreasing contributions of products facing waning demand, whether due to age or any other reason. Such reasoning, which is analogous to the relationship that Burns saw between national output and the output of individual industries, would lead to the view that the basic growth entity is the individual product rather than individual industries.

There is nothing in Burns's monograph to imply acceptance of such a transformation in his basic focus. But one comment: 'it is possibly of some significance that industries engaged in the production of rather specific commodities show often the highest rates of retardation' [4, p. 173] suggests that single product industries might have been considered purer examples of his prototype of industries in general than the complex multi-product processing and manufacturing industries which were almost entirely absent from his study (with a few exceptions such as rolled iron and steel). Stigler made a similar point in saying, 'We are not surprised to find evidence of retardation in the outputs of virtually all established industries making a relatively narrow range of products' [25, p. 26]. It should be emphasised, however, that all of the empirical findings which have been presented in this paper also relate to Burns's individual-product-dominated series. Hence, Burns's expectations are not widely supported even by such single product series, despite intuitive urging to the contrary. And the difficulties of analysis at the industry level are also intensified by the problems of effectively measuring physical output when the new products are being added and old ones dropped, when individual products are undergoing constant alterations in size, functions and quality, and when the relative volumes and prices of various products are subject to fluctuation.*

Attention should also be given to the implications of Burns's essential undertaking: to search for widely applicable, if not universal, patterns of change in economic activities such that the path of past adjustment over a period of time permits reasonably accurate forecasting of future segments of that path. This widely prevalent procedure may well continue to prove more successful in ballistics than in economics so long as the former is guided by a rigorous theory covering the physical forces involved, while the latter seems virtually devoid of supporting theories of the economic processes involved [15]; and so long as the former operates under unchanging conditions, while industrial groups intensify their efforts and mobilise new forces in actively fighting back against unfavourable pressures and prospects. Might it not be more precise to describe such an approach to economic prediction as backcasting rather than forecasting? Instead of moving forward from some past period through analytical evaluations of successive periods which lie ahead as a means of testing the framework for assessing alternative future paths, the process usually begins by looking backward to rationalise the 'average' path which led to the present and then projects this backward vision into the future. Not only is this philosophical principle of reverse destiny—what has been, will be—unappealing, but the shakiness of the pragmatic basis for this approach is attested by the wide deviations among past adjustment paths determined at successively earlier periods (as illustrated by the gross linear linkages used in this paper and by the still wider array of combinations which would result from using shorter linkages).

At any rate, are such efforts to delineate production paths designed to estimate what is likely to happen if the industry submits passively to whatever may befall, or to estimate the outcome regardless of the industry's counter measures? One can hardly rule out the possibility that adverse adjustments in profits or markets or factor supplies often engender the very reactions which tend to alter future adjustments. Indeed, it is conceivable that processes of this kind help to explain the dominance of growth patterns which seemed unlikely to Burns twenty-five years ago—

---

* But problems connected with the special purposes of this study should not be allowed to obscure the usefulness of the industry level of aggregation for many other forms of economic analysis [2].

thereby emphasising the need for fuller understanding of these potentials for altering past growth patterns and, hence, future expectations.

11.4 PRODUCTS AND FIRMS IN THE STRUCTURE OF ECONOMIC GROWTH

Perhaps the most fundamental question raised by the preceding discussion concerns the nature and relative influence of the growth forces and hindrances to be confronted at levels of aggregation above and below that represented by industries. Whether one is concerned with forecasting growth, or promoting it, or harnessing its prospective benefits—in the interest of enhancing profitability or the social welfare—such questions as the following emphasise major gaps in our knowledge. Do firms, industries and regions vie with one another merely to divide up the growth increments generated solely at the national level? Or is the growth of the total economy itself largely the by-product of natural resources discoveries, technological advances, new marketing techniques and other innovations generated within firms and industries? And, at the other extreme, to what extent is the growth of firms and industries merely derived from the forces of growth and decline exerted directly at the level of individual products?

As was noted earlier, most economic theorists have focused their analytical models of growth on the economy as a whole, seemingly implying that such forces are uniform throughout the economy, or that growth forces operating at lower levels of the economy are either unimportant or irrelevant. Within the past fifteen years, there has been increasing interest in growth models of subregions of national economies.* And even more recently, some evidences of concern with the analytical determinants of the growth of firms have appeared.†

Perhaps the continuing serious shortcomings of the national models is helping to redirect interest towards a fuller exploration of growth factors at other levels of aggregation in the structure of the economy. At any rate, the need is great, not only for economic theory, but for corporation executives and government officials whose decisions may prove to be more influential than is now recognised and whose bases for making strategic choices might benefit from analytical advances.

* The more limited attention given thus far to regional models is indicated roughly by a recent survey of economic theory covering both: Hahn and Mathews devoted 124 pages to aggregative growth models compared with Meyer's 31 pages covering regional models [15, 22].

† Economic studies with some bearing on the growth of firms include: Baumol [3], Hymer and Pashigian [16], Marris [21] and Penrose [23]. The only major studies encountered so far which are substantially concerned with the generalised growth patterns of a variety of products are those by Burns [4], Kuznets [18] and Gaston [11].

Some of the theoretical needs and empirical prospectives which may be opened up by such undertakings can be illustrated by summarising a recent study of the growth patterns of firms and products [13]. No formal theoretical models of the expected growth patterns of firms were found in the economics literature, but three hypotheses may be deduced from managerial expectations discussed in business publications:

(1) the growth pattern of the firm is dominated by that of its industry, except for short-term variations in market shares;
(2) the growth pattern of the firm is determined by those of its products, allowing for new products to offset declining growth in older products; and
(3) when faced by unfavourable prospects, the growth pattern of the firm is subject to successive increments through the acquisition of other firms.

Such formulations identify three different sources of influence and they may even reflect significant disparities in the experience of different sectors of business. But they are obviously too loose either to define meaningful alternatives or to permit rigorous testing.

To clarify the analytical issues involved, one may begin by noting that the growth in output of an industry or a firm must be identical with the growth in aggregate output of all of its products. However, this leaves unsettled the nature and relative influence of industry-wide pressures as compared with developments concentrated on particular products, and also leaves unclear the relative influence on individual product output of external market pressures as compared with intra-firm stimuli. Nor do these hypotheses say anything about the likelihood that new product output will offset declines in the output of older products, or about the costs and advantages of this course as compared with the acquisition of other firms. In short, these do not represent penetrating hypotheses so much as partial listings of factors which may prove relevant, leaving a largely uncultivated field for theoretical development.

Empirical findings based on the analysis of output data for 107 firms within sixteen industries (102 covering at least twenty years and 67 at least thirty years) [13] suggested the following hypotheses (Figure 11.2):

(1) that most industries seem to be characterised by strong 'gravitational' or 'tidal' forces as a result of which there is much less variation among their constituent firms in the *direction* of their movements than in their *rates*; (in other words, few firms seem to have declining trends when most are increasing and *vice versa*, but their rates of change tend to cover a wide range);

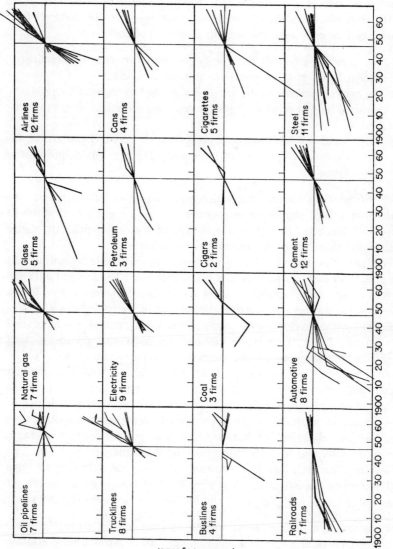

Fig. 11.2 Firm growth patterns by industry

(2) that the timing and direction of such increasing and decreasing trends seem to differ markedly among industries;

(3) that the differentiating pressures generated within individual industries seem to be substantially offset in their effects on the adjustment patterns of their constituent firms by the externally-imposed pressures of such national emergencies as the depression of the 1930s and the Second World War; and

(4) that the long-term adjustment patterns of individual firms seem to be more flexible than those found for industry aggregates: the former yielding shorter periods of stable growth rates and more frequent cases of reversals in direction [13, p. 153.]

Such preliminary soundings seem to reinforce expectations that growth pressures may be generated at various levels of aggregation and that their relative influences are subject to change. Thus (1) suggests that industry-wide forces have more pervasive effects on constituent firms in the short run than over longer periods; (2) suggests that industry patterns differ from one another in the short as well as the longer run; and (3) suggests that national, or supra-industry, forces are more powerful than differentiated industry forces during certain emergency periods. Finally, (4) raises the interesting question of the extent to which the greater stability of industry as compared with firm growth rates reflects the common effects of higher levels of aggregation or the greater consistency of industry-level growth forces (as against the pressures generated at the level of firms in the interest of gaining market advantages relative to their competitors).

With respect to the growth patterns of individual products, evidence was presented earlier which raised doubts about the universal applicability of Burns's progressive retardation model as well as of Gaston's Gompertz model. Nor is this surprising in view of the array of factors suggested by economic theory as affecting the prospective output of individual products, including the possible expansion of current markets through lower costs and prices, product improvements, increased population and incomes, as well as the creation of new markets through geographical extensions and the development of new uses for the product.

In the recent empirical study being cited, output series for fifty-eight product categories in seventeen industries, most covering forty years or more, were found to present a wider array of adjustment patterns than either individual firms or industries (Table 11.3). 'Of particular interest here are the patterns indicating that extended periods of no growth and even of declining input have been followed by renewed upsurges. It should also be emphasised that in the industries for which numerous product series could be obtained (steel (7), glass (9) and petroleum (11)), growth patterns were widely dissimilar—as illustrated in Figure 11.4(a). The latter suggests a far more complex managerial problem than is implied in the view that essentially similar life cycle patterns for each product need merely be

TABLE 11.4   Product growth patterns

Pattern	Total No.	Product identification
	12	Oil pipelines, Cement, Natural gas (residential, commercial, industrial), Steel sheets and strips, Steel plates, Electricity (residential, commercial and industrial), Asphalt, Window glass.
	15	Trucklines, Cans, Cigarettes, Autos (high, medium, and low priced), Airlines (freight, passenger, and mail), Petroleum (gas, distillate and still gas). Electricity (other public authorities).
	1	Glass beverage containers.
	7	Buslines, Coal, Railroad freight ton-miles, Steel bars, Wire rods, Petroleum lubricating oil, Glass polished plate.
	3	Street and highway lighting electricity, Petroleum wax, Petroleum coke.
	3	Cigars, Structural steel, Steel skelp.
	1	Kerosene.
	5	Manufactured gas (industrial, commercial and residential), Glass lamp chimneys.
	5	Railroad and railway electricity, Petroleum residual, Petroleum road oil, Glass tumblers, Glass tubing.
	1	Glass milk bottles.
	2	Railroad passenger-miles, Steel rails.
	1	Chewing and pipe tobacco.

superimposed upon one another with appropriate time lags, as shown in Figure 11.4(b). Indeed, our findings indicate that the commonly conceived life cycle pattern is applicable to few products in this sample [13, p. 154].

Three additional findings have a bearing on relative growth rates at different levels of aggregation. One fails to support the tendency

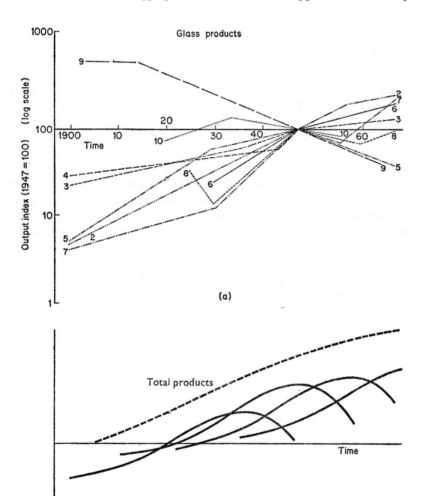

Fig. 11.3 Actual and speculative product growth patterns

found by others for market shares to be more unstable, or for company growth rates to vary more widely, in rapidly growing than in slowly growing industries [14, 16, 17]. The second indicates that product growth patterns in multi-product industries tend to be more variable than firm growth patterns, which tend in turn to be more variable than industry growth patterns. In addition, the analysis found that, 'contrary to the myth that loss of market share over extended periods tends to impair recovery permanently, shifts in relative growth rates among major companies are common and frequently reversed' [13, p. 155].

And a final stimulus to theoretical work, as well as to the reconsideration of widespread managerial beliefs, is provided by the finding of 'little or no consistent relationship between the average growth rates and the average rates of profit after taxes on total investment' over the extended periods studied. Nor were the faster-growing firms (i.e., those increasing their market shares) found to have achieved relatively higher profit rates.

Perhaps it should be re-emphasised before closing that the material in this final section has been presented not because of any certainty about the empirical findings—exploratory studies rarely warrant this—but in order to illustrate the interesting perspectives which may be uncovered and to indicate their potential value for broadening understanding of the structure of economic growth by economic analysts and by decision makers.

TABLE 11.5 Rates of change of fitted linear linkages and of Burns's log parabolas

| Series | Period | Linear linkages[1] | | Burns's estimates[2] | |
		Slope	95% confidence limits	Begin-ning	End
Petroleum	85–51	3·19	3·33 3·05	7·19	5·11
Cigarettes	85–55	4·07	4·25 3·89	*	*
Tobacco, raw	85–55	0·77	0·84 0·69	2·31	0·33
Cattle	90–52	0·68	0·76 0·61	6·00	−4·36
Hogs	90–52	0·60	0·70 0·50	3·05	0·60
Natural gas	95–55	2·83	2·92 2·74	10·72	−2·51
Aluminium	95–55	4·30	4·62 3·98	42·52	−31·53
Barley	02–55	0·65	0·83 0·47	3·50	−0·42
Wheat	70–97	1·19	1·50 0·88	2·79	1·52
	97–55	0·39	0·51 0·28	1·52	−1·49
Potatoes	70–04	1·06	1·29 0·83	4·01	1·49
	05–55	0·16	0·25 0·07	1·49	−2·02
Iron ore	80–05	2·88	3·29 2·47	9·86	4·71
	05–55	0·60	0·98 0·21	4·71	−4·87
Coke	80–05	3·66	4·01 3·31	11·52	5·48
	05–51	0·57	0·83 0·31	5·48	−4·56
Pig iron	70–05	3·11	3·35 2·87	9·21	4·69
	05–51	0·61	0·98 0·25	4·69	−0·84
Steel	72–05	6·01	6·59 5·43	20·54	8·66
	05–52	1·17	1·47 0·87	8·66	−7·01
Rolled steel	85–05	3·00	3·57 2·43	6·00	4·52
	05–55	1·16	1·43 0·89	4·52	0·92
Beet sugar	92–05	11·30	12·98 9·62	20·54	14·44
	05–55	1·11	1·28 0·94	14·44	−3·73
Railway ton-miles	70–05	3·17	3·32 3·02	10·69	5·36
	05–51	0·86	1·09 0·64	5·36	−1·12
Rice	16–35	0·05	0·51 −0·41	4·42	3·59
	35–55	2·38	2·64 2·12	3·59	2·76
Corn	70–05	1·07	1·28 0·86	4·73	1·11
	05–40	−0·28	−0·07 −0·49	1·11	−2·38
	40–55	0·51	1·01 0·01	−2·38	−3·84
Fish	80–28	0·47	0·52 0·41	1·95	1·44
	28–37	2·98	4·47 1·49	1·44	1·34
	37–52	0·18	0·51 −0·16	1·34	1·24
Cotton	70–11	1·45	1·60 1·30	5·09	1·78
	11–54	0·01	0·22 −0·20	1·78	−1·83
Oats	70–12	0·14	0·33 −0·05	6·61	1·58
	12–55	0·06	0·26 0·15	1·58	−3·79
Bituminous coal	70–18	3·05	3·18 2·92	10·68	2·12
	18–55	0·01	0·23 −0·22	2·12	−3·49
Total coal	70–18	2·60	2·70 2·50	9·13	1·71
	18–54	−0·06	0·12 −0·31	1·71	−3·19

Footnotes on next page.

10

TABLE 11.5 (*continued*)

Series	Period	Linear linkages[1]			Burns's estimates[2]	
		Slope	95% confidence limits		Begin-ning	End
Copper	70–16	4·23	4·48	3·98	15·04	4·09
	16–55	0·41	0·91	−0·10	4·09	−4·78
Buckwheat	70–05	0·51	0·69	0·32	3·83	−0·11
	05–55	−1·43	−1·19	−1·67	−0·11	−5·43
Anthracite coal	70–17	1·51	1·63	1·39	6·69	0·14
	17–54	−0·99	−0·77	−1·21	0·14	−5·35
Rye	70–22	1·06	1·21	0·91	5·00	0·36
	22–55	−1·32	−0·79	−1·85	0·36	−2·76
Sheep	80–43	1·02	1·98	0·06	9·86	2·24
	43–52	−4·08	−2·93	−5·23	2·24	1·11
Lead	70–28	2·16	2·36	1·96	10·70	0·49
	28–37	−2·90	0·66	−6·46	0·49	−0·32
	37–51	−0·19	0·60	−0·98	−0·32	−2·70
Railway passenger-miles	82–20	2·03	2·15	1·91	6·62	1·18
	20–32	−2·39	−1·66	−3·12	1·18	−0·78
	32–44	5·64	7·93	3·35	−0·78	−2·07
	44–51	−7·43	−4·93	−9·93	−2·07	−2·71
Cane sugar	75–08	2·09	2·47	1·71	8·25	−1·97
	08–27	−3·21	−1·71	−4·71	−1·97	−6·06
	28–55	1·75	2·24	1·26	−6·06	−13·73
Wool	85–25	0·02	0·11	−0·07	2·52	−0·72
	25–31	2·78	2·95	2·61	−0·72	−1·12
	31–43	0·15	0·34	−0·04	−1·12	−2·30
	43–50	−3·94	−3·45	−4·43	−2·30	−3·08

[1] Slope of line fitted by least squares to *unadjusted* actual data, expressed as average annual percentage rate of change. For graph of original data as well as these trend lines, see Fig. 11.4. Note that omission of adjustments for cycles and certain extreme data tend to increase the dispersion around our trend lines in proportion to the amplitude of the cycles in individual series and hence to broaden the confidence limits relative to the slope magnitudes especially for slopes approximating the horizontal.

[2] These were determined as follows: (a) Burns determined the average annual rate of change per decade—for decades with successive five-year overlaps—after adjusting the actual data in each series to remove cycles and certain extreme values; (b) he then fitted a log parabola to these rates of change and used the equation (not published) to estimate both the year when this equation would reach a maximum and its average rate of retardation; (c) these findings were published and hence were used to define the parameters of our approximation to his log parabola for each series; (d) this surrogate equation was then used to estimate the average annual rates of change per decade for every fifth year in Burns's unpublished equation; and (e) the rates in the above table are for the decade mid-point closest to the beginning and end of the period specified for each line.

* Average annual rate of growth (1880–1929) was 11·6 per cent. Rate of growth was increasing, i.e. retardation rate was slightly negative (0·3 per cent per decade).

TABLE 11.6 Timing of production peaks

	Burns's estimate	Actual	Prior peaks
	(1)	(2)	(3)
Petroleum	2116	1955+	
Cigarettes	No Max.	1952	96
Tobacco, raw	1966	1951	20, 31
Cattle	1924	1947	10, 18, 36
Hogs	1965	1944	90, 01, 08, 16, 23
Natural gas	1943	1955+	88, 17, 30
Aluminium	1924	1955+	29, 43
Barley	1949	1942	06, 14, 28
Wheat	1925	1947	86, 91, 98, 15
Potatoes	1926	1946	95, 12,22, 28
Iron ore	1929	1953+	92, 16, 42
Coke	1929	1951+	92, 18, 29, 44
Pig iron	1943	1951+	90, 16, 29, 43
Steel	1929	1951+	17, 29, 44
Rolled steel	1968	1955+	90, 17, 29, 44
Beet sugar	1944	1954+	15, 20, 33, 40
Railway ton-miles	1942	1944	93, 18, 29
Corn	1916	1948	91, 96, 06, 16
Rice	2023	1954+	20
Fish	2073	1941	90, 03, 17
Cotton	1932	1937	98, 14, 26
Oats	1923	1945	05, 17
Bitumin. coal	1933	1947	18
Total coal	1932	1947	18
Copper	1933	1955+	18, 29, 42
Buckwheat	1904	1905	
Anth. coal	1916	1917	
Rye	1924	1922	96, 03
Sheep	1926	1943	02, 12, 31
Lead	1933	1926	17
Railway pass-miles	1929	1944	20
Cane sugar	1903	1953+	94, 08, 38
Wool	1916	1942	85, 93, 09, 32
Vessels	1898	1943	91, 01, 08, 20
Mercury	1867	1877	

(1) Burns's estimate represents the year in which the logarithmic parabola which he fitted to each series reaches its maximum (A. F. Burns, *Production Trends in the U.S. Since 1870*, N.Y.: National Bureau of Economic Research, 1934, Tables 22–55).

(2) Highest peak reached during period covered by this study. A plus sign signifies still higher peaks beyond that period.

(3) Lists prior peaks followed by declines of at least five years which might have encouraged contemporary judgment that an all-time peak had been passed.

Based on sources cited in Appendix.

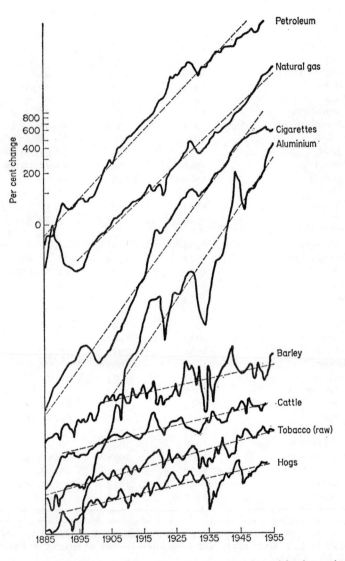

Fig. 11.4 Detailed industry growth patterns, rates, logarithmic vertical scale;
(a) Series with constant growth

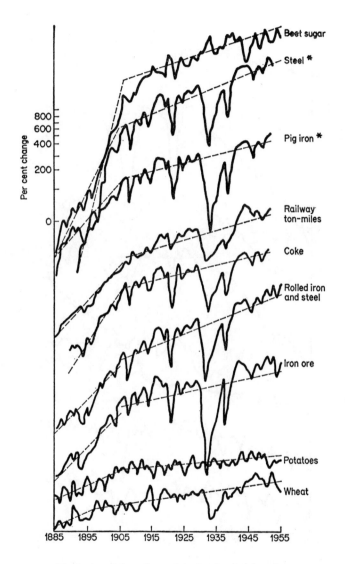

Early trend based on data beginning in 1870
(b) Series with rapid growth followed by slower but steady growth

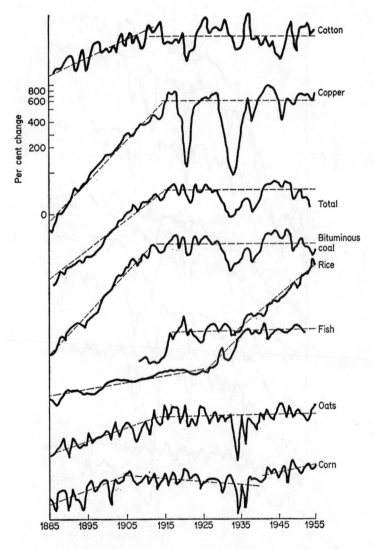

(c) Series exhibiting growth and extended horizontal trends

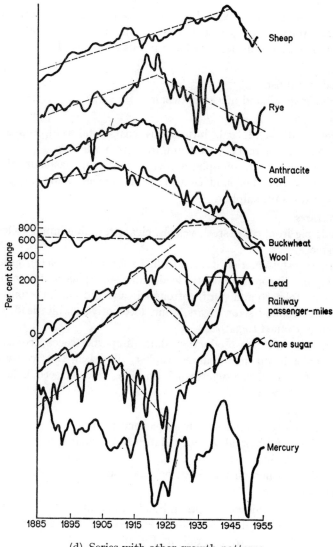

(d) Series with other growth patterns

APPENDIX

COMPARISON OF SERIES USED BY BURNS AND PRESENT STUDY
(From [4, 24])

Agriculture

16 used: barley, beet sugar, buckwheat, cane sugar, corn, cotton, oats, rye, tobacco (raw), wheat, wool, cattle, hogs, rice, potatoes, sheep.

4 omissions: hay, molasses and syrup, raisins, flaxseed.

Fisheries

1 used: total fish.

2 omissions: cod and mackerel, whales.

Mining

9 used: anthracite coal, bituminous coal, total coal, copper, lead domestic, mercury, petroleum, iron ore, natural gas.

13 omissions: gold, phosphate rock, silver, zinc, asphalt, Portland cement, non-Portland cement, total cement, fluorspar, gypsum, pyrites, salt, sulphur.

Manufactures

7 used: pig iron, coke, steel, vessels, cigarettes, aluminium, rolled iron, steel.

17 omissions/production data: distilled spirits (incomplete), fermented liquors (incomplete), total lead, rails, superphosphate, antimonial lead, tobacco and snuff, cottonseed cake and meal, cottonseed oil, nails, roofing slate, cigars, flour, locomotives, white lead, canned corn, canned tomatoes.

21 omissions of non-production data: imports (cocoa, coffee, jute, Manila hemp, minor fibres, rubber, silk, sisal, tin); consumption (cotton, lead, raw sugar, wool, tin plate, zinc, flaxseed, gold, silver, tobacco, copper).

Transportation

2 used: railway ton-miles, railway passenger-miles.

3 omissions of physical activity data: N.Y. canal traffic, S.S. *Marie* canal traffic, coastal trade.

2 omissions of non-output data: postage stamps, postal money orders.

Other Omissions

2 construction: rail consumption, building permits.

5 trade: agricultural exports, deflated clearings, tonnage entered and cleared, shares traded, railway freight.

Total production series used:	35
Total production series omitted:	39
Non-production series omitted:	30
	104

References

CHAPTER I

[1] Blyth, C. A., *American Business Cycles 1945-50* (London: Allen and Unwin, 1969).
[2] Burns, A. F., *The Business Cycle in a Changing World* (New York: Columbia Univ. Press, 1969).
[3] Cohen, M. R., *Reason and Nature* (New York: Harcourt, Brace, 1931).
[4] Cyert, R. M. and March, J. G., *A Behavioral Theory of the Firm* (New York: Prentice-Hall, 1963).
[5] Ehrenberg, A. S. C., 'American Marketing Association Meetings', *Operations Research Quarterly*, p. 411, September 1965.
[6] Eilon, S., 'What Is a Decision?', *Management Science, 16*, no. 4, 1969.
[7] Gifford, J. K., 'Correlationism: A Virulent Disease in Economic Sciences', *Journal of Political Economy*, p. 1091, September 1968.
[8] Gold, B., 'Exploring Management in its Native Habitat', *Pittsburgh Business Review*, August 1963.
[9] Harrod, R. F., *The Life of John Maynard Keynes*, p. 137 (New York: Harcourt, Brace, 1952).
[10] Liu, T. C., 'Underidentification, Structural Estimation and Forecasting', *Econometrica*, October 1960.
[11] Morgenstern, O., 'Limits to the Uses of Mathematics in Economics', in J. C. Charlesworth (ed.) *Mathematics and The Social Sciences* (Philadelphia: The American Academy of Political and Social Sciences, June 1963).
[12] Schumpeter, J. A., *History of Economic Analysis* (New York: Oxford Univ. Press, 1954).
[13] Simon, H. A., 'Theories of Decision Making in Economics and Behavioral Science', *Surveys of Economic Theory:* III Resource Allocation (London: Macmillan, 1966).

CHAPTER 2

[1] Chamberlain, N. W., *The Firm: Micro-Economic Planning and Action* (New York: McGraw-Hill, 1962).
[2] Gold, B., *Foundations of Productivity Analysis* (University of Pittsburgh Press, 1955).
[3] Horrigan, J. O., 'A Short History of Financial Ratio Analysis', *The Accounting Review*, April 1968.

[4] *Improved Tools of Management* (New York: American Management Association, Financial Management Series, No. III, 1956).

[5] Jerome, W. T., *Executive Control*, Ch. 13, 14 (New York: John Wiley, 1961).

[6] Kline, C. A. and Hesler, H. H., 'The DuPont Chart System for Appraising Operating Performance', *N.A.C.A. Bulletin* (National Association of Cost Accountants, 1952).

[7] Weston, J. F. and Bingham, E. F., *Managerial Finance*, Chapter 4 (New York: Holt, Rinehart and Winston, 1968).

[8] 'How a big company controls itself', *Business Week*, December 6, 1952.

CHAPTER 3

[1] Amey, L. R., 'The Allocation and Utilization of Resources', *Operational Research Quarterly*, **15**, 1964.

[2] Barger, H., *Distribution's Place in the American Economy* (Princeton University Press, 1955).

[3] Blaug, M., 'The Productivity of Universities', in *Universities and Productivity* (Background Papers for a Conference of the Joint Consultative Committee of Vice Chancellors and the Association of University Teachers, London, 1967).

[4] Boulding, K. E., 'Some Difficulties in the Concept of Economic Input', in [9].

[4a] Fabricant, S., *The Output of Manufacturing Industries, 1899–1937* (New York: National Bureau of Economic Research, 1940).

[5] Gold, B., *Foundations of Productivity Analysis* (University of Pittsburgh Press, 1955).

[6] ——, *Wartime Economic Planning in Agriculture* (New York: Columbia University Press, 1949).

[7] Gould, J. and Kolb, W. L., (eds.), *A Dictionary of the Social Sciences* (New York: The Free Press, 1964).

[7a] Grossman, G., 'Notes for a Theory of the Command Economy', in M. Bornstein (ed.), *Comparative Economic Systems*, p. 145 (Homewood, Ill.: Richard D. Irwin, 1965).

[8] Hirschman, A. O., *The Strategy of Economic Development* (Yale University Press, 1958).

[9] *Input, Output and Productivity Measurement* (Princeton University Press, 1961).

[9a] Kendrick, J. W., *Productivity Trends in the U.S.* (Princeton University Press, 1961).

[10] Kuznets, S. S., *Commodity Flow and Capital Formation* (New York: National Bureau of Economic Research, 1938).

[11] *Measuring the Productivity of Federal Government Organizations* (Washington, D.C.: U.S. Government Printing Office, 1964).

[12] Salter, W. E. G., *Productivity and Technical Change* (Cambridge University Press, 1960).

[13] Sanders, B. S., 'Some Difficulties in Measuring Inventive Activity' in *The Rate and Direction of Inventive Activity: Economic and Social Factors* (Princeton University Press, 1962).

[14] Schmookler, J., 'The Changing Efficiency of the American Economy', *Review of Economics and Statistics*, 1952.

[15] Siegel, I. H., 'On the Design of Consistent Output and Input Indexes for Productivity Measurement', in [9].

[16] ——, 'Wage–Price–Productivity Statistics: Old Gaps and New Needs', *1968 Proceedings of the Business and Economics Section, American Statistical Association* (Washington, D.C.: American Statistical Association, 1968).

[17] Solow, R. M., 'Education and Economic Productivity', in S. Harris and A. Levensohn (eds.) *Education and Public Policy* (Berkeley, California: McCutcheon, 1965).

[18] Thorelli, H. B., 'Productivity—A Tantalizing Concept', *Productivity Measurement Review*, August, 1960.

CHAPTER 5

[1] Andrews, P. W. S., *Manufacturing Business* (Landow: Macmillan, 1949).

[2] *General Electric 1959 Annual Report* (New York: General Electric Company, 1960).

[3] Gold, B., *Foundations of Productivity Analysis* (University of Pittsburgh Press, 1955).

[4] Mills, F. C., *Economic Tendencies in the United States* (New York: National Bureau of Economic Research, 1932).

CHAPTER 6

[1] Fabricant, S., *The Output of Manufacturing Industries, 1899–1937* (New York: National Bureau of Economic Research, 1939).

[2] Manne, A. S., *Economic Analysis for Business Decisions* (New York: McGraw-Hill, 1961).

[3] Mills, F. C., *Economic Tendencies in the United States* (New York: National Bureau of Economic Research, 1932).

CHAPTER 7

[1] Alchian, A., 'Costs and Output', in M. Abramovitz *et al.*, *The Allocation of Resources* (Stanford University Press, 1959).

[2] Andrews, P. W. S., 'Industrial Analysis in Economics', in *Oxford Studies on the Price Mechanism*, p. 161 (Oxford: Clarendon Press, 1951).

[3] ——, *Manufacturing Business*, pp. 271–2. (London: Macmillan, 1949).

[4] ——, *On Competition in Economic Theory*, pp. 60–1, (London: Macmillan, 1964).

[5] Bain, J. S., *Pricing, Distribution and Employment*, pp. 75–7, (New York: Henry Holt, 1948).

[6] Burns, A. F., *Production Trends in the United States Since 1870*, pp. 90–102 (New York: National Bureau of Economic Research, 1934).

[7] Committee on Price Determination, *Cost Behaviour and Price Policy*, pp. 90–102 (New York: National Bureau of Economic Research, 1943).

[8] Fabricant, S., *Output of Manufacturing Industries, 1899–1937*, Appendix A (New York: National Bureau of Economic Research, 1939).

[9] ——, *Employment in Manufacturing*, pp. 47–53 (New York: National Bureau of Economic Research, 1942).

[10] Gold, B., *Foundations of Productivity Analysis*, pp. 109–55 (University of Pittsburgh Press, 1955).

[11] Grant, E. L. and Norton, P. T., Jr., *Depreciation*, p. 267 (New York, Ronald Press, 1949).

[12] Hall, R. L. and Hitch, C. J., 'Price Theory and Business Behaviour', in [2], pp. 113 and 126–36 (column B).

[13] Harrod, R., *Economic Essays*, pp. 154, 170 (New York: Harcourt, Brace, 1952).

[14] Heflebower, R. B., 'Full Costs, Cost Changes and Prices', *Business Concentration and Price Policy*, p. 370 (Princeton University Press, 1955).

[15] Hultgren, T., *Changes in Labor Cost During Cycles in Production and Business* (New York: National Bureau of Economic Research, 1960).

[16] Johnston, J., *Statistical Cost Analysis* (New York: McGraw-Hill, 1960).

[17] Knauth, O., *Managerial Enterprise*, p. 136 (New York: W. W. Norton, 1948).

[18] Spencer, M. H. and Siegelman, L., *Managerial Economics*, p. 267 (Homewood, Ill.: Richard D. Irwin, 1959).

[19] Staehle, H., 'The Measurement of Statistical Cost Functions: An Appraisal', *American Economic Review*, June 1942.

[20] Stigler, G. J., *The Theory of Price*, pp. 162–4 (New York: Macmillan, Revised, 1952).

[21] Triffin, Robert, *Monopolistic Competition and General Equilibrium Theory*, especially Chapter II. (Harvard University Press, 1940).

[22] Walters, A. A., 'Production and Cost Functions', *Econometrica*, January 1963.

[23] Wilson, T. and Andrews, P. W. S. (eds.), *Oxford Studies in the Price Mechanism* (Oxford: Clarendon Press, 1951).

CHAPTER 8

[1] Creamer, D., *et al.*, *Capital in Manufacturing and Mining* (Princeton University Press, 1960).

[2] Gold, B., *Foundations of Productivity Analysis* (University of Pittsburgh Press, 1955).

[3] Gold, B. and Kraus, R. M., 'Integrating Physical and Financial Measures for Managerial Control', *Journal of the Academy of Management*, June 1964.

[4] Kraus, R. M., *Empirical Testing of New Managerial Control Ratios* (Unpublished dissertation, University of Pittsburgh, 1967).

[5] Reps, D. M., *Operational Requirements for Planning and Control Models in a Large Diversified Industrial Company* (Unpublished dissertation, University of Pittsburgh, 1967).

CHAPTER 9

[1] Abramovitz, M., 'Economics of Growth', in B. F. Haley (ed.) *A Survey of Contemporary Economics* (Homewood, Illinois: Richard D. Irwin, 1952).

[2] ——, *cf.* p. 277 Ch. 7 [2] and [3] 'Resource and Output Trends in the U.S. Since 1870', *American Economic Review*, May 1956.

[3] Adelman, M. A., 'Steel, Administered Prices and Inflation', *Quarterly Journal of Economics*, February 1961.

[4] Anthony, R. N., *Management Accounting* (Homewood, Illinois: Richard D. Irwin, 1960).

[5] Andrews, P. W. S., 'Industrial Analysis in Economics', in T. Wilson and P. W. S. Andrews (eds.), *Oxford Studies in the Price Mechanism* (Oxford: Clarendon Press, 1951).

[6] Andrews, P. W. S. and Brunner, E., *Capital Development in Steel* (Oxford: Blackwell, 1952).

[7] Arrow, K. J., 'Comment', in [38].

[8] Babbage, C., *On the Economy of Machinery and Manufactures* (London: Knight, 3rd Edition, 1833).

[9] Bierman, H., Jr. and Smidt, S., *The Capital Budgeting Decision* (New York: Macmillan, 1960).

[10] Böhm-Bawerk, E. V., *Positive Theory of Capital* (London: Macmillan, 1891).

[11] Brozen, Y., 'Determinants of the Direction of Technical Change', *American Economic Review*, May 1953.

[12] Carter, C. F. and Williams, B. R., *Investment in Innovation* (Oxford: Oxford University Press, 1958).

[13] Cyert, R. M. and March, J. G., *A Behavioral Theory of the Firm* (New York: Prentice-Hall, 1963).

[14] Dean, J., *Capital Budgeting* (New York: Columbia University Press, 1951).

[15] Douglas, P. H., 'Are There Laws of Production?', *American Economic Review*, March 1948.

[16] Enos, J. L., 'Invention and Innovation in the Petroleum Refining Industry', in [38].

[17] Fabricant, S., *The Output of Manufacturing Industries, 1899–1937* (New York: National Bureau of Economic Research, 1940).

[18] ——, *Employment in Manufacturing* (New York: National Bureau of Economic Research, 1942).

[19] Fellner, W., 'Does the Market Direct the Relative Factor-Saving Effects of Technological Progress?', in [38].

[20] Gold, B. *Foundations of Productivity Analysis* (University of Pittsburgh Press, 1955).

[21] Gourvitch, A., *Survey of Economic Theory on Technological Change and Employment* (Philadelphia: U.S. Works Progress Administration—National Research Project, 1940).

[22] Grant, E. L., *Principles of Engineering Economy* (New York: Ronald, 1959).

[23] Griliches, Z., 'Hybrid Corn: An Exploration in the Economics of Technical Change', *Econometrica*, October 1957.

[24] ——, 'Comment', in [38].

[25] Habakkuk, H. J., *American and British Technology in the Nineteenth Century* (Cambridge University Press, 1962).

[26] Hahn, F. H. and Matthews, R. C. O., 'The Theory of Economic Growth: A Survey', *Surveys of Economic Theory: Growth and Development* (New York: St. Martin's Press, 1967).

[27] Hicks, J. R., *Value and Capital* (Oxford: Clarendon Press, 1939).

[28] Hitch, C. J., 'Comment', in [38]
[29] Jerome, H., *Mechanization in Industry* (New York: National Bureau of Economic Research, 1934).
[30] Kuznets, S. S., *Secular Movements in Production and Prices* (New York: Houghton Mifflin, 1930).
[31] Machlup, F., 'The Supply of Inventors and Inventions', in [38].
[32] Manne, A. S., *Economic Analysis for Business Decisions* (New York: McGraw-Hill, 1961).
[33] Mansfield, E., 'The Speed of Response of Firms to New Techniques', *Quarterly Journal of Economics*, May 1963.
[34] Marshall, A., *Principles of Economics* (London: Macmillan, Eighth Edition, 1920).
[35] Massell, B. F., 'Capital Formation and Technological Change in U.S. Manufacturing', *Review of Economics and Statistics*, May 1960.
[36] Minasian, J. R., 'The Economics of Research and Development', in [38].
[37] Mueller, W. F., 'The Origins of the Basic Inventions Underlying Du Pont's Major Product and Process Innovations, 1920 to 1950', in [38].
[38] Nelson, R. R. *et al.*, *The Rate and Direction of Inventive Activity: Economic and Social Factors* (Princeton University Press, 1962).
[39] ——, 'The Link Between Science and Invention', in [38].
[40] Norton, F. E., 'Administrative Organization in Capital Budgeting' in Ezra Solomon (ed.), *The Management of Corporate Capital* (Glencoe, Illinois: The Free Press, 1959).
[41] Peck, M. J., 'Inventions in the Postwar American Aluminum Industry', in [38].
[42] Reder, M. W., 'Alternative Theories of Labor's Share', in M. Abramovitz *et al.*, *The Allocation of Resources* (Stanford University Press, 1959).
[43] Scheuble, P. A., Jr., 'How to Figure Equipment Replacement', *Harvard Business Review*, September 1953.
[44] Schmookler, J. 'The Changing Efficiency of the American Economy, 1869–1938', *Review of Economics and Statistics*, August, 1952.
[45] ——, 'Changes in Industry and in the State of Knowledge as Determinants of Industrial Inventions', in [38].
[46] Schumpeter, J. A., *The Theory of Economic Development* (Cambridge, Mass: Harvard University Press, 1934).
[47] Solow, R., 'Technical Change and the Aggregate Production Function', *Review of Economics and Statistics*, August 1957, and 'A Reply', *ibid.*, November 1958.
[48] ——, 'A Skeptical Note on the Constancy of Relative Shares,' *American Economic Review*, September, 1958.
[49] ——, 'Investment and Technical Progress', in K. J. Arrow *et al.* (eds.), *Mathematical Methods in the Social Sciences* (Stanford University Press, 1960).
[50] Sraffa, P., *Production of Commodities by Means of Commodities* (Cambridge University Press, 1960).
[51] Strassman, W. P., *Risk and Technological Innovation* (Cornell University Press, 1959).
[52] Terborgh, G., *Business Investment Policy* (Washington, D. C.: Machinery and Allied Products Institute, 1958).

[53] Veblen, T., *The Theory of Business Enterprise* (New York: Chas. Scribner's, 1904) and *The Engineers and the Price System* (New York: Harcourt, Brace and World, 1963).

[54] Walters, A. A., 'Production and Cost Functions', *Econometrica*, January 1963.

[55] *Return on Capital as a Guide to Managerial Decisions* (New York: National Association of Accountants, 1959).

[56] U.S. Works Progress Administration—National Research Project in Co-operation with the National Bureau of Economic Research, Series on *Productivity and Employment in Selected Industries*, Philadelphia, Pa.

CHAPTER 10

[1] Abramovitz, M., 'Resource and Output Trends in the U.S. Since 1870', *American Economic Review*, May 1956.

[2] Andrews, P. W. S. and Brunner, E., *Capital Development in Steel* (Oxford: Blackwell, 1952).

[3] Anthony, R. N. and Day, J. S., *Management Controls in Industrial Research Organizations* (Cambridge: Harvard University Press, 1952).

[4] Arrow, K. J., 'Economic Welfare and the Allocation of Resources for Invention', in [94].

[5] Babbage, C., *On the Economy of Manufactures* (London: Charles Knight, 3rd edition, 1833).

[6] Bloom, G. F., 'Union Wage Pressure and Technological Discovery', *American Economic Review*, September 1951.

[7] Bridgman, P. W., *Reflections of a Physicist* (New York: Philosophical Library, 1950).

[8] Bross, I. J., 'Algebra and Illusion', *Science*, June 3, 1966.

[9] Brown, W. H., 'Innovation in the Machine Tool Industry', *American Economic Review*, May 1951.

[10] Brozen, Y., 'Invention, Innovation, and Imitation', *American Economic Review*, May 1951.

[11] ——, 'Determinants of the Direction of Technical Change', *American Economic Review*, May 1953.

[12] ——, 'Trends in Industrial Research and Development', *Journal of Business*, July 1960.

[13] ——, 'The Future of Industrial Research and Development', in [94].

[14] Burns, A. F., *Production Trends in the United States Since 1870* (New York: National Bureau of Economic Research, 1934).

[15] Carter, C. F. and Williams, B. R., *Industry and Technical Progress* (London: Oxford University Press, 1957).

[16] ——, *Investment in Innovation* (London: Oxford University Press, 1958).

[17] Cherington, P. W., Peck, M. J. and Scherer, F. M., 'Organization and Research and Development Decision Making within a Government Department', in [94].

[18] Coales, J. F., 'Financial Provision for Research and Development in Industry,' *Journal of Industrial Economics*, July 1957.

[19] Comanor, W. S., 'Research and Competitive Product Differentiation in the Pharmaceutical Industry in the United States', *Economica*, November 1964.

[20] Comanor, W. S., 'Research and Technical Change in the Pharmaceutical Industry', *Review of Economics and Statistics*, May 1965.

[21] Cyert, R. M. and March, J. G., *A Behavioral Theory of the Firm* (New York: Prentice-Hall, Inc. 1963).

[22] Denison, E. F., 'Theoretical Aspects of Quality Change, Capital Consumption and Net Capital Formation', in *Problems of Capital Formation* (Studies in Income and Wealth, XIX) (Princeton: Princeton University Press, 1957).

[23] Domar, E., 'On Measurement of Technological Change', *Economic Journal*, December 1961.

[24] Enos, J. L., 'Invention and Innovation in Petroleum Refining Industry', in [94].

[25] Fellner, W., 'Does the Market Direct the Relative Factor-Saving Effects of Technological Change', in [94].

[26] Feynman, R. P., 'The Development of the Space-Time View of Quantum Electrodynamics', *Science*, August 12, 1966.

[27] Freeman, C., 'Research and Development: A Comparison Between British and American Industry', *National Institute Economic Review*, May 1962.

[28] Galbraith, J. K., *American Capitalism* (Cambridge, Mass.: Houghton Mifflin, 1952).

[29] Gass, J. R., 'The Human Element in the Application of Science', *Impact of Science on Society*, June 1954.

[30] Godfrey, M. D., 'Certain Problems in the Application of Mathematical Economics', in [117].

[31] Gold, B., *Wartime Economic Planning in Agriculture* (New York: Columbia University Press, 1949).

[32] ——, *Foundations of Productivity Analysis* (Pittsburgh: University of Pittsburgh Press, 1955).

[33] Gordon, R. A., 'Differential Changes in the Prices of Consumer's and Capital Goods', *American Economic Review*, December 1961.

[34] ——, statement: Senate Hearings on *Technology in the Nation's Economy* [124].

[35] Graham, B., 'The Nonprofit Research Institute: A Nonuniversity Approach', in B. R. Keenan (ed.) *Science and the University* (New York: Columbia University Press, 1966).

[36] Griliches, Z., 'Comment', in [94].

[37] Hahn, F. H. and Matthews, R. C. D., 'The Theory of Economic Growth', in *Surveys of Economic Theory: II Growth and Development* (New York: St. Martin's Press, 1967).

[38] Harrel, C. G., 'Selecting Projects for Research', in C. C. Furnas (ed.), *Research in Industry*, Chapter 8 (New York: D. Van Nostrand Co., Inc., 1948)

[39] Hershey, R. L., 'Finance and Productivity in Industrial Research and Development', *Research Management*, July 1966.

[40] Hertz, D. B., *The Theory and Practice of Industrial Research* (New York: McGraw-Hill, 1950).

[41] Hicks, J. R., *The Theory of Wages*, Chapter 6 (London: Macmillan & Co. Ltd., 1932).

[42] ——, *Value and Capital* (Oxford: Clarendon Press, 1939).

[43] Hitch, C. J., 'Character of Research and Development in a Competitive Economy', *Proceedings of a Conference on Research and Development and Its Impact on the Economy* (National Science Foundation, 1958).

[44] ——, 'Comment', in [94].

[45] Holland, M., *Management's Stake in Research* (New York: Harper & Bros., 1958, Chapter 2.

[46] Hollomon, J. H., in [124].

[47] Jewkes, J., Sawers, D. and Stillerman, R. *The Sources of Invention* (New York: St. Martin's Press, 1959).

[48] Jones, C., 'Criteria used by Industrial Research in Evaluating a Specific Research Project', in [124].

[49] Jorgenson, D. W., 'The Embodiment Hypothesis', *Journal of Political Economy*, February 1966.

[50] Kaplan, A., *The Conduct of Inquiry* (San Francisco: Chandler Publications, 1964).

[51] Keezer, D. *et al.*, *New Forces in American Business* (New York: McGraw-Hill, 1959).

[52] ——, 'The Outlook for Expenditures on Research and Development during the Next Decade', *American Economic Review*, Papers and Proceedings, May 1960.

[53] Kendrick, J. 'Productivity Trends: Capital and Labour', *Review of Economic Statistics*, August 1956.

[54] Kennedy, C., 'Induced Bias in Innovation and the Theory of Distribution', *Economic Journal*, September 1964.

[55] Keynes, J. M., *The General Theory of Employment, Interest and Money* (London: Macmillan, 1936).

[56] Klein, B. H., 'Reply and Rejoinder', in [94].

[57] ——, 'The Decision Making Problem in Development', in [94].

[58] Klein, B. H. and Meckling, W., 'Application of Operations Research to Development Decision', *Operations Research*, May 1958.

[59] Kornhauser, A. W., *Scientists in Industry* (Los Angeles: University of California Press, 1962), Chapter 3.

[60] Kuznets, S., *Economic Change*, (New York: W. W. Norton and Company, Inc., 1953), Chapter 9.

[61] ——, 'Inventive Activity: Problems of Definition and Measurement', in [94].

[62] Lamberton, D. M., *The Theory of Profit* (Oxford: Blackwell, 1965), Chapter 5.

[63] Larrabie, W. M. *et al.*, *Profit, Performance and Progress* (New York: American Telephone and Telegraph Co., 1959), in [109].

[64] Leontieff, W., *Essays in Economics* (New York: Oxford University Press, 1966).

[65] Littauer, S. B., 'Conceptualization and Formalization—The Impossible and The Obvious', *Management Science*, October 1965.

[66] Machlup, F., 'The Supply of Inventors and Inventions', in [94].

[67] Maclaurin, W. R., 'Federal Support for Scientific Research', *Harvard Business Review*. March–April 1947.

[68] ——, 'The Process of Technological Innovation: The Launching of a New Scientific Industry', *American Economic Review*, March 1950.

[69] Maclaurin, W. R., 'The Sequence from Invention to Innovation and Its Relation to Economic Growth', *Quarterly Journal of Economics*, February 1953.

[70] ——, 'Technological Progress in Some American Industries', *American Economic Review*, 1954.

[71] Mansfield, E., 'Technical Change and Rate of Imitation', *Econometrica*, October 1961.

[72] ——, 'Entry, Gibrat's Law, Innovation and the Growth of Firms', *American Economic Review*, December 1962.

[73] ——, 'Speed of Response of Firms to New Techniques', *Quarterly Journal of Economics*, May 1963.

[74] ——, 'Industrial Research and Development Expenditures: Determinants, Prospects, and Relation to Size of Firm and Inventive Output', *Journal of Political Economy*, August 1964.

[75] ——, 'Rates of Return from Industrial Research and Development', *American Economic Review*, May 1965.

[76] March, J. G. and Simon, H. A., *Organizations* (New York: John Wiley & Sons, 1958), Chapter 7.

[77] Markham, J. W., 'Inventive Activity: Government Controls and the Legal Environment', in [94].

[78] Marris, R., *The Economic Theory of Managerial Capitalism* (New York: Free Press of Glencoe, 1964).

[79] Marquard, C., *Costs in the Electrical Machinery Industry* (Unpublished M. A. Thesis, University of Pittsburgh, 1960).

[80] Marshall, A. W. and Meckling, H. W., 'Predictability of the Costs, Time and Success of Development' in [94].

[81] Massell, B. F., 'A Disaggregated View of Technical Change', *Journal of Political Economy*, December 1961.

[82] Minasian, J. R., 'The Economics of Research and Development', in [94].

[83] Motley and Newton, 'The Selection of Projects for Industrial Research', *Operations Research Quarterly*, November–December 1959.

[84] Mueller, W. F., 'The Origins of the Basic Inventions Underlying Du-Pont's Major Product and Process Innovations, 1920 to 1950', in [94].

[85] ——, 'Case Study of Product Discovery and Innovation Cost', *Southern Economic Journal*, July 1957.

[86] Nelson, R. R., 'The Background for the Conference', in [94].

[87] ——, 'The Link Between Science and Invention: The Case of the Transistor', in [94].

[88] ——, 'Economics of Invention—A Survey of the Literature', *Journal of Business*, April 1959.

[89] ——, 'The Simple Economics of Basic Scientific Research', *Journal of Political Economy*, June 1959.

[90] Peck, M. J., 'Inventions in the Postwar American Aluminum Industry', in [106].

[91] Penrose, E. T., *The Theory of the Growth of the Firm* (New York: John Wiley, 1959).

[92] Piore, E., 'Is System Science a Discipline?', in [117].

[93] Quinn, J. B. and Cavanaugh, R. M., 'Fundamental Research Can Be Planned', *Harvard Business Review*, January–February, 1964.

[94] *The Rate and Direction of Inventive Activity: Economic and Social Factors*, National Bureau of Economic Research Special Conference, Series No. 13 (New Jersey: Princeton University, 1962).

[95] Ricardo, D., *The Principles of Political Economy and Taxation* (New York: E. P. Dutton, Everyman's Library, 1933).

[96] Rosenberg, N., 'Capital Goods, Technology and Economic Growth', *Oxford Economic Papers*, 1963.

[97] Rubenstein, A. H., 'Organization and Research and Development Decision Making within the Decentralized Firm', in [94].

[98] ——, 'Setting Criteria for Research and Development', *Harvard Business Review*, January 1957.

[99] Ruggles, R. and N., 'Concepts of Real Capital Stocks and Services', in *Output, Input and Productivity Measurement*, Conference on Income and Wealth, No. 25 (New Jersey: Princeton University Press, 1961).

[100] Salter, W. E. G., *Productivity and Technical Change* (Cambridge: Cambridge University Press, 1960).

[101] Sanders, B. S., 'Some Difficulties in Measuring Inventive Activity', in [94].

[102] Sayers, R. S., 'Springs of Technical Progress in Britain, 1919–1939', *Economic Journal*, June 1950.

[103] Schmookler, J., 'The Level of Inventive Activity', *Review of Economic Studies*, May 1956.

[104] ——, 'The Economic Sources of Inventive Activity', *Journal of Economic History*, March 1962.

[105] Schumpeter, J., *Capitalism, Socialism and Democracy* (New York: Harper, 1950).

[106] Shaw, W. H., *The Value of Commodity Output Since 1869* (New York: National Bureau of Economic Research, 1947).

[107] Shonfield, A., *Modern Capitalism* (London: Oxford University Press, 1965).

[108] Siegel, I. H., 'Conditions of American Technological Progress', *American Economic Review*, May 1954.

[109] Silk, L., *The Research Revolution* (New York: McGraw-Hill, 1960).

[110] Smith, V. L., 'Engineering Data and Statistical Techniques in the Analysis of Production and Technological Change: Fuel Requirements of the Trucking Industry', *Econometrica*, April 1957.

[111] Solow, R. M., 'Technical Change and the Aggregate Production Function', Review of *Economic Statistics*, August 1957.

[112] ——, 'Investment and Technical Progress', K. J. Arrow et al. (eds.), *Mathematical Methods in the Social Sciences* (California: Stanford University Press, 1960).

[113] ——, 'Technical Progress, Capital Formation and Economic Growth', *American Economic Review*, Proceedings, May 1962.

[114] Spengler, J. J., 'Comment', in [94].

[115] Strassmann, W. P., 'Interrelated Industries and the Rate of Technological Change', *Review of Economic Studies*, October 1959.

[116] Sutherland, A., 'Diffusion of an Innovation in Cotton Spinning', *Journal of Industrial Economics*, March 1959.

[117] *System Theory*, Microwave Research Institute Symposia Series, Vol. XV (New York: Polytechnic Press, 1965).

[118] Terleckyj, N. E., 'Research and Development Funds: Sources and Applications', in Peter M. Gutmann (ed.), *Economic Growth* (New York: Prentice-Hall, 1964).

[119] Ulin, R. P., 'Thinking Ahead: What Will Research Bring About?' *Harvard Business Review*, January–February 1958.

[120] U.S. Congress House. Select Committee on Government Research, *Summary of Hearings, Federal Research and Development Programs*, 88th Congress, First and Second Sessions, 1964.

[121] U.S. Congress House. Select Committee on Government Research, *Report, National Goals and Policies*, Study No. 10, 88th Congress, Second Session, 1964.

[122] U.S. Congress Senate. Subcommittee of the Select Committee on Small Business, *Hearings: The Role and Effect of Technology in the Nation's Economy*, 88th Congress, First Session, 1963 (Part 1).

[123] U.S. Congress Senate. Subcommittee of the Select Committee on Small Business, *Hearings: The Role and Effect of Technology in the Nation's Economy*, 88th Congress, First Session, 1963 (Part 2).

[124] U.S. Congress Senate. Subcommittee of the Select Committee on Small Business, *Hearings: The Role and Effect of Technology in the Nation's Economy*, 88th Congress, First Session, 1963 (Part 3).

[125] U.S. Congress Senate. Subcommittee of the Select Committee on Small Business, *Hearings: The Role and Effect of Technology in the Nation's Economy*, 88th Congress, First Session, 1963 (Part 5).

[126] Villard, H. H., 'Competition, Oligopoly and Research', *Journal of Political Economy*, December 1958.

[127] Williams, B. R., 'Information and Criteria in Capital Expenditure Decisions', *Journal of Management Studies*, September 1964.

[128] Woodruff, W., 'Origins of Invention and Inter-Continental Diffusion of Techniques of Production in the Rubber Industry', *Economic Review*, December 1962.

[129] Worley, J. S., 'The Changing Direction of Research and Development Employment Among Firms', in [94].

CHAPTER 11

[1] Abramovitz, M., 'Economics of Growth', in Bernard F. Haley (ed.), *A Survey of Contemporary Economics*, p. 144 (Homewood, Illinois: Richard D. Irwin, 1952).

[2] Andrews, P. W. S., 'Industrial Analysis in Economics with special reference to Marshallian Doctrine', in T. Wilson and P. W. S. Andrews (eds.), *Oxford Studies in the Price Mechanism*, pp. 141–8 (Oxford: Clarendon Press, 1951).

[3] Baumol, W. J., *Business Behavior, Value and Growth* (New York: Macmillan, 1959).

[3a] Bruton, H. J., 'Contemporary Theorizing on Economic Growth', in B. F. Hoselitz (ed.), *Theories of Economic Growth*, p. 263 (Glencoe, Illinois: The Free Press, 1961).

[4] Burns, A. F., *Production Trends in the U.S. Since 1870* (N.Y.: National Bureau of Economic Research, 1934; Reprinted, N.Y., Augustus M. Kelley, 1950).

[5] Burns, A. F., 'Frickey on the Decomposition of Time Series', *The*

Frontiers of Economic Knowledge (Princeton University Press, 1954), pp. 277 *et seq.*

[6] Crum, W. L., *Quarterly Journal of Economics*, August 1934, pp. 742–8. Also see Burns comments on this in [5].

[7] Dade, E. B., *American Economic Review*, June 1934, pp. 357–9.

[8] Fabricant, S., 'Study of the Size and Efficiency of the American Economy', in E. A. G. Robinson (ed.), *Economic Consequences of the Size of Nations* (N.Y.: St. Martin's, 1960), p. 52.

[9] One of the few notable exceptions was E. Frickey, *Economic Fluctuations in the United States* (Cambridge: Harvard University Press, 1942).

[10] Frickey, E., 'The Problem of Secular Trend', *Review of Economics and Statistics*, October 1934, pp. 199–203 and [9, p. 42 *et seq.*].

[11] Gaston, J. F., *Growth Patterns in Industry: A Re-examination* (New York: National Industrial Conference Board, 1961).

[12] Gold, B., *Foundations of Productivity Analysis* (University of Pittsburgh, 1955), p. 279.

[13] Gold, B., Huettner, D., Mitchell, R. W. and Skeddle, R., 'Long Term Growth Patterns of Industries, Firms and Products', *1968 Proceedings of the Business and Statistics Section of the American Statistical Association* (Washington, D.C., 1968).

[14] Gort, M., 'Analysis of Stability and Change in Market Shares', *Journal of Political Economy*, February 1963, p. 51.

[15] Hahn, F. H. and Matthews, R. C. O., 'The Theory of Economic Growth: A Survey', in *Surveys of Economic Theory: II Growth and Development* (New York: St. Martin's Press, 1967).

[16] Hymer, S. and Pashigian, B. P., 'Firm Size and Rate of Growth', *Econometrica*, **27**, No. 2, p. 315.

[17] Jacoby, N. H., 'The Relative Stability of Market Shares . . .', *Journal of Industrial Economics*, XII, No. 2, March 1964, pp. 83–107.

[18] Kuznets, S. S., *Secular Movements in Production and Prices* (New York and Boston: Houghton Mifflin, 1930).

[19] ——, 'Concepts and Assumptions in Long Range Projections of National Production', *Long Range Economic Projection* (Princeton University Press, 1954), pp. 10–17.

[20] For example, see H. H. Landsberg, L. L. Fischman and J. L. Fisher, *Resources in America's Future* (Baltimore: Johns Hopkins Press, 1963).

[21] Marris, R., *The Economic Theory of Managerial Capitalism* (New York: Macmillan, 1964).

[22] Meyer, J. R., 'Regional Economics: A Survey', in *Surveys of Economic Theory: II Growth and Development* (New York: St. Martin's Press, 1967).

[23] Penrose, E., *The Theory of the Growth of the Firm* (New York: John Wiley, 1960).

[24] Rowland, T. L., *A Critical Examination of Arthur F. Burns' Theory of Retardation in the Rate of Growth of Individual Industries* (M. A. Thesis, University of Pittsburgh, 1960), Appendix A.

[25] Stigler, G. J., *Trends in Output and Employment* (N.Y.: National Bureau of Economic Research, 1947), p. 26.

[26] Vining, R., 'Methodological Issues in Quantitative Economics: A Rejoinder', *Review of Economics and Statistics*, May 1949, p. 94.

[27] Woytinsky, W. S., 'Trends in Production', in W. S. Woytinsky and Associates, *Employment and Wages in the United States* (N.Y.: Twentieth Century Fund, 1953), pp. 32, 34.
[28] Yntema, T. O., *Journal of the American Statistical Association*, XXX (1935), p. 124.

Index

289

Authors Cited

Abramovitz, M.   179, 278, 281, 286
Adelman, M. A.   207n, 278
Alchian, A., 277
Amey, L. R.   276
Andrews, P. W. S., 85n, 139, 205, 277, 278, 281, 286
Anthony, R. N.   214n, 278, 281
Arrow, K. J.   203, 278, 281

Babbage, C.   179, 237, 279, 281
Bain, J. S.   277
Barger, H.   276
Baumol, W. J.   260n, 286
Bierman, H., Jr.   279
Bingham, E. F.   276
Blaug, M.   276
Bloom, G. F.   281
Blyth, C. A.   275
Böhm-Bawerk, E. V.   179, 279
Bornstein, M.   276
Boulding, K. E.   32n, 276
Bridgman, P. W.   212n, 281
Bross, I. J.   212n, 281
Brown, W. H.   213n, 281
Brozen, Y.   212n, 213n, 223n, 279, 281
Brunner, E.   278, 281
Bruton, H. J.   286
Burns, A. F.   147, 223n, 247–60, 263, 267–9, 274, 275, 277, 281, 286

Carter, C. F.   208n, 212n, 213n, 223n, 229n, 279, 281
Cavanaugh, R. M.   217n, 284
Chamberlain, N. W.   275
Charlesworth, J. C.   275
Cherington, P. W.   231n, 281
Coales, J. F.   213n, 281
Cohen, M. R.   14, 275
Comanor, W. S.   215n, 217n, 281
Creamer, D.   278
Crum, W. L.   286
Cyert, R. M.   222n, 223n, 275, 279, 281

Dade, E. B.   286
Day, J. S.   214n, 281
Dean, J.   200, 279
Denison, E. F.   240n, 281
Domar, E.   281
Douglas, P. H.   179n, 279

Ehrenberg, A. S. C.   275
Eilon, S.   275
Enos, J. L.   203, 279, 282

Fabricant, S.   54, 56, 122, 183, 276, 277, 279, 286
Fellner, W.   212n, 214n, 279, 282
Feynman, R. P.   229n, 282
Fischman, L. L.   287
Fisher, J. L.   287
Freeman, C.   212n, 215n, 282
Frickey, E.   251, 286
Furnas, C. C.   282

Galbraith, J. K.   211n, 214n, 282
Gass, J. R.   282
Gaston, J. F.   256, 260n, 263, 286
Gifford, J. K.   275
Godfrey, M. D.   240n, 282
Gold, B.   240n, 275, 276, 277, 278, 279, 282, 287
Gordon, R. A.   240n, 282
Gort, M.   287
Gould, J.   276
Gourvitch, A.   179, 279
Graham, B.   282
Grant, E. L.   277, 279
Griliches, Z.   182, 214n, 215n, 217n, 279, 282
Grossman, G.   42, 276
Gutman, P. M.   215n, 285

Habakkuk, H. J.   279
Hahn, F. H.   180, 260n, 279, 282, 287
Hall, R. L.   277
Harrel, C. G.   214n, 282

Siegel, I. H.   32n, 39, 214n, 277, 285
Siegelman, L.   278
Silk, L.   213n, 215n, 285
Simon, H. A.   245, 275, 284
Skeddle, R.   287
Smidt, S.   279
Smith, V. L.   285
Solomon, E.   280
Solow, R. M.   36n, 199n, 277, 280, 285
Spencer, M. H.   278
Spengler, J. J.   214n, 285
Sraffa, P.   205, 280
Staehle, H.   278
Stigler, G. J.   258, 278, 287
Stillerman, R.   211n, 222n, 227n, 229n, 282
Strassman, W. P.   213n, 280, 285
Sutherland, A.   213n, 285

Terborgh, G.   181, 193n, 209n, 280
Terleckyj, N. E.   215n, 285

Thorelli, H. B.   277
Triffin, R.   139, 278

Ulin, R. P.   213n, 215n, 285

Veblen, T.   179, 280
Villard, H. H.   286
Vining, R.   287
von Braun, W.   229n, 229

Walters, A. A.   121n, 278, 280
Weston, J. F.   276
Wiesner, J. B.   211n, 222n, 243n
Williams, B. R.   208n, 212, 212n, 213n, 222n, 223n, 229n, 231n, 279, 281, 286
Wilston, T.   278, 286
Wirtz, W. W.   211n
Woodruff, W.   213n, 286
Worley, J. S.   286
Woytinsky, W. S.   287

Yntema, T. O.   287